ON EXHIBIT

Victorian Literature and Culture Series
Karen Chase, Jerome J. McGann, *and* Herbert Tucker, *Editors*

—

ON EXHIBIT
Victorians and Their Museums

———❦———

Barbara J. Black

UNIVERSITY PRESS OF VIRGINIA
Charlottesville and London

The University Press of Virginia
© 2000 by the Rector and Visitors of the University of Virginia
All rights reserved
Printed in the United States of America

First published in 2000

∞ The paper used in this publication meets the minimum requirements of the American National Standard for Information Sciences—Permanence of Paper for Printed Library Materials, ANSI Z39.48-1984.

Library of Congress Cataloging-in-Publication Data
Black, Barbara J., 1962–
    On exhibit : Victorians and their museums / Barbara J. Black.
      p.   cm. — (Victorian literature and culture series)
    Includes bibliographical references (p.   ) and index.
    ISBN 0-8139-1897-9 (cloth : alk. paper)
    1. Museums—England—London—History—19th century.   2. London
(England)—Intellectual life—19th century.   3. London (England)—
Civilization—19th century.   4. Literature and society—England—
London—History—19th century.   5. Popular culture—Great Britain—
History—19th century.   6. Great Britain—History—Victoria, 1837–1901.
I. Title.   II. Series.
AM43.L6B53   2000
069'.09421—dc21   99-16415
                                                                                              CIP

Contents

Illustrations

Acknowledgments

THERE ARE MANY people I wish to thank. First, I am grateful to Karen Chase-Levenson and Paul Cantor, the directors of this project when it was a dissertation. With their wisdom, encouragement, and support, they helped to transform the arduous years of graduate school into a wonderfully idyllic time. In ways that may surprise them, they have continued to strengthen my commitment to and deepen my pride in our profession. I cannot thank them enough for their guidance and their intellectual energy and generosity.

I am indebted to the capacious knowledge of Herbert Tucker, who, with characteristic incisiveness, provided me with a file of citations and many suggestions. I am also grateful to the late Edgar Shannon for long ago eloquently and gracefully defending my work. This book would not stand completed without the insight and encouragement of Michael Chase-Levenson and my fellow Londonists; whatever luminosity my writing might achieve owes much to this marvelous group of scholars and that summer in London when this nineteenth-century metropolis was our focus.

Parts of this book were written with the financial support of several institutions: the Bradley Foundation, the University of Virginia, the National Endowment for the Humanities, and the dean's office at Skidmore College. I thank my department, too, for financial assistance but also for much more: with their intellectual rigor and genuine, tough-minded interest, they have provided a fine community in which to teach and think for the past seven years.

I have enjoyed working with the University Press of Virginia, and I am particularly grateful to Ellen Satrom and to Cathie Brettschneider, whose interest in my project was quick and whose patience regarding its completion was great. I must also thank Louise Black for her keen eye and my student assistants Ellen Hock and Rosemary Whalen for their diligence. I am indebted to the quick and able assistance Phyllis MacDonald provided me, in both London and Vermont. I am grateful to the editors of the journals in which earlier versions of the following chapters originally appeared: chapter 2, in *In-Between: Essays and Studies in Literary Criticism,* 5, no. 2 (1996): 161–86; chapter 5, in *Victorian Poetry,* 32, no. 1 (1994): 1–20; chapter 6, in *Nineteenth-Century Contexts,* 2, no. 2 (1999): 235–38. I thank the following archives for permission to reproduce and quote materials from their collections: the National Art Library at the Victoria and Albert Museum; Sir John Soane's Museum; the Owen Collection in the Library of the Natural History Museum, London; the Bethnal Green Museum; the British Library; the University of London Institute of Historical Research; the University of London; the Special Collections Department at the University of Virginia Library; the Adler Collection at Skidmore College; the Guildhall Library, Corporation of London; the Illustrated London News Group; the Freud Museum, London; the Hirshhorn Museum; and the Cincinnati Historical Society.

Because my arguments repeatedly point to the connections among museums, childhood and adulthood, and home, I dedicate this book to my family. The memorial work of museums has kept me thinking about my childhood and the memories embedded in the childhood places of (re)collection. So to a maternal grandmother's teacups, a paternal grandmother's troves stored in cinnamon barrels, a father's cut-edged cruets in serried rows always in attendance at family dinners, a mother's bureau drawer of clove-scented chiffon scarves, a brother's cicada collection, to trips made to the North Museum at Franklin and Marshall and the walk-through heart at the Franklin Institute, and to the summer of Picassos at the Art Institute of Chicago, I dedicate this book. And to my new family, Jim—with your Caesars, Tabriz, and guillotines—I am most grateful.

ON EXHIBIT

Introduction

We live in the age of Omnium-Gatherum; *all the world's a museum, and men and women are its students.*

—Robert Kerr, *The English Gentleman's House*

AN ARCHITECT'S WORDS begin this study because I wish to emphasize that the nineteenth century was an age of builders who reconstructed the cityscape of London as much as they constructed their cultural identities. With the rise of speculative builders and the codification of architecture as a profession, Victorian London's docks, palaces, parliaments, model dwellings, department stores, and railways epitomized that "perfect fury of building in the thirties, forties, and fifties" that H. G. Wells describes in *Tono-Bungay* (1909) and that historians ever after have attempted to chronicle—most recent and most successful among them, Roy Porter in *London: A Social History.* This Victorian appetite for the built environment boasts no grander record than the three-volume *Official Descriptive and Illustrated Catalogue of the Great Exhibition* of 1851. In its first one hundred pages this massively detailed, impressively arranged text showcases a pride that resides less in the material it exhibits than in the construction of the Crystal Palace itself and of its textual counterpart, the catalog. This text praises "English constructive power" by enumerating the men and materials needed for the job, delighting in the "patented machine process" that rapidly and efficiently built the Crystal Palace, and taking pages to extol the engineering feat of the Paxton gutter.[1] Imagining the day when the Crystal Palace no longer stands, the catalog commends its own construction as a permanent monument to the work of arrangement and display of 1851. Today, both this building and this catalog serve as eloquent memorials to what I believe is the greatest constructive project of the nineteenth century—the civic museum.

Even as it mythologizes the home as the construction that is the inalienable right of refined English folk, Robert Kerr's *The English Gentleman's House* suggests a deeper enchantment with the museum. Redolent of his ceaseless energy for partitions that multiply rooms and specialize their functions, Kerr's plans bring the site of the museum home, whether it be in his recommendations for collection and display in the library, gallery, and winter garden or the designs and lighting of the South Kensington Museum's galleries he wishes to emulate. But the length and nature of his domestic plan reveal the museum's influence to be more deeply embedded in his vision of the British domestic space. After 350 pages of British domestic-design history and plans, Kerr ponders the question that does not vex: "In what *Style of Architecture* shall you build your house?" What follows is a reverie of all that is available exclusively to England in the nineteenth century. To his readers Kerr offers a menu of choices: "You can have Classical . . . you can have Elizabethan in equal variety; Renaissance ditto; or . . . Mediaeval—the Gothic . . . in any one of its multifarious forms—of the eleventh century, twelfth century, thirteenth, fourteenth, whichever you please."[2] Such an embrace of eclecticism allows Kerr to construct a museal, or museum-like, compendium that erects a building fantasy for an age that saw all previous centuries and styles as its legacy, an age in which all the world was a museum.

Kerr's vision of having it all was not unique. In cataloging the insistent variety of sites in London, Gustave Doré and Blanchard Jerrold's *London: A Pilgrimage* showcased in deluxe fashion the panoramic abundance that characterized London in 1872. In their penultimate chapter Doré and Jerrold turn to "London at Play" and open with the definitive statement: "There is the British Museum." Following this declaration, Jerrold's narrative proceeds to enumerate the marvels within: "The wonders of Nineveh; the Elgin Marbles; the mummies, the Natural History rooms, the geological collections, the matchless reading-room."[3] Then the text hurries on to identify other, equally lauded collections: "There is the South Kensington Museum. . . . There are, the Zoological and Horticultural Gardens; the Museum of Practical Geometry in Jermyn Street; the India, and College of Surgeons, Museums; the Houses of Parliament; the Tower of London; the Mint; and there is the National Gallery" (162). Jerrold's syntax is revealing: only lists, only numerous appositions can capture the grandeur of these London sites. Indeed, Jerrold ends *London: A Pilgrimage* with the topic of museums, as if the final gesture must be to grant their undeniable magnitude.[4] Here he heightens his prose yet further, using a fairy-tale rhetoric to spin a closing, beatific vision of London's museal pleasure domes: "The northern and southern boundary lines of the great metropolis glitter with two Crystal Palaces, beautiful as any jewelled halls that have been conceived by Eastern imagination" (190).

This aerial view—itself a kind of fantasy of supremacy—grants us perspective on how museums, these earthly paradises, enchanted Victorian culture. Museums promised so much to the observing eye. They bewitched with their abundance. When Doré and Jerrold visit the museum's sister institutions, the zoo and the botanical gardens, they create yet another panoramic view: "As in the Regent's Park the holiday-maker can study the animal life of every clime; so at Kew, in the palm-house, he can transport himself from the vapoury richness of English park scenery, to the climes where the banana spreads its festoons of luscious food" (111). Both visions transform the site of collection into utopia. Here one has access to every clime in one park and every scene in one garden. Here the West can compete with the East for the beautiful and exotic, as if the march of civilization had done an about-face. Here one can be transported through a kind of ecstasy, in all the senses of these rich words. The imaginary time travel a museum affords—particularly in that most ambitious of Victorian museal projects, the universal survey museum— allows a culture to stand outside itself within itself, to leave the realm of the merely familiar while staying at home. Jerrold's reliance on effusive expressions and romanticized visions captures the age's avidity for its museum culture; civic pride, the root of the Victorian museum enterprise, helped make *London: A Pilgrimage* "the most splendid gift book of the season" in 1872.[5]

In the same year the French journalist Hippolyte-Adolphe Taine published *Notes on England,* which originally appeared the previous year as a series of articles for the Paris *Temps* and contemporaneously in translation in the *Daily News.* These observations functioned as "mirror journalism"—that is, as a textual mirror shining from across the Channel in which the British could admire their own form.[6] Indeed, Taine seems to endorse Doré and Jerrold's fantasy vision. When he comes to praise what is perhaps the greatest space of Victorian England, the Crystal Palace, Taine defers to its ineffability: "It is gigantic, like London itself, and like so many things in London, but how can I pourtray the gigantic? All the ordinary sensations produced by size are intensified several times here."[7] But Taine does not maintain this posture of obeisance long. He quickly drops simple wonderment for a pragmatic defense of the museum as a tool of the regime. He sees in such institutions as the museum, what he calls "masterpieces of good arrangement and of ordered comfort," proof of a well-run, smoothly managed society (230). In his chapter "The Clubs, the British Museum, the Crystal Palace," Taine cleverly classifies together spaces known equally for luxury or luxuriating and regulation. In these institutions that monitor even as they seem to indulge, Taine sees a slick enterprise of efficiency and control at work. He exclaims, "How well they know how to organise comfort!" (229). He describes the commodious arrangements in the library of the British Museum in deliberate detail: "All the lower stage of shelves is filled with works of reference . . . which can be consulted on the spot, and are excellently arranged" (230). As the place of humanity's realized power, museums, Taine concludes, are the hallmarks of Victorian advancement (as evident in his following string of infinitives): "Man has been able to become master of Nature, to reform society, to ameliorate his condition, to adjust things to his wants, to establish a society" (230).

Such praise of, such investment in, and such commitment to the museum mark the departure point for my own study. The following chapters enter the Victorian museum in order to illuminate nineteenth-century British culture and the texts that generated it and were, in turn, generated by it. At times in my argument I will construe the museum as emblem, as historical event, as institution, as image, as practice—but always as what Eugenio Donato calls a "master pattern" that illuminates the ideological workings of Victorian society and literature.[8] Although I do not wish to claim that a unified Victorian response to the museum existed (and the following readings will represent the dissensus), the museum did possess a centripetal force; it was the age's great enterprise, realized in the opening of the National Gallery in 1824, the South Kensington complex in 1857, the National Portrait Gallery in 1859, the Natural History Museum in 1881, and the Tate Gallery in 1897. Victorian society constructed museums, celebrated and criticized museums, attended museums, worked in museums, wrote about museums, and collected in homage to museums. In a sense, one may perceive the museum as an impulse or spirit that infused the age and many of its projects: the triple-decker novel; collected works; encyclopedias and dictionaries; and phenomena as ordinary as keepsakes, dollhouses, and rock collections or a theory as cataclysmic as Darwin's panoramic evolutionism. Great and small, these system-building projects involved compilation, organization, and display—the three activities fundamental to a museum's work.

The spirit of the museum has also guided this book. It is decidedly expansive in order to capture the magnitude of the museum enterprise. My time frame ranges from the house-museum of Sir John Soane, which opened in 1837, to the collection-filled study of Sigmund Freud, which was erected in London in 1938, spanning the history of the museum from what I argue is its birth in the post–French Revolution era to its uncertain reign in Edwardian England. Along the way I will make deliberate museal leaps, curating what I consider important associations across time and space: thus Jean Baudrillard might yield rich commentary on Victorian collecting; Steven Spielberg's films may shed light on Rudyard Kipling's fiction; and Los Angeles's Museum of Jurassic Technology might profitably stand alongside Richard Owen's Natural History Museum. My primary focus, however, will be on the Victorian age as marking the great efflorescence of the phenomenon I call museum culture. My argument presents a mix of cultural critique and literary analysis, aiming to expand our notions of worthy texts. In order to produce the readings that follow, I rely on both cultural criticism—the Frankfurt School, New Historicism, and contemporary French theory—and social history. My aims include historical retrieval, literary interpretation, and theoretical discussion in the process of exploring the relations between museums and cultural production as well as the relentless production of text that the sites of collection generate, from labels to mission statements to fantasy fiction.

Because I situate this project firmly within the context of cultural studies, two classic works have been fundamental to it: Richard Altick's monumental *Shows of London* and Asa Briggs's *Victorian Things*. Altick's conviction that the movement from eighteenth- to nineteenth-century visual culture was marked by a rupture, a shift from the "age of exhibitions" to the "age of public museums," and Briggs's sense, in the spirit of Marx, that objects rivaled personal relations in importance in the nineteenth century are foundational to my study.[9] Both catalogic works capture the age's exuberance for its rich visual culture; both share the presiding spirit of cultural studies in their interest in everyday life, material culture, and cultural settings. My work intersects with studies on the urban environment and urban projects, restructurings, and experiences—a diverse body of scholarship that includes Judith Walkowitz's examination of Victorian urban sexuality, *City of Dreadful Night,* Christine Boyer's more expansive *City of Collective Memory,* Susan Buck-Morss's *Dialectics of Seeing,* and Deborah Nord's study of women in the city, *Walking the Victorian Streets.* My work shares with these studies a curiosity about the individual in history, the subject within the context of the collective and communal. Of course, my work is indebted to museum studies, and here the Smithsonian Press has been invaluable. In particular, *Exhibiting Cultures,* edited by Ivan Karp and Steven Lavine, and *Museums and Communities,* edited by Karp, Lavine, and Christine Kreamer, have clarified for me the central issues in museology today. I have also turned to studies on curatorial practice and the museum's history: Kenneth Hudson's *Museums of Influence,* Peter Vergo's *New Museology,* Daniel Sherman and Irit Rogoff's *MuseumCulture,* Andrew McClellan's *Inventing the Louvre,* Eilean Hooper-Greenhill's *Museums and the Shaping of Knowledge,* Paula Findlen's *Possessing Nature,* and Tony Bennett's *Birth of the Museum.*

This study is distinctive, however, in its concentration on nineteenth-century London and its museums. My combined interest in the social functions and the literary representations of Victorian museums also marks fresh terrain this book will travel. I hope my reader will hear both less familiar voices, such as those of Moncure Conway, Thomas Greenwood, and the curator Henry Cole, and more recognizable voices in new ways, for the museum offers a broadly ranged register for the age. Its influence can serve to contextualize John Ruskin's educative mission in *Deucalion* (1886), in which he outlines his ideal geology museum "for working men at Sheffield"[10]—a plan that would inform his founding of Saint George's Museum in Sheffield, which partially realized Ruskin's larger hope for a world rich in museums: "I heartily wish there were already, as one day there must be, large educational museums in every district of London, freely open every day, and well lighted and warm at night, with all furniture of comfort, and full aids for the use of their contents by all classes."[11] But the work of the museum can also help to explain Henry Mayhew's sheer delight in the Crystal Palace's ordered abundance, a delight that produced his delirious novelistic rendering of the Great Exhibition, *1851: or, The Adventures of Mr. and Mrs. Cursty Sand-*

boys. The cultural optimism invested in museums, it might be argued, fuels even the countercultural Oscar Wilde in his rare poetic creation, the catalogic Sphinx that lurks in the corner of his college room, as well as in his construction of Dorian Gray's collector's house, a rarefied palace of art carefully transposed from the pages of South Kensington guidebooks. Certainly the earnest dicta in "Advice to Collectors," which Charles Darwin appended to his *Narrative of the Surveying Voyages of Adventure and Beagle* (1839), stand in endless negotiations with the larger context of nineteenth-century museum culture. As one of the age's most celebrated collectors, Darwin appropriately ends his travel romance offering practical advice on such matters as the numbering of specimens, boxing, preserving, cataloging, and storing—a formula, in effect, for ensuring a nation of collectors, a collective identity fashioned after the collector's own image.

The central dilemma of all scholarly projects—what to include, what to exclude—was intensified for mine, the very topic of which heightens the complexities of selection and organization. Because of the proliferation of museums in the nineteenth century, I have had to limit discussion to certain key London museums, despite the very real, very Victorian commitment to founding museums in the provinces and the colonies. Although many museums will arise in the literary texts I examine, I focus on the house-museum of Sir John Soane, the Natural History Museum, and the exemplary South Kensington; Kenneth Hudson has identified the Natural History Museum and the South Kensington as two of the three "museums of influence"—and the only two that remained on site in London—that arose during Victoria's reign.[12] Furthermore, these three institutions represent a range of types of museums, with nuances among their missions and interests, yet in their shared metropolitan site they permit me to explore connections among museums, urbanism, and modernity. My intent is not to provide a full history of each institution but to study patterns of development and isolate issues that preoccupy museum enthusiasts. Arguments are like museums in that they function as exhibited collections, as select appropriations that serve partially obscured and partially admitted agendas; thus an overview of my interests here may help to guide my reader.

In chapter 1 I contextualize the museum within the rich visual culture of Victorian London. Edward FitzGerald's *Rubáiyát of Omar*

Khayyám, as both a cultural object and a literary text, is the focus of my second chapter. As that characteristically nineteenth-century figure, the collector, FitzGerald offers a distinct inroad into the phenomenon of a collecting culture. In chapters 3 and 4, I examine how the concerns of nineteenth-century fiction, particularly realism, collide with the ambitions of the museum in order to produce new readings of such texts as *Jane Eyre, Our Mutual Friend,* and *Middlemarch.* As narrative attempts to represent and use the museum for its own purposes, elective affinities emerge: a preoccupation with the individual, an investigation into crises of identity, a study of the construction of suitable homes and home cultures as well as the founding of communities. Chapter 5 treats Victorian poets who saw in the museum, in the very collection of works of art, an analogy with their plight as artists in the marketplace. In this chapter and throughout the book, although the genres discussed shift, the space of the museum repeatedly links itself to other, key interlocking spaces—home, empire, city, and marketplace. Indeed, empire provides the focus of chapter 6, where I return to narrative to discuss the charged fantasy of the museum in imperialist boy fiction. The museum's role in the construction of imperial myth allows me to examine more fully what I have introduced here as the essential ties between museums and utopia, a kinship that stands in rich counterpoint to other, dystopic representations of museums that I discuss in chapter 7. The project concludes with a coda on Sigmund Freud, who—as a cusp figure—shows that the enterprise of collecting is as suggestive about modernism as it is about Victorianism. This coda underscores a foundational point of my entire study: that museums and modernity are inextricable, that museums represent an institutional response to—or a collective making sense of—the immensity of a radically and rapidly changing world order. Perhaps within the collection-filled space of Freud's study, we can tease out the implications of Henry James's fondness for "the hard *modern* twinkle of the roof of the Crystal Palace" (emphasis mine).[13]

In determining what a museum is, I prefer the modern definition in the *Oxford English Dictionary,* "a building . . . used as a repository for the preservation and exhibition of objects," to the antiquated and literal rendering, "house of the Muses." The British Museum, founded in 1753, was the latter kind, a gentlemen's retreat that for much of the nineteenth century resisted becoming a Victorian or modern (that is, accessible) museum. Indeed, I concur with Philip Fisher's sense of the museum as a "form of access" to "the critical history and display of the total past," for access is the defining feature of modern museums.[14] My working definition of the museum, however, continues beyond these minimal descriptions to identify it as a complex civic space, open to the people and often endorsed by the government, that purports to be the site of origins, continuities, and traditions yet is equally the site of ruptures, fractures, and conflicts. At times I will move outside the museum's walls, to explore what André Malraux calls the "museum without walls," to investigate the collecting enterprises of the street, the home, and the empire. More often, however, I stay within the museum's walls to determine the meaning of those very boundaries and of the many encoded messages within. The museum offers a visual experience, made possible by its constituent parts—paths, rooms, crowds, displayed objects, frames, labels, cordons, lighting, guards, and guides—that invariably becomes a cultural experience. Thus the institution contributes to the life of the individual, altering the formulations for family, romance, childhood, gender—that is, culture.

This book has a central premise: the nineteenth century gave birth to the modern museum. Victorian culture was a museum culture brought to fruition by key political events and social and cultural forces: the British involvement in imperialism, exploration, and tourism; advances in science and changing attitudes about knowledge; the nationalist commitment to improved public taste through mass education; the growing hegemony of the middle class and the subsequent insurgence of bourgeois fetishism and commodity culture; and the democratization of luxury engendered by the French Revolution and the industrial revolution. As Georges Bataille has provocatively claimed, "The origin of the modern museum is . . . linked to the development of the guillotine."[15] Bataille makes a crucial point here: the museum, as much as the guillotine, was the people's instrument of power. It was a symbol of the new order, another specular site around which the people rallied. Indeed, in 1793 Napoleon's renovations transformed the king's palace into the Louvre, the "people's palace," as contemporary sources so aptly renamed it. The archive's doors swung wide, and many people and many nations, Britain included, could now witness, better yet own, and even reproduce the formerly untouchable masterpieces of aristocratic Europe. Whether through the tour package, the art market, or the assembly line, Britain could enjoy the pleasures of having. If Britain could not buy it, Britain could manufacture it. So museums, particularly the South Kensington, often functioned not only as the house of Britain's new properties but also as the showcase of Britain's confidence in its own industrial and mechanical ingenuity.[16] Here was the dawn of reproducibility.

Techniques of reproduction were one of the main achievements of the industrial revolution; and the Great Exhibition of 1851, the pre-eminent palace of industry, was a shrine to manufactured things. The Great Exhibition taught the public how to see the world in a new way, through things and the value of things. In this earthly paradise industry became a kind of art and commerce a kind of culture; and the exhibition was the apogee of this culture industry. The exhibition demonstrated that bigger and more were better and that power was shifting along country lines. In large measure, this British-cum-international exhibition was a nationalist attempt to surpass the earlier French exhibitions, which had been merely national in scope. The Society of Arts, led by Prince Albert, planned the Great Exhibition as a showcase for Britain's rich, infinite productions and reproductions. To many of its 6,039,195 visitors, the Great Exhibition must have appeared as it did to their queen in her thirty-four visits: "a wonderful spectacle," "one of the wonders of the world," "a dream."[17] As the prototype for many Victorian museums and as the precursor to the South Kensington Museum, the Great Exhibition—and its fetishizing of commodities—promoted museum culture.[18] After the exhibition's five-and-a-half-month reign, the public and officials alike clamored for this temporary exhibit to become a permanent dimension of their lives and culture. And permanent it became, providing the seed money and core collection for the South Kensington, influencing the museology of other institutions, and reopening its own doors in the suburbs of London. Until 1937, when it was destroyed by fire, the transported Crystal Palace provided edification and entertainment to countless visitors in Sydenham.

But the museum's affiliation with the guillotine also exposes its foundations in fear, fear of the mob. The new order was magnificent, but was it unruly? Increasingly powerful lower classes were cause for consternation: Could an insurrection like the French Revolution happen on British shores? Would the age, as its greatest sages wondered, witness culture or anarchy? Revolution (Chartism and reform in England) had resulted in a class system that needed to be constructed, legitimated, and monitored. In "On the Extent and Aims of a National Museum of Natural History" (1862) the curator Richard Owen argued that museums were the best means by which to stave off revolution in England. So too does it seem significant that Madame Tussaud began her waxworks in England exhibiting the victims and leaders of the French Revolution. Owen and Tussaud seemed to know that turning political threat into a spectacle would disarm it. Public collections could be a safety valve, an elaborate crowd-control device that became part of Victoria and Albert's master plan of mass education in taste. The museum's ability to consolidate the mob into the public did not elude *Punch* when, in 1851, it allowed Young Mob, "the better-behaved son of a wild and ignorant father," Old Mob, to speak for himself and attest to his newly found civility: "Am I not seen with my wife and children wondering at MR. LAYARD'S Nineveh Marbles—wondering quietly, and I will add, if you please, reverently? Have I, in fact, chipped the nose of any statue? Have I wrenched the little finger from any mummy? Have I pocketed a single medal? . . . Do I scratch RAPHAEL in the National Gallery?" [19] Again, Taine's understanding of the museum as a tool of the regime is germane. The museum is the space in which humankind masters nature, as Taine readily acknowledges; however (and this is his subtler point), it is also the space in which men master other men. [20] Although the museum seemed democratic in ethos, it generated new oppressions in its wake. It is a central paradox of the museum that, like a stern but beneficent god, it both giveth and taketh away.

The museum served to legitimate Britain's power at home and across the globe. It grew complicit with British imperialism, housing the spoils of colonization and guarding the growing perimeter of the British empire. One thinks of the enriching of the British Museum's African collections following the Benin Raid, showcased in the museum's 1897 exhibit of ivories and bronze plaques; the 1890 *Stanley and African* exhibition; or the 1899–1900 *British, Boer, and Black in Savage South Africa* exhibition. [21] But perhaps the ties between collecting and empire are nowhere more strongly felt than in Victorian Britain's possession of India. For example, the South Kensington both inaugurated a program of art schools and museums in India and, beginning in 1879, showcased the collections transferred from the defunct India Museum in well-timed, official fashion to Queen Victoria's having become empress of India three years earlier. Henry Cole's preface to the *Catalogue of the Objects of Indian Art Exhibited in the South Kensington Museum* (1874) opens boldly: "Apart from any other consideration the possession of British India will always place England among the foremost nations of the world." Cole goes on to argue that the British must come to the South Kensington's India collections to learn more about their empire in order to rule more effectively. Nor can England ignore that, according to Cole, "a knowledge of the artistic resources of India may bear not inconsiderably on the commercial interests of this country and of the East." For many, there was "no better university in which to study India" than this London collection. Moncure Conway, whose *Travels in South Kensington* (1882) I now quote, could believe with impunity that "it is wonderful, indeed, that it should be left to this age and to England to appreciate the romance of the East, and to revise, correct, and estimate the traditions of the Oriental world." Whenever a culture travels, it collects. Whenever a culture tours, it appropriates—whether it be Lord Elgin and his pilfered marbles or an anonymous citizen back from Cook's Tours with souvenirs in his or her pocket. As the age of expeditions both grand and humble, the nineteenth century fulfilled its nouveau noblesse oblige in its museums. Most curators of the age readily acknowledged that it was Britain's imperial obligation to collect in order to exhibit. Owen claimed, "The greatest commercial and colonizing empire of the world can take her own befitting course for ennobling herself with that material symbol of advance in the march of civilization which a Public Museum of Natural History embodies."[22] And when Taine states that the Crystal Palace consists "of a museum of the Middle Ages; of a Revival museum; of an Egyptian museum; of a Nineveh museum; of an Indian museum; of a reproduction of a Pompeian house; of a reproduction of the Alhambra," he is characterizing Britain's collections as a virtual embarrassment of riches (232).[23]

The museum is an expression of an age equally giddy and anxious, an age that succeeded many revolutions (and that assimilated the revolutionary programs of literary romanticism, as we shall see in chapter 5), had access to many old things, and produced many new things. Such is

Fig. 1. "All the World Going to See the Great Exhibition," 1851, by George Cruikshank for *1851: or, The Adventures of Mr. and Mrs. Cursty Sandboys* by Henry Mayhew. (Courtesy of Norman Fox, Adler Collection, Skidmore College)

the trajectory implied in the space between George Cruikshank's opening and closing illustrations for Mayhew's *1851* (figs. 1 and 2). One might say that, together, these images construct a fable for museum culture. Cruikshank's first illustration offers a geopolitical vision of the world commercially and imperially remapped, with London playing host. As the Union Jack flies over the North and South Poles (for the British have the world covered), London becomes the "Crystal focus" of the world, the crown of the globe's literally brighter and hence implicitly better

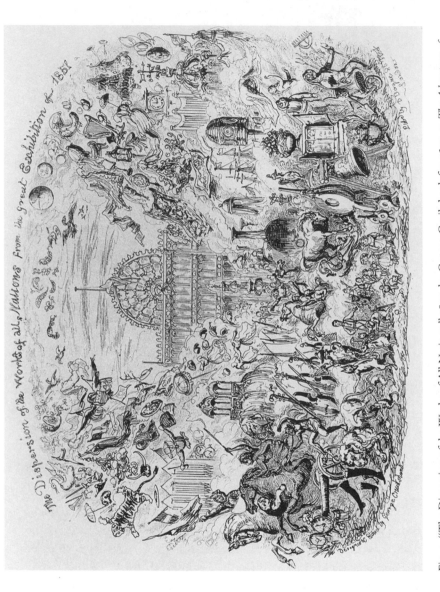

Fig. 2. "The Dispersion of the Works of All Nations," 1851, by George Cruikshank for 1851: or, The Adventures of Mr. and Mrs. Cursty Sandboys by Henry Mayhew. (Courtesy of Norman Fox, Adler Collection, Skidmore College)

hemisphere to which all races—in all manner of conveyance and forsaking all type of abode—run. Working one's way up the globe from the South Pole, one can chart the march of civilization: the exhibition hall itself replaces pyramids and pagodas; tribes become crowds, and native dress becomes westernized; the steamer supplants camels and elephants—only itself to be replaced farther north by the train. With all the world gone to the Great Exhibition, a new vision of that world emerges, a world of objects produced, collected, and consumed. Hence Cruikshank's final virtuosic strokes envisioning a globe peopled by things give us a visual rendering of the commodity fetishism, the fascination with plenitude and surplus, at the heart of Victorian material culture. Behind the museum lies the exciting and unnerving question: what does one do with all the things of the world?

Perhaps this was the question most fully embraced by Darwin and by Victorian science more broadly. Like museology, Victorian positivism and Darwinism represent a response of control and order to the specter of chaos. Beyond his encouragement of the nineteenth-century cult of collecting and his assistance in stockpiling civic collections, Darwin had strong ties to the museum. When he writes in *On the Origin of Species by Means of Natural Selection* (1859) that "the crust of the earth with its embedded remains must not be looked at as a well-filled museum, but as a poor collection made at hazard and at rare intervals," Darwin makes room for his science to become the museum, the archive that will "clear away the mist" and illuminate "that mystery of mysteries." It is precisely the rich, mysterious variations in orchids that promise them to be an intriguing object of study for Darwin; in short, their inscrutable intricacy makes them a delight to see and to know. Darwin's expertise in morphology permits him to detect time and again the form, the kind, the origin of species; moreover, his focus on homology enables him to uncover "the connecting links" that help explain, make sense of, and order the seemingly teeming abundance of the unknown natural world. Darwin's rallying cry to the would-be collector—"as long as due steps are taken that the harvest may not be spoiled, let him not be disheartened, because he may for a long time be labouring by himself; let him work hard from morning to night"—arises from the pleasures of knowing that he articulates so eloquently: "The map of the world ceases to be a blank; it becomes a picture full of the most varied and animated figures. Each part assumes its true dimensions. . . . Africa, or North and South America, are well-sounding names, and easily pronounced." [24] Such delight in the production and organization of knowledge resembles Owen's turn to John Milton in order to liken his Natural History Museum to "the Paradise in which Adam"

> *Beheld each bird and beast*
> *Approaching two and two . . .*
> *He named them as they passed and understood*
> *Their nature; with such knowledge God endued*
> *His sudden apprehension.*[25]

Victorian science, boasting its epistemological triumph over the immensity of the world, makes all the world a map, a collection of museum labels or exotica familiarized.

Many treatments of the Great Exhibition focus too narrowly on specific items on display—for example, gadgets in Thomas Richards's *The Commodity Culture of Victorian England* and machines in Mayhew's *1851.* But a careful reading of *The Official Descriptive and Illustrated Catalogue of the Great Exhibition* yields the more expansive account of the museum's genealogy that this introduction has attempted to chart. Individual items were less important than what they said about British culture at the time. In other words, exotics were the particular province of the colonies and thus confirmed Britain's position as an imperial power; novelties ensured Britain's right to productive prosperity; gadgets and gimcracks proclaimed Britain's skills in reproduction. Furthermore, the concurrent display of raw materials and machines underscored Britain's supremacy as an industrial power. In short, the birth of the modern museum is historically conditioned. Indeed, such scholars as Germain Bazin in *The Museum Age* and Oliver Impey and Arthur MacGregor in *The Origins of Museums: The Cabinet of Curiosities in Sixteenth and Seventeenth Century Europe* have attributed the invention of museums to other ages, while some scholars—like Warren Muensterberger in *Collecting: An Unruly Passion*—argue that humankind has always collected and will continue to do so. One can construe humankind's existence as a sequence of collections—from the library of Alexandria, to medieval church collections, to Renaissance curiosity cabinets, to the eighteenth-century scholarly collections of Oxford. One can attest to the museum's connections to various forms of imperialism across time, whether they be political, cultural, or intellectual. To insist on the transhistorical nature of collecting, to construe it as impulse or instinct, is certainly fruitful. And I do at times psychologize human acquisitiveness, exploring our need for order or the connections between eroticism and collecting or collecting and anality. But my dominant approach to the museum combines the forces of history with the workings of psyche and culture in order to explore the psychocultural instead of the purely psychological, for a purely psychological approach does not convey the discontinuity the Victorian museum enterprise represents on this continuum of collecting. No other age collected with such a vengeance and to such spectacular proportions. No other age treated the museum as an enterprise. Indeed, only we as collectors today rival the nineteenth century, for the museum is our legacy. An investigation of the museum thus grants us not only historical understanding but also many important self-revelations. In nineteenth-century England we may witness the birth of the modern museum, but in twentieth-century America we watch it endure.

Today in America we live in a culture steeped in Barnum, the Peales, world's fairs, and Disney. In the last few years we have seen highway museums proliferate, rock and roll museumified in Cleveland, the Coca-Cola Museum open in Atlanta, *Batman*'s Joker slash museum masterpieces in countercultural rage (and Batman's later nemesis, Mr. Freeze, target the antiquities wing of the Gotham Museum), the presidential aspirant Ross Perot boast an office-museum that serves to construct the narrative of "the self-made man/cultural hero," the Museum Shop come to infiltrate our malls, the Museum Channel come to enhance our cable packages, and both Holocaust survivors and Native Americans move to occupy space in the center of the museum establishment in order to display their collective histories. What we will come to see is difficult to predict, as computer technology enables museums to go virtual, Bill Gates continues to build the Corbis Collection of reproducible photography and fine-art images—a postmodern museum of copies housed on the Net and in his home "telemuseum"—London's National Gallery becomes accessible on CD-ROM (what Jed Perl in the *New York Times* called "a museum at your fingertips"), and the Louvre opens its doors on the World Wide Web, coming home to us in ways unfathomable to the nineteenth century.[26] But I suspect—or hope—that nothing will

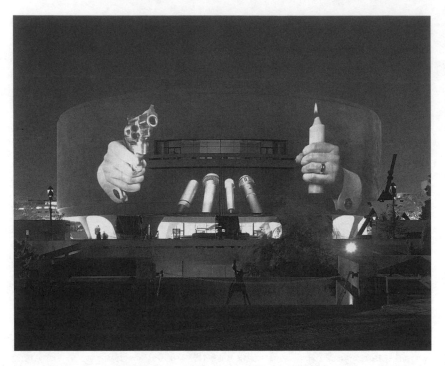

Fig. 3. Projection on the Hirshhorn Museum, October 1988, *Works: Krzysztof Wodiczko.* (Courtesy of the Hirshhorn Museum and Sculpture Garden, Smithsonian Institution. Photograph by Lee Stalsworth)

replace visits to museums, and we will never stop talking about them. Since I began this study of Victorian museums, articles, essays, and books wrestling with the phenomenon of museum culture have multiplied. The gallery is no longer empty. Many know that the museum is a force to be reckoned with, understood, revised, discarded, embraced. As Krzysztof Wodiczko's public-space installation shows (fig. 3), the museum is the keeper of the cultural faith, the bride of the politician, the long arm of the law, the enforcer of opinion. A space such as the facade of the Hirshhorn Museum marks the spot in which we should examine how we vow, affiliate, and commit ourselves to institutional(ized) culture.

The first chapter of this book begins to unearth how complex a force the museum was and continues to be. Here I present a series of anecdotes about specific objects constructed for or as museums in nineteenth-century London, a sort of collection before the main collection, that establishes and clarifies my two central arguments about museums. Here I have also assembled some of the first critical analyses of museums—musings on museums from an array of nineteenth- and twentieth-century thinkers who have speculated on the purposes of museums in both the private and public spheres. These writers form a fascinating "museum crowd," contributing to the frenzy and furor that surround the museum. So, in essence, this book begins with clarification and then moves to deliberate confusion because it is in these many voices, in this avalanche of utterances and equivalences, that the museum's ambiguities become startlingly evident. As the collective voice of these thinkers would conclude, the museum is a whorehouse is a mausoleum is a department store is a secular cathedral is a disease is a glory . . .

I

The Museum Crowd: Fragments Shored against Their Ruin

With conscious proide
I stud insoide.

—William Makepeace Thackeray, "Mr. Molony's Account of the Crystal Palace"

ON 31 DECEMBER 1853 Richard Owen, a scientist and the director of the Natural History Museum in London, invited twenty-one colleagues to a celebratory dinner to take place inside the reconstruction of a dinosaur. This thirty-five-foot-long Iguanodon, one of several dinosaurs built to adorn the grounds at the permanent Crystal Palace in Sydenham, served Prince Albert's plan to memorialize the great achievements of Victorian paleontology. On islands in a six-acre man-made lake equipped with an artificial tide, the dinosaurs posed in simulated habitats in order of their appearance in Britain two hundred to seventy million years earlier. Having discovered the species and named them dinosauria in 1841, Owen was consultant to the sculptor Benjamin Hawkins, who built the dinosaurs to Owen's specifications. The Iguanodon alone required 4 iron columns, 600 bricks, 1,550 tiles, 38 casks of cement, 98 casks of stone, 100 feet of iron hooping, and 20 feet of iron bar. This simulated dinosaur was an immense scientific, technological, and cultural triumph for all concerned. Humankind had resuscitated the dead, and so the fete was planned to mark this great act of salvage.

That evening from the belly of the Iguanodon the geologist Edward Forbes toasted,

The jolly old beast
Is not deceased,
There's life in him again.

An article in *Punch* praised "the company on the era in which they live; for if it had been an early geological period, they might have occupied the Iguanodon's inside without having any dinner there." Victorian science had, in effect, not only rescued but also revised history, replacing the ravages of nature and animal with the triumphs of culture and humankind. Those who would have been devoured could now ingest with relish. As the great chain of being was turned on its head, the *London Quarterly Review* asked the crucial gastronomical question, "Potentates of the Wealdon and Oolite! Saurians and Pterodactyls all! dreamed ye ever, in your ancient festivities, of a race to come . . . dining on your ghosts?" That night in 1853 the scientists, sated with dinner and success, reposed in the belly of the Iguanodon as Owen delivered his after-dinner speech from the dinosaur's skull. The celebration continued late into the night.[1]

This tableau is emblematic of the conquest central to the museum enterprise: through acts of collecting, humankind eviscerates the other and arrogates the seats of life and the mind unto itself.[2] Just as the scientists usurp the space of the prehistoric interior, people repeatedly place themselves in the center of their exhibited collectibles. As Georges Bataille has argued, "The museum is the colossal mirror in which man, finally contemplating himself from all sides, and finding himself literally an object of wonder, abandons himself to the ecstasy expressed in art journalism."[3] Substitute "museology" for "art journalism," and Bataille has paved the way for an understanding of the ecstasy expressed in the museum. This ecstasy relies on a key paradox: the self initially collects out of a curiosity for an other—be it animal, female, primitive, or exotic—yet possession ultimately empowers the self because the very act of collecting demystifies the unknown. Within the museum's walls, the other ultimately serves to reflect the self's glory, as numerous and desirable transformations transpire. Culture triumphs over nature, the mind surpasses the body, the outsider, in all senses of the word—the unprivileged, the marginal, the uninformed—becomes the insider or initiated.

The scientific disemboweling of the Iguanodon suggests yet another, related process central to the Victorian museum enterprise—

montage. The Natural History Museum reconstructs with clay the skull of primitive man based on two "true" fragments; the magnificent Egyptian faces in the British Museum reveal on closer inspection their chipped noses, their fragile ligatures, their missing eyes; in general, museums construct wholes from parts.[4] Owen's reconstruction of the Iguanodon was culturally determined and socially significant—a whole beast, an entire species based on fragmentary knowledge. Although scientists have since outlined Owen's numerous misconstruings and misconstructions, his most curious fabrication lay in the religious imperative that underscored his theory: he believed the dinosaurs to be antediluvian creatures, which, too large for Noah's ark, drowned in the flood instigated by God's potent wrath. Owen hoped that spectators would stand in subdued awe before the spectacle of the doomed prehistoric beast. But his greater ambition was that spectators would understand the beast's doom to be humankind's glory. In this redemptive discovery of dinosaurs humankind had come to know—and be blessed by—the mysterious workings of God and prehistory. Humankind shored up the Iguanodon's ruin against its own ruination, transforming the ruin into the runic. Owen identified the ecstasy located within the reconstituted body—"Crystallised bodies . . . have always attracted the eye and excited the desire of possession"—and claimed, "No triumph of science has appeared more marvelous to the intelligent mind than the reconstruction of a form of life that has passed away long ages ago, and the representation to the visual sense of such [an] animal by its framework, so as to leave little to the imagination in realising a complete idea of the once living figure of the extinct beast."[5] Similarly, whenever humans collect and exhibit, they appropriate the ruins of other times, species, and cultures in order to ensure the survival and transcendence of their own. As Christine Boyer has stated, "to save the past, to turn it inside out, is simultaneously to rescue the present from alienation, boredom, and distraction," for, to quote Roland Barthes, "inventory is never a neutral idea."[6]

The scientists' invasion of the Iguanodon's body—an outsider's attempt to invade the previously unknown interior—presents a configuration that appeared time and again throughout the nineteenth century. On 2 July 1831 the *Times* issued the following announcement: "GIGANTIC WHALE.—There is now exhibiting, in a Pavilion erected for the purpose at Charing-Cross, the skeleton of a whale, of larger dimensions than any that is known ever before to have fallen into the possession of man."[7] Although the *Times* goes on to complain about the steep admission price of two shillings, what became known as the Whale-bone Lounge at Charing Cross Road proved to be a popular attraction (fig. 4). The whale's bony interior boasted a twenty-four piece orchestra, chairs and tables for relaxing conversation, and relevant reading material—copies of Lacépède's *Natural History*.[8] In effect, for the price of admission, one could enter the whale's body transformed into the site of a new body, the human body, and of an alternate intelligence, the human mind. This usurped interior, this fortification for a new master, also housed the new text, the scientific discourse that had mastered nature. Visitors were encouraged to sign a guest book and pen into its annals their own witticisms, new texts all the time multiplying. With Jonah's ordeal far behind, the narrative now stood revised, and Victorian men and women could fearlessly permit the whale to swallow them.

Such an anatomy of spectacle marks an entryway into the Victorian museum and its promised ecstasy. The Iguanodon and the Whale-bone Lounge capture the intense visuality of Victorian London life; these spectacles introduce us to a way of seeing, to the "museum effect," and to museums as they modernized existence in the nineteenth century. Like the city, its inevitable setting, the museum—which Lewis Mumford called "the most typical institution of the metropolis"—was born in a vortex of spectacular growth, erected in the face of the unexampled expansion of the world and the growing unintelligibility of life. In response, the Victorian museum operated on the unshakable intimacy between the urban and the urbane, providing new information to combat new and mounting problems. Like the city in relation to its inhabitants, the museum fed the curiosity of its visitors; given its heterogeneity, the museum could—like a city—satisfy the appetite for novelty as well as for nostalgia. It was, like a city, a site of sociability where—and this seems particularly so at the Whale-bone Lounge—people journeyed to see and be seen. But unlike that metonymic representative of the city, the street, the museum was more than paths, something distinctive from the chaos of city streets, for the museum experience was monitored and controlled.[9] The antithesis of the city, the museum was well-ordered, beautiful, quiet. People went to museums to fight the alienation and isolation that characterized modern urban existence; here the socioeconomic fragments of

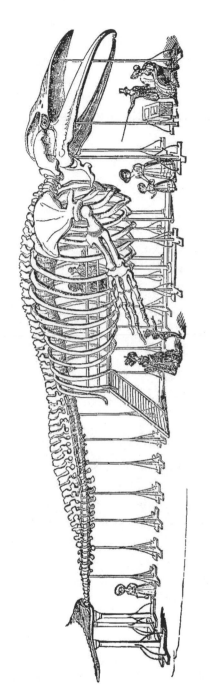

Fig. 4. The Whale-bone Lounge at Charing Cross, 1831, *Mirror of Literature*. (Courtesy of the Guildhall Library, Corporation of London)

class came together as that whole called the public, if one only relinquished a defining feature of the streets, one's autonomy. So much like
the city, so dissimilar to it—either way, the museum is inconceivable
without its modern-city setting. Although I will examine elsewhere the
museum both as utopia and dystopia, it seems necessary to see it initially
for all its complexities, as what Michel Foucault would call a heterotopia.
Foucault explains:

> *Heterotopia is capable of juxtaposing in a single real place several*
> *spaces, several sites that are in themselves incompatible . . . they have a*
> *function in relation to all the space that remains. This function unfolds*
> *between two extreme poles. Either their role is to create a space of illu-*
> *sion that exposes every real space, all the sites inside of which human*
> *life is partitioned, as still more illusory. . . . Or else, on the contrary,*
> *their role is to create a space that is other, another real space, as perfect,*
> *as meticulous, as well arranged as ours is messy, ill constructed, and*
> *jumbled.*

Indeed, Foucault makes the connection explicit: "the idea of accumulat-
ing everything, of establishing a sort of general archive, the will to enclose
in one place all times, all epochs, all forms, all tastes, the idea of consti-
tuting a place of all times that is itself outside of time and inaccessible to
its ravages, the project of organizing in this way a sort of perpetual and
indefinite accumulation of time in an immobile place, this whole idea
belongs to our modernity. The museum and the library are heterotopias
that are proper to western culture of the nineteenth century." [10]

In 1851, London's year of exhibitions, James Wyld, a map and globe
seller as well as geographer to the queen, was justified in hoping that the
outsider would, once again, wish to step inside. Knowing that London
would enjoy a steady stream of sightseers in 1851, Wyld hired one hundred men to build to his specifications a globe seventy feet high and
eighty-eight feet in diameter (fig. 5). Originally planned for inclusion in
the Great Exhibition, Wyld's globe proved too large for the Crystal Palace and was erected at Leicester Square instead. Its interior boasted four
viewing galleries connected by staircases, all surrounded by a ground-
level circular corridor that housed Wyld's maps, models, and plans
(fig. 6). For one shilling a visitor entered this globe turned inside out
through Antarctica and journeyed first to the center of the earth and then

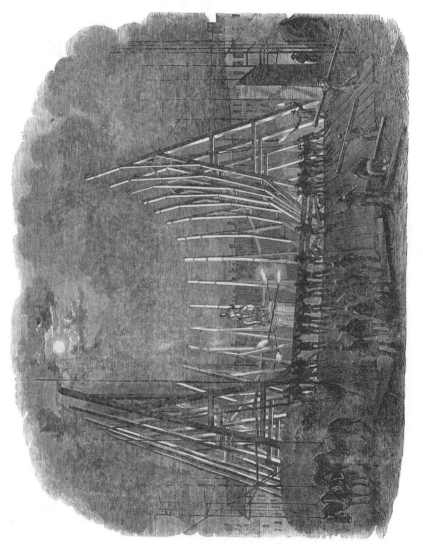

Fig. 5. "Raising the Trusses of the Building in Leicester-Square, for Mr. Wyld's Large Model of the Earth," 1851. (Courtesy of the Illustrated London News Picture Library)

Fig. 6. "Mr. Wyld's Model of the Earth," 1851. (Courtesy of the Illustrated London News Picture Library)

to the top of the globe, enjoying on a scale of ten miles to an inch a vision of the world with topographical detail and tinted hues. Contained within was also a range of temporary exhibits—at times, a diorama of Russia or a simulated gold mine—that attested to Wyld's mixed ambitions to amaze and instruct. Opened a month after the Great Exhibition began and in business for ten years, Wyld's globe was one of the most popular attractions of 1851, second only to the Crystal Palace.

Wyld's globe shared in the spirit of the Great Exhibition. The *Illustrated London News,* for example, praised the swift and ingenious construction of the edifice, claiming that its progress reminded the editors "of that effected in the Great Industrial Palace."[11] Much as the Great Exhibition generated a fast and furious production of text alongside the spectacle, Wyld produced *Notes to Accompany Mr. Wyld's Model of the Earth,* which confirmed and validated his engineering triumph: "Now, for the first time in the annals of English geography, these obstacles to the representation of the earth's surface have been overcome. In MR. WYLD'S GREAT MODEL OF THE GLOBE, the surface being seen from the inside, the eye may take in, by a rapid survey, the whole extent, figure, magnitude, and multifarious features of the world we live in, as if it were one vast plain."[12] Moreover, like the Great Exhibition itself, Wyld's globe seemed to owe its existence to the largesse of a powerful, international England. *Punch's* imagination was drawn to travel Wyld's globe several times, praising it as additional evidence of England's ability to play "host-country" to the world: "The interior should be fitted up as lodgings for foreigners, who . . . might find accommodation on those parts of MR. WYLD'S globe, which correspond with their own places of residence. By this arrangement a foreigner would feel himself perfectly at home, though really abroad."[13] By contrast, Wyld's *Notes* focused on Britain's role as teacher to its own people. With ceremonial seriousness, Wyld maintained that an empire must know the world; thus a defense of his "annotated" globe reads: "As the chief seat of a race to which the largest portion of the earth's surface . . . belongs; as the link between the Old World and the New; and as the centre of the arts of peace London would rightly be chosen as the scene of such an essay. The habits, too, of our population qualify them to appreciate such an undertaking. In London all the wanderers meet, and form part of a vast fluctuating population. And London, as by its population it is the greatest, so, by its situation, it has become the most frequented of the cities of the world" (xii). More than promotional material, Wyld's *Notes* offer a lesson in British imperial geography: we learn about the Hindustan, about the missionaries in Polynesia, about Africa "too little known," "too little civilized," too uninteresting. In a move that would turn out to be prophetic of the century's shift in power, Wyld's *Notes* prove their mettle on demystifying the topography of the United States, particularly the magic of the Mississippi. The States generate more text than any other country except England, which Wyld maps in a way consistent with the construction of England's self-image in 1851 as the country of unsurpassed "internal communication" yet pastoral beauty ("a vast garden"), as a country of cosmopolites, as the "great workshop of the world" (31–33).

But *Punch* found most wondrous the phantasmic excursions made possible by the fact that the world could be found in Leicester Square. Like a museum and much like the century's most enduring spectacle, the panorama, Wyld's globe operated on a dialectic of the miniature and the gigantic. As contemporary accounts suggest time and again, the wonder lay in the exchanges between the singular—that which could be taken in with one glance—and the abundant—that which required a larger scope, such as an "entire range of mountains." In panoramic fashion, Wyld's globe horizontalized experience (all here, all now), collapsing time and space as the "here" became an "everywhere."[14] Thus, with a nod to Milton, *Punch* claimed, "It is most agreeable to stand in the centre of the Earth, and to see yourself surrounded by oceans and continents . . . to drink in with your eyes a whole Atlantic-full of water. . . . All the World is before you; you have only to choose where to go to." The *Times* concurred: "The eye reaches downwards in all directions, and is able to embrace almost the whole surface of the globe. . . . The spectator . . . [is] thus endowed with a kind of ubiquity."[15] Such testimony identifies multiple satisfactions—time travel, fantastic adventure, godlike omniscience. In effect, Wyld's illusion appeared to undo the Copernican revolution: humankind was once again at the center of the universe. The immense, unknowable world was merely the backdrop or container for humanity's "world"-making talents. Encoded within Wyld's successful transformations of the city into the world and London into a world city lies the function of monumentality in city life.[16] That Wyld replaced a sense of placelessness with place is even more fully charged when one considers his globe's site, Leicester Square. In obvious ways, Leicester Square was uncongenial; contemporary accounts commonly called it a "wilderness" or "desert" littered with garbage and haunted by stray cats and ne'er-do-well youths. Wyld's replacing the urban dustheap with a solid foundation of bricks on which to build the world was a literal act of sanitation that, in turn, enabled London to reimagine itself. Here London constructed London for itself and for the world.[17] In effect, Wyld's construction of the globe was surpassed only by his construction of London as a global city.

It is significant that Wyld was a mapmaker by trade. Like other spectacles that promised to map out the world—the Iguanodon, the Whale-bone Lounge, the panorama, Wyld's globe—the museum offered a vision of the world to scale, a one-to-one correspondence between unknown reality and culturally generated representation. The museum wielded the power to transform the terrain of the world so that all territory was knowable and familiar to the home culture, allowing a culture to call the world its own. Thus empires were built on a museum's foundations. Erecting museums is, therefore, always a political act and a hybrid one at that—egalitarian and hegemonic, for even as the museum grants art to the many, it dictates the conquest and appropriation of innumerable, alien others. As Pierre Bourdieu and Alain Darbel claim, "If this is the function of culture, and if the love of art is the clear mark of the chosen, separating, by an invisible and insuperable barrier, those who are touched by it from those who have not received this grace, it is understandable that in the tiniest details of their morphology and their organization, museums betray their true function, which is to reinforce for some the feeling of belonging and for others the feeling of exclusion."[18] The museum both opens up the world and contracts it by assimilating it under one aegis.

By mapping out the world, museums become synonymous with culture. The phrase "museum culture" is thus a tautology, though not an entirely useless one. The collections of a regime are one of the most effective tools of what Norbert Elias has called the "civilizing process." Culture is a relational construct that establishes the boundaries by which a community comes to know itself as distinct from another. The map or the museum not only delineates the lay of the land but also reassures that, at one point, "You Are Here." Elias defines civilization as "the self-consciousness of the West." Later he adds, "The concept of *Kultur* mirrors the self-consciousness of a nation which had constantly to seek out and constitute its boundaries anew, in a political as well as a spiritual sense, and again and again had to ask itself: 'What is really our identity?'" This question articulates Victoria and Albert's central agenda in encouraging their subjects to attend museums and collect in their homes. Museum culture was for the people's own good: possession promised self-possession, or civility. Such cultural optimism informed the lifework of Henry Cole, the first director of the South Kensington Museum. Cole's curatorial aim was to promote what he called "National Culture" and thus repair the low self-esteem of the British.[19] Concerned about Britain's uneducated working classes and its philistine middle classes, Cole believed that his museum would correct the yoked problems of poor production and tasteless consumption. Nowhere was his didactic mission more overt than in the museum's *False Principles,* an exhibit of "samples of decorations of the most costly kind, which had no principles of decoration about them."[20] Known as the museum's "chamber of horrors," this mini-antimuseum of 1853 showcased tastelessness in design in order to admonish the potential producer and consumer alike.

The focus of the South Kensington's collections was what Prince Albert had called "Fine Art Applied to Industry." More specifically, the division of collections, as presented in the museum's first guidebook, illustrates an eclecticism that typifies the institution to this day:

> *The Museum of Ornamental Art*
> *The Educational Collections*
> *The Commissioners of Patents Museum*
> *The Architectural Museum*
> *Sculpture of the United Kingdom*
> *Gallery of British Fine Arts*
> *The Trade Collection [with its focus on imports and exports of the*
>   *world, this section was like a permanent Great Exhibition]*
> *The Economic Museum [familiar objects]*

This list paints a picture of Britain at the time and its preoccupations—Britain, in other words, under construction. The "connexion between art and manufacture," claims the Honorable Robert Lowe, was important "to us, a peculiarly manufacturing nation." Museum officials admitted that the special attention paid to British painting and sculpture helped to correct the notion "that the English have no native taste for art." In 1868 a workingman named Thomas Conolly spoke to the House of Lords about the government's duty to erect more London museums in order to "educate the working classes, making one Englishman equal to two of any other country." [21] In its commitment to founding local museums and in its satellite program, the South Kensington was influential beyond its walls; the museum emerged as a kind of rescue work, an act of social intervention.[22] Known as "a circulating museum," the collections of the South Kensington traveled to the industrial centers of England's north: between 1854 and 1870 Birmingham requested loans from South Kensington's Special Exhibitions ten times; Leeds, seven; Liverpool, eight; Manchester, five; Nottingham, eight; and Sheffield, fourteen.[23]

But at no point did muscology more closely resemble philanthropy than when the South Kensington's continuous renovations literally sent its discarded parts to be reassembled in London's poorest district. Demolition of the Brompton Boilers, the museum's original glass-and-iron structure, had begun in 1864, and on 24 June 1872 the South Kensington opened in East London, rechristened the Bethnal Green Branch. In its new working-class milieu, the museum competed directly with the public house by offering evening hours and specially targeted exhibits that provided "an excellent antidote" to the "peculiar temptations" of the bank holiday.[24] Curious as to the institution's effect, one newspaper sent a "West End flaneur," another a "pilgrim to the Far East," to study the poor in their museum and offer such reports as the following: "There would be hope for the British workman if he took to collecting." [25] As the museum's guidebooks indicate, the focus was on both the relevant and the improved. Thus exhibits featured the principal local trades of weaving and furniture making, and the purpose of the Food Collection, the museum's most popular exhibit, was "to show the nature and sources of the food which we daily use" and to answer the question "what are the substances or elements which, together, constitute my body?" By the turn of the century, for free and daily, visitors could come to the Bethnal Green to learn details about criminal life; they could marvel at the front hall's tiled floor crafted by female prisoners to replicate the design used in the Sheepshanks Gallery in the West End's South Kensington, or they could see "exact specimens of [the criminal] diet."[26] They could also study the mysteries of commerce and trade. Progressive exhibits demonstrated the wonders of production: how to make goods out of waste or how an animal becomes a product. The museum's second most popular collection, Animal Products, featured such items as sharkskin boxes, hair jewelry, feather ornaments, shellwork, and bone chess pieces. Although the basement housed a few exhibits on the rest of the world's cultures, the most important exhibits focused on the body: in addition to the Food Collection, there were exhibits on physiology; the Thames, clean versus dirty water, and disease (especially cholera); London's sewer system, which was replete with filters, chemicals to test for impurities, and residue. This diligent showcasing of hygiene to London's dirtiest— whom one newspaper called "the great unwashed"—facilitated a larger dream of an England consolidated in prosperity. Thus the guidebooks proudly allude to "our national wealth and vast commerce," a key lesson in citizenship offered at the Bethnal Green.[27]

In *Suggestions for Establishing Cheap Popular and Educational Museums of Scientific and Art Collections* (1885) Thomas Laurie claimed that a museum belonged in every town of five hundred or more inhabitants, in every district in London, and throughout the colonial empire. Not surprisingly, his business supplied entire museum outfittings, the centerpiece of which was an enormous diagrammatic display case on the human body—seven feet high, fifteen feet long, one foot deep, and raised one foot from the ground, with simple, large-typeface explanations—which he sold for £75. Laurie explains how the display "stimulates" the observers "in forming aspiring ideals of what might yet be accomplished"; it teaches them the grace and proportion of the human form, contrasting an athlete's arm with a sedentary person's, the stomach of a healthy person with that of a drunkard, the human nervous system with the system of a lower animal species, a Chinese foot distorted through binding with the foot of the Venus de Medici. A magnified model of the skin, moreover, puts dirt itself on display and showcases the importance of frequent cleansing. Laurie's "living temple," much like the (social) body under construction at Bethnal Green, recalls the sanitized bodies of the Iguanodon, the whale of Charing Cross, and Wyld's globe. If the history of civilization is, as Elias suggests, a long-range attempt to discipline the body, the museum's role in perpetuating culture is to regulate the body.

Strewn with incarcerated and antiseptic bodies, the museum becomes for many a house of the dead, a mausoleum. As Theodor Adorno writes, "Museum and mausoleum are connected by more than phonetic association. Museums are like the family sepulchres of works of art." Jean Baudrillard, too, sees the intimacy between collecting and death: "For ethnology to live, its object must die."[28] By shattering the sanctum of the body, the preserve of the hypernatural, the museum asserts the supremacy of the mind. It also asks how best to disinfect the past to serve the present. The bodies of the museum visitors become regulated, disciplined by example and by the codes of conduct the museum enforces. We learn to refrain from touching the works of art, to whisper, to leave the umbrella behind, to respect the cordon, to walk this way or that for best effect, to read the corporate-benefactor plaques. In short, we learn to read and see alike in the museum, which, as a setter of standards, heralds the advent of standardized existence.[29] Perhaps, then, the museum is as powerfully panoptic as it is panoramic. Its ecstasy is a dream not only of comprehensive survey but of total surveillance as well. Indeed, the museum goer goes to see all, but the museum official sees more.

Although Foucault never wrote extensively about the museum, his work offers ample models for a critique of institutionality and an exploration of the history of individual institutions. The museum functions as a pastiche of the institutions Foucault researched—madhouse, school, prison, death house. Critics such as Eugenio Donato and Douglas Crimp have delineated a Foucauldian critique of the museum. Donato explores how the museum is interested in *archēs,* in the origin and order of things. Crimp argues that the museum is one more institution of confinement that constructs one more usable discourse of power. However, in "On the Museum's Ruins," he argues that the museum's love for order is always already undermined. Both writers, in fact, view the museum as an enterprise debased and discredited from its inception. Donato maintains that the museum does not tell us what its function demands it should—information about the objects it exhibits. Rather the museum represents the wish fulfillment of the curator; his order reveals what he wishes it to show. Donato explains that, resting on a central, fragile fiction, the system-building wholes we construct within museums always threaten to fracture back into shards: "The set of objects the Museum displays is sustained only by the fiction that they somehow constitute a coherent representational universe. The fiction is that a repeated metonymic displacement of fragment for totality, object to label, series of objects to series of labels, can still produce a representation which is somehow adequate to a nonlinguistic universe. . . . Should the fiction disappear, there is nothing left of the museum but 'bric-a-brac,' a heap of meaningless and valueless fragments." [30]

Donato and Crimp use this subversion of the museum to prepare the way for their larger critiques of the Enlightenment. Thus their critiques capture the moment when the museum totters between the shrine of Enlightenment thought and the fun house of postmodernism. Certainly, museums rely on the power of reason to make sense of and to order existence. The Great Exhibition of 1851 expressly stood in homage to Victorian progressivism. The displays abundantly revealed England's national prosperity as well as its global patronage. In the Crystal Palace life was good, utopic; things arranged stood for something real and political and magnificent. But the things—the fans, the music boxes, the epergnes—soon ceased to be referents and instead were transformed into things to be reproduced. In its marketing of the "look and feel" of luxury, the Crystal Palace displayed simulation and technique as two of its main attractions. And—as we know in our culture today—debris and wreckage became the necessary, potential risks in a commodity-based, image-saturated culture, for the Crystal Palace displayed not just things but things manufactured quickly and easily—that is, not just the luxurious divan but the papier-mâché luxurious divan. Given the Victorian love of marbleizing, veneering, trompe l'oeil, and plaster, one can see how resonant Donato's sense of the exhibition as bric-a-brac or as a heap truly is. The crucial question arises again: what does one do with all the things of the world?

When Hippolyte-Adolphe Taine discusses the Crystal Palace in *Notes on England,* he, too, sees that simulation is key to its displays. He catalogs the many manufactured points of interest within—the imitation Sphinx, the Iguanodon, the Colosseum-like concert room—and lingers on a reconstructed exotic from America, "the bark of a Sequoia California 450 feet in height and measuring 116 feet in circumference." Taine goes on to describe his fascination with how "the bark is arranged and fastened to an inner framework in such a manner as to give an idea of the tree itself" (233). Based on these exhibitions, Taine draws a comparison between ancient Rome and Victorian Britain that suggests an even more fascinating distinction: "In truth, Rome enriched herself with these things by conquest, England by industry. Thus it is that at Rome the paintings, the statues, were stolen originals, and the monsters, whether rhinoceroses or lions, were perfectly alive and tore human beings to pieces; whereas here the statues are made of plaster and the monsters of goldbeater's skin" (233). Taine's ending phrase, "monsters of goldbeater's skin," recalls the many spectacles mentioned so far—the Iguanodon, the Whale-bone Lounge, and Wyld's great globe—foregrounding the museum's kinship with kitsch and image culture. Goldbeater's skin, the treated animal membrane that allows craftsmen to pound out extra-fine, extra-thin gold leaf, is emblematic of a museum's simulation. It shows how the museum uses and then discards nature (the animal's body) in the service of culture (the artifice of craft). Even though our primary sense of the museum's function is as the house of the eternal, original, and sacred, the museum invariably participates in the culture industry, transforming high culture into low culture in the process of making the unique accessible and domesticated. Such a transformation should not surprise us, living as we do in a culture where museums have become big business, where anyone can purchase his or her own computer-generated *Water Lilies* at the Museum Shop, where the relentless replication of images makes the visual violence of a British Museum visitor's simultaneous view of the Parthenon and, say, the Mona Lisa on the T-shirt of another sightseer a common occurrence. Such logic also informs, for example, many contemporary accounts of Wyld's great globe as providing an adventure that is also "safe" and "easy." Based on Marshall Berman's distinction between modernization as routine and modernization as adventure, one senses here the museum's proximity to postmodernism, which heralds the collapse of the two into routinized adventure. In effect, museums can serve not only a culture's dignity but also its desire for mediated, hence pleasurable frights. (Here the rhinoceros will not tear you.)

When in *Simulations* Baudrillard places the age of the simulacrum after the age of production—that is, after the nineteenth century—his argument misses its temporal mark. The age of the museum's birth, when panoramas could be found even inside cigarette papers, is the true age of the emergent hyperreal. As we have seen, the museum, with its powers of reproducibility, can obscure the distinction between authentic and

sham. This is why Baudrillard uses the museum as a powerful metaphor for existence: "The museum, instead of being circumscribed in a
geometrical location, is now everywhere, like a dimension of life itself"
(15–16). The museum, according to Baudrillard, encapsulates the ascen-
dant artificiality of existence; life itself undergoes a process he coins
"museumification": "It is here, everywhere, in the metropolis, among
the whites, in a world completely catalogued and analysed and then *arti-
ficially revived as though real,* in a world of simulation" (16). Baudrillard's
only mistake is arguing that the museum is a dimension of the "now"
rather than the "now and then," for the Victorian era was the first age of
museumification.

Baudrillard moves on to discuss how psychologically essential museums are to modern culture, but, again, I would argue that his comments
are equally relevant to Victorian culture. Museums are necessary, he
writes, because "we need a visible past, a visible continuum, a visible
myth of origin to reassure us as to our ends" (19). Museums construct
narratives, replete with necessary beginnings and much-cherished end-
ings, that enable cultures to continue. Victorian museums relied on the
stories told by labels, on the linear messages embedded in pediments, on
the progression that tours *through* a collection and *up to* modern times
implied. Furthermore, Victorian museums depended on the assumptions
of nineteenth-century literary realism, on the fidelity to circumstantial
evidence and empirical data (seeing is believing) that makes a culture
avow, "This is how it really happened." In the spirit of montage, the
museum, as it goes *piece by piece,* promises to reveal the *whole* story. The
ramification of not collecting, Baudrillard concludes, is cultural death:
"Our entire linear and accumulative culture would collapse if we could
not stockpile the past in plain view" (19). Cultures rely on "culture-
collecting," to use James Clifford's term.[31] We insist on the death of the
other so that the self can live. As Baudrillard states, "Mummies do not
decay because of worms: they die from being transplanted from a pro-
longed symbolic order, which is master over death and putrescence, on
to an order of history, science and museums." Baudrillard maintains that
we transplant mummies because of an "irreparable violence towards all
secrets, the violence of a civilisation without secrets" (21). Such psychocultural analysis echoes one of my central arguments about museum culture: we envy the insider ("all secrets") and usurp his privileged position,

hoping to forget that we are outsiders ("without secrets"). The museum for Baudrillard is one giant panic attack, an excrescence of our paranoia.

Friedrich Nietzsche turned to the nineteenth century when, in *On the Advantage and Disadvantage of History for Life* (1874), he too viewed museum culture in pathological terms. Nietzsche argues that late-nineteenth-century Germany suffered from an excess of history and from the threat "of perishing through 'history.'"[32] This overdeveloped historical sense not only regulates the body but severely enervates it, disabling it from desiring and acting. The disease of antiquarianism, according to Nietzsche, suppresses the healthy effects of instinct and youth. It turns man into the hollow man, into the man without qualities—a mere spectator at "the feast of a world exhibition" (28). The malaise of modern man is his status as epigone, which fuels his unhealthy love for memory and legacy. Museums satisfy modern man's appetite for memento mori, for he will always construe his race as descendants, "filling and overfilling ourselves with alien ages" and thus transforming ourselves into "walking encyclopedias" (24). The century's museum culture is for Nietzsche a nightmare: "You may well witness the repugnant spectacle of a blind lust for collecting, of a restless raking together of all that once has been" (21). The gallery creates a frisson in him: "So we moderns run through art galleries," and "it is the same absurd method which leads our young painters and sculptors into salons and art galleries" (41, 60). The spectator is a specter: modern men are "pale and feeble late arrivals . . . who eke out a frosty life as antiquarians and grave diggers" (46). The museum becomes for Nietzsche a central expression of his horror, a key constituent in his dystopic vision of modernity and urbanity.

Paul Valéry in "The Problem of Museums" (1923) seems to agree with Nietzsche on the deathly essence of museums. Valéry invites us to accompany him on a very intimate and painful tour through the museum. As his confidants, we must listen to his malaise: "Presently I lose all sense of why I have intruded into this wax-floored solitude, savoring of temple and drawing room, of cemetery and school."[33] Along with Valéry, we too must feel the "cold confusion" of the museum qua charnel house—"I am lost in a turmoil of frozen beings, each of which demands, all in vain, the abolition of all the others" (202). In the museum, which turns all art into relics, Valéry feels overwhelmed by mortality. To him the museum is the house of violence, the repository of "rarities whose creators wanted each one to be unique. *That picture,* people sometimes say, *KILLS all the others around it*" (204). Just as the art object is violated, so too is the museum visitor, as we witness in the opening of this narrative of assault: "At the first step that I take toward things of beauty, a hand relieves me of my stick, and a notice forbids me to smoke" (202). But Valéry dreads most the later ravagings—what the visitor feels within the walls as the "crushing burden" of a museum's abundance. His first sight of "a dazzling bust appear[ing] between the legs of a bronze athlete" is a deliberately jarring grotesquerie (202). He goes on to describe his exhaustion in "such a domain of incoherence" and finally concludes that "our wealth is a burden and a bewilderment" (205).

Valéry articulates the paradox that has become so central to our own, postmodern existence: in having so much, we have come to have so little; abundance has, in effect, flattened out existence. "Modern man," Valéry writes, is "impoverished by the sheer excess of his riches" (204). Like a thriving whorehouse, the museum insists on promiscuity in its visitor; in turn, like a succubus, the museum inevitably seduces him. Valéry's capitalistic metaphor underscores his sense of the paucity of options, the ineluctability of his destiny: "The museum exerts a constant pull on everything that men can make. It is fed by the creator and the testator. All things end up on the wall or in a glass case. . . . I cannot but think of the bank at a casino, which wins every time" (204–5). Such fatalism leaves Valéry at the end of his tour in extreme fatigue, a fatigue unrelieved by the shock of the street that mingles too readily with his chaotic museum visit; however, he cannot let the paradox or the seduction go.

In another extremely personal essay, "The Fabre Museum" (1938), Valéry almost seems to acknowledge that he may be the beneficiary of a museum's abundance. Here he expresses much of the same dread and horror; however, now such feelings are mingled with love. This essay opens with a sentimental recollection: "It is many a year since I visited the museum at Montpellier where, as a boy, I was to learn my first love of painting."[34] Although Valéry goes on to use many of his characteristic adjectives—"dreary," "dark," and "terrible"—to describe the museum, he recognizes that the museum saved him from the "boredom" of the lycée and its printed texts. Accordingly, his language soon changes to the "lighter and much livelier," the "agreeable," the "delightful." Most

importantly, he confesses that he "lingers," for in the museum he experiences "the joys of wordless contemplation." To the museum where he
has come to life and come of age, Valéry dedicates an essay that resembles
a Wordsworthian return to a formative place, lovingly and lyrically described, or a Proustian immersion in subjectivity. Here, of course, the
force described is not the River Derwent, Tintern Abbey, or a *petite made-
leine;* it is the museum, meticulously recalled by Valéry—for its rooms,
arrangements, picture titles, what he last looked at ("Going out, I would
always give a glance at a charming *Stratonice* by Ingres" [210]).[35] Although
Valéry ended "The Problem of Museums" imagining works of art in a
museum culture as orphaned children, here he conceives of the museum
as a guardian for whom he has "developed a special love."

Valéry's ambivalence toward the museum becomes Adorno's concern in his essay "Valéry Proust Museum." When scholars quote from
this essay, they usually cite the same passage, a passage I have already used
in this chapter: "Museum and mausoleum are connected by more than
phonetic association. Museums are like the family sepulchres of works of
art. They testify to the neutralization of culture. Art treasures are hoarded
in them, and their market value leaves no room for the pleasure of looking at them."[36] Yet the very next lines complicate Adorno's position:
"Nevertheless, that pleasure is dependent on the existence of museums.
Anyone who does not have his own collection (and the great private
collections are becoming rare) can, for the most part, become familiar
with painting and sculpture only in museums" (175). Adorno's "only"
signals that he is far from simply agreeing with Valéry's condemnation
of the museum. In fact, he wants to recognize the beneficence essential
to the museum: it gives all individuals, Valéry included, personal encounters with magnificent art. It seems as if Adorno wants us to recall more
fully the tenderness of Valéry's "Fabre Museum." His own essay is dialogic, presenting the debate about museums as it pits the voice of Valéry
against Valéry's opponent in this case, Marcel Proust—the museum's
advocate. Adorno carefully summarizes each man's feelings, identifying
the strengths of each and insisting at the essay's end that neither is correct
in what he calls "the litigation" and that any compromise between the
positions is impossible. Nevertheless, Adorno leaves such decorous form
behind and goes on to imply where his sympathies lie. He identifies the
dangers inherent in Valéry's rage: "Modernizing the past does it much

violence and little good. But to renounce radically the possibility of experiencing the traditional would be to capitulate to barbarism out of devotion to culture" (176).

Adorno seems to adopt a draconian stance: What choice do we have? Do not the advantages of the museum far outreach its deficiencies? He finds greater truth in Proust's belief that "it is only the death of the work of art in the museum which brings it to life" (182). Later he returns to this paradox: "Works of art can fully embody the *promesse du bonheur* only when they have been uprooted from their native soil and have set out along the path to their own destruction" (185). Adorno agrees with Valéry that works of art are orphaned, yet he reminds us that all classical heroes were motherless: it is precisely this tragic status that yields epic greatness. Adorno concludes that the museum should never be shut and always be taken seriously, for it is often the very force that revitalizes art and culture. The museum seems to function for Adorno as the very center of life, the forum for our struggles and characters. And he begs us not to be ingenuous. Returning to the assault that begins Valéry's essay, Adorno ends with a stern admonishment: "The evil Valéry diagnoses can be avoided only by one who leaves his naïveté outside along with his cane and his umbrella, who knows exactly what he wants, picks out two or three paintings, and concentrates on them as fixedly as if they really were idols" (185).

We thus see that the museum draws its advocates and can stand as the site of potent cultural affirmation. Valéry—at least indirectly—acknowledges some ambivalence toward the museum, while Adorno embraces the conflict wholeheartedly, becoming the museum's champion in the end. Here Walter Benjamin and Adorno form an alliance. Without the essential tragedy—Benjamin might call it the essential comedy—of the museum, our existence would be impoverished. The museum realizes the kind of hope Benjamin sees glimmering in the advance of reproducibility. The public museum opens art to the many, freeing it from the shrine and the ritual, insisting that the masterpiece be copied and possessed many times over. It invites student-copyists into its galleries, photographers into its halls, buyers into its shops. For many Victorian writers museums were the great sign of cultural health. The museum was the space not of the dead body, the regulated body, the specular body, the hollow body but of the productive and reproductive social body. Many Victorian men and women felt that the museum was cause for pure optimism. About her own "world exhibition," Queen Victoria exclaimed, "The triumph is immense!" And *The Official Descriptive and Illustrated Catalogue of the Great Exhibition* opens with the proclamation: "It may be said without presumption, that an event like this Exhibition could not have taken place at any earlier period, and perhaps not among any other people than ourselves." Even in the twentieth century, André Malraux argued most unequivocally that "a museum is one of the places that show man at his noblest." [37]

My hope is that the writings of this museum crowd of critics begin to chart the complexities of the museum enterprise. Indeed, museums can be the site of cultural pessimism, even cultural despair, as well as cultural confidence. They can be held responsible for both the disenchantment and the enchantment of the world. In *Worthy Monuments* Daniel Sherman grants museums this complexity: the museum "would in the long run embody the imperfections as well as the highest aspirations of its creators." [38] Accordingly, I aim to explore the museum as a complex civic space involved in the exotic, the urban, the collective, the maneuverings of politics and desire, and the workings of the past, present, and future. The museum's paradoxical functions within the public and private spheres will become increasingly apparent through my readings, and I can only suggest them now through a catalog of oppositional terms: inclusion and exclusion, preservation and dissemination, the aura and what Benjamin identifies as the withering of the aura, recollection and effacement, the monumental and the miniature, order and abundance, death and life, colony and home, egalitarianism and hegemony. In the midst of these shifting functions, however, my central argument persists: museums are fragments shored against a culture's ruin. In other words, whether nurturing the nostalgia of Sir John Soane or showcasing the progressivism of the South Kensington, whether they be home to silver or dinosaurs, museums generate a sense of belonging; part of a culture's strategy of survival, museums participate in the construction of national identity. Of course, I am not the first to make this argument. Carol Duncan has written a book-length study on museums and "the ritual of citizenship"; Hans Haacke has conceived of museums as "managers of consciousness."

Benedict Anderson has argued for the connections between museums
and nationalism and has claimed that in the museum one witnesses "political inheriting at work." But it is the profound vision of the nineteenth-
century bourgeoisie in Marx's *Communist Manifesto* that most compels
us to take a close look at the cultural function of museums. As much as
it is explicitly concerned with manufacture, the *Communist Manifesto* is
implicitly concerned with institutions of cultural production like the
museum. In the museum the bourgeoisie "creates a world after its own
image." Here we have "intercourse in every direction, universal inter-
dependence of nations" where "national one-sidedness and narrow-
mindedness become more and more impossible."[39] On the steps of the
museum arises the first global, modern society.

Certainly, Thomas Hardy understood this when in "The Fiddler of
the Reels" (1893), his tale set during the Great Exhibition, he called 1851
"a precipice in time," "a sudden bringing together of ancient and modern
in absolute contact."[40] And it seems fitting that the last public ceremony
performed by Queen Victoria, the first monarch of a modernized society,
was laying the cornerstone in the newly expanded South Kensington,
renamed for posterity the Victoria and Albert Museum. Avid museum
goer and presiding genius alongside Prince Albert of the Great Exhibition, Queen Victoria, whose image was often replicated and collected by
her subjects, was most significantly a collector herself. Biographies and
letters describe the leisure time she devoted to gallery hunting in Florence, her attendance at Madame Tussaud's and various shows of freaks
and the bizarre, and her purchases at Royal Academy exhibitions of miniatures, which she used to outfit the interiors of her residences, and of
paintings, which she and Albert loved to exchange.[41] But it is Lytton
Strachey's infamous portrait of Victoria that most powerfully construes
her as a collector within her home, having begun her most urgent collecting for therapeutic reasons after the death of Prince Albert. Strachey
portrays a domestic Victoria ensconced in her acquisitions:

> *There, in drawer after drawer, in wardrobe after wardrobe, reposed*
> *the dresses of seventy years. But not only the dresses—the furs and*
> *the mantles and subsidiary frills and the muffs and the parasols and the*
> *bonnets—all were ranged in chronological order, dated and complete.*
> *A great cupboard was devoted to the dolls; in the china-room at Wind-*

sor a special table held the mugs of her childhood, and her children's
mugs as well. Mementoes of the past surrounded her in serried accumu-
lations. In every room the tables were powdered thick with the photo-
graphs of relatives; their portraits, revealing them at all ages, covered the
walls; their figures, in solid marble, rose up from pedestals, or gleamed
from brackets in the form of gold and silver statuettes. The dead, in
every shape—in miniatures, in porcelain, in enormous life-size oil-
paintings—were perpetually about her.[42]

Strachey deliberately overwrites this passage because, having identified collecting as definitively Victorian, he chooses it as a target for his
invective against the Victorians. To Strachey the enterprise of collecting
captures the excesses of an unattractive age, yet he in turn seems capti-
vated by a particular sense of time and history that informs the work
of his Victorian collector. Despite his bias, Strachey portrays a Victoria
who illuminates the dialectic of past and present at play within Victorian
museum culture. "Over this enormous mass," Strachey continues, "she
exercised an unceasing and minute supervision, and the arrangement
and the contemplation of it, in all its details, filled her with an intimate
satisfaction" (239). Strachey identifies how the collected mass satisfies a
curator's compulsion to order and control, thereby suggesting that collection is an allegory of memory, an experiment in recollection in which,
as Robert Harbison has pointed out, "reverence for the past cannot disguise
the present's power over it," for, as Christine Boyer has argued, monuments and commemoration "are the past we still experience in the present."[43] Strachey concludes that Victoria was obsessed with collecting her
life in order to preserve her life: "Nothing should ever move—neither
the past nor the present—and she herself least of all!" (240). Recollecting
was endurance—"Might even death itself be humbled, if one could recall
enough?" (242). And recollecting was erotic, even necrophiliac. (We all
have heard accounts of how, after Albert's death, Victoria placed a photograph of her husband above every bed she slept in and how she insisted
his meals be arranged each day and his clothes laid out each evening.)
Through a pursuit that seems simultaneously her pathos and her glory,
her sickness and her cure, Victoria continued to sleep, eat, and live with
Albert. Strachey implicitly insists that her collections were a source of
narcissistic pleasure: "When she considered the multitudinous objects

which belonged to her, or, better still, when, choosing out some section of them as the fancy took her, she actually savoured the vivid richness of their individual qualities, she saw herself deliciously reflected from a million facets, felt herself magnified miraculously over a boundless area, and was well pleased" (239–40).

This wondrous reflection of Queen Victoria in her collectibles, her godlike pleasure with her creation, is this chapter's final emblem of the usurped interior and the reconstituted fragment. The detail of the million identical images thrown back by a million facets suggests simultaneously the fracture and the totality central to the museum enterprise. It also suggests the museum's ecstasy, a word I privilege in this chapter for its richness, for its lighter and darker nuances. Furthermore, this icon of the cultural narcissist radiates with both wonder and resonance, two key terms I borrow from Stephen Greenblatt's apologia for New Historicism, "Resonance and Wonder"—an apologia that ends up being a meditation on museums. By *resonance* Greenblatt means "the intertwining voices," the "historical memory," the "ethnographic thickness" that we have come to identify as the New Historicist's discovery. *Wonder,* by contrast, is the "enchanted looking" that "stills all murmuring voices."[44] In an unacknowledged nod to Thomas Carlyle, Greenblatt seems eager to retrieve the retrograde value of sheer wonder. In fact, he argues, wonder is the very desire that generates one's search for resonance, and, thus he concludes, wonder must come first. In effect, this book on Victorian museum culture begins by upholding Greenblatt's defense of wonder in order to return to Carlyle's celebration of wonder, wonder that fired the faith and eagerness of Thomas Macaulay's historiography, *History of England,* a text that cannot resist curating the past and praising the present as the copia—as the museum with its commemorative pageants, memorial records, and monumental taxonomies—of all that has come before. It begins by upholding wonder in order to match the wonder Victorian society felt for the spectacular Iguanodon, the Whale-bone Lounge, Wyld's great globe, the queen's collections, for its own mirror image in contrast to Macaulay's England of 1685. These visions were the secular miracles of the age. It then moves through resonance, directed by New Historicism itself, to investigate the museum as the site of cultural negotiations. In fact, this chapter's museum crowd constitutes the "murmur-

ing voices" that will be "still[ed]" by wonder. But the book ends recom-
mitted to wonder, insisting that readers become even more fascinated
with the museum precisely because of its multivalence. This is the ecstasy
of the museum, and it necessitates not only our skepticism but also our
enthusiasm.

II

Fugitive Articulation of an
All-Obliterated Tongue: Edward
FitzGerald's *Rubáiyát of
Omar Khayyám* and the
Politics of Collecting

Or whether I am Omar.
Have I a country at all?

—Ezra
Pound,
Letters

*Omar Khayyám's position as a poet is curious. He
was never very popular in his native Persia; and he
exists in the West in a translation that is really a complete reworking of his verses, in many cases very different from the spirit (to say nothing of the content) of
the original. I, too, am a translated man. I have been
borne across.*

—Salman
Rushdie,
Shame

IN 1934 EZRA POUND issued a challenge: "Try to find out why the
FitzGerald *Rubáiyát* has gone into so many editions after having lain un-
noticed until Rossetti found a pile of remaindered copies on a second-
hand bookstall."[1] Yet another challenge lies in understanding this poem's
status in the academy today. Infrequently taught, rarely discussed, Edward FitzGerald's *Rubáiyát of Omar Khayyám* now lies, once again, "un-
noticed." For many academics today the proverbial wisdom of the
Rubáiyát has grown clichéd, and its literary and cultural significance is
as too well known as the legend of its discovery.[2] But, as the *Rubáiyát* has

become a predictable text to us, our response to it has turned predictable. Most readers explain its undeniable popularity by contextualizing it within the increasingly nihilistic and decadent culture of late-Victorian society—the product, in other words, of a protoaesthete's sensibility. For example, Frank Kermode writes, "These are G. M. Young's 'years of division,' the frontier between two Victorian ages; and the *Rubáiyát* belongs to the hither, nastier side." The poem's early admirers were the Pre-Raphaelites and their sympathizers, premature souls of the fin de siècle who, overwhelmed by the aged world, saw in FitzGerald's translation an invitation to escape. In his 1985 biography of FitzGerald, Robert Bernard Martin upholds this standard explanation of the *Rubáiyát's* popularity, calling the poem "a repudiation of traditional religious morality and the attempt to find an alternative to it." Daniel Schenker, in "Fugitive Articulation: An Introduction to the *Rubáiyát of Omar Khayyám,*" identifies the poem's appeal to its readers as "infinite resignation made simple."[3]

Schenker grants this standard reading new life, however, when he assesses the *Rubáiyát* as a cultural compendium of the age. In short, the poem's comprehensiveness—not merely its ennui—ensures its popularity: "The *Rubáiyát* is perhaps the archetypal Victorian poem. Those 101 quatrains have a little bit of everything from the nineteenth century: dramatic speech, mysticism, *Weltschmerz,* sentimentality, Manfred, epicureanism, the palette of Rossetti and Burne-Jones, the 'melancholy, long, withdrawing roar' of the sea in Dover Beach."[4] Schenker's sense of the age's archetype is, however, incomplete. Like most critics, Schenker overlooks how the *Rubáiyát* may be the manifestation of the equally compelling Victorian enthusiasm most pertinent to this study—not the love of sadness but the love of collecting. FitzGerald's *Rubáiyát* draws our attention to a central cultural enterprise in the nineteenth century, the erecting of grand civic collections or museums. It is this context of Victorian museum culture that, bolstered by an imperious and often imperial sense of its own mission, can recharge the *Rubáiyát's* legendary appeal. For the *Rubáiyát,* in its status as both translation and collected text, illustrates the fate of the acquisition in Victorian museum culture. Initially, the Victorian man of letters FitzGerald is drawn to Khayyám's rubaiyat for their strangeness; yet, ultimately, he proceeds to transfigure the quatrains, preparing them for popular consumption. The *Rubáiyát,* then, as both an exotic wonder and a tamed, familiarized object, becomes one of the age's most vivid examples of the domesticated exotic. Serving the paradoxical purpose of collectibles, it at once satisfies the possessor's curiosity for the strange and confirms his superiority. In his self-professed violent co-optation of the Oriental, FitzGerald offers a case study of the Victorian collector that illuminates the activities of the nineteenth-century collecting populace at large and, ultimately, demonstrates how the *Rubáiyát,* as curiosity or curio, can become once again for us a curious piece.

As such titles as *With Friends Possessed,* by Robert Bernard Martin, and *FitzGerald to His Friends,* edited by Alethea Hayter, suggest, it has long been a critical commonplace to situate FitzGerald among friends. A study of his correspondence, however, reveals him more at home among objects, on which he loved to gaze and which he desired to possess. His letters document with what unceasing delight he attended, and paid attention to, public collections—he refers to visits to London's National Gallery, assesses each year's Royal Academy Exhibition, and expresses his affection for "my dear Crystal Palace," where he could go in pursuit of "just the thing!"[5] His exchanges with his dear friend Bernard Barton read like a tireless cataloging of art purchases and reviews of individual paintings, painters, exhibitions, and museums. And the great homes did not fail to tantalize him with their collections: FitzGerald could not resist the duke of Bedford's Woburn Abbey and its Canaletti or Corsham Court, whose pictures are in his view "well worth seeing" (2:515). But best of all, FitzGerald enjoyed Luton Park: "I have been to see Lord Bute's place. . . . The collection of pictures is almost the best I have seen" (1:259). Such endless discriminations, such expressions of wonder characterize a way of life made possible by the Victorian fascination with the accumulation and display of material culture. The rival delights found in excess and order inform both FitzGerald's life as a collector and the culture rich with museums in which he lived.

Representative of his class, FitzGerald eagerly brought the enterprise of the museum home with him. A haunter of pawnshop, department store, and gallery, he boasted that his house, Little Grange, was "a wonderful Museum of such scraps"; and his correspondence confirms how thrilled he was with every purchase of art for the home, which gave him what he calls in one letter "all the throes of imprudent pleasure." As a collector, FitzGerald nurtured a passion for things exotic. From the Chi-

nese flowering trees at Sydenham Palace to the Eastern texts he translated, the Oriental fueled a fire in FitzGerald that had started long before
when a childhood friend, the Anglo-Indian Major Moor, introduced
him to the allure of the East. Moor would recount his Eastern adventures
to the young FitzGerald and boast about his collections of Oriental god
figures, "which he eventually immured in a pyramidal mausoleum near
his front drive." [6] Throughout his life FitzGerald preferred fantastic and
exotic literature, shunning the writers of home epics, marriage plots, and
everyday life in a country village: "I never could read Miss Austen, nor
(later) the famous George Eliot. Give me People, Places, and Things,
which I don't and can't see" (3:642). About his translations of Eastern
texts, FitzGerald often expressed the need to keep the "Oriental *Forms*"
authentic, uninfected by Europe or by the nineteenth century (2:164). [7]

   To George Crabbe the younger in 1862 FitzGerald described a trip
to London's Baker Street Bazaar: I "spent what Time and Money I had
in the new Chinese Department, where I bought a heap of Things. . . .
[I] like Oriental Things: their quaint shapes, fine Colours, and musky
sandal-wood Scents; and though I do not so much look at these things
individually, yet their Presence in the Room creates a cheerfulness which
is good as one grows old, blind, deaf, and dull." [8] FitzGerald's use for these
acquisitions is suggestive: acquired to be gazed on, the collection promises the collector a new scene, a better world, or at least an improved
atmosphere; and the heap, the sheer quantity, affords greater satisfaction.
Elsewhere FitzGerald boasts: "You should see my little Room—filling
with the most wonderful Gewgaws. . . . I shall have samples of China,
Greece, Italy, etc., all mixed" (2:425). His home acquisitions reveal Fitz-
Gerald to be a striking composite of the provincial and the cosmopolitan.
His mix is international, yet the scene of his pleasure is always one's little
room. [9] In effect, his life aspired to be what his translation of the *Rubáiyát*
so successfully embodied: exotic domesticity. Although he traveled little,
was intensely nationalistic, and lived a circumscribed existence, FitzGerald demanded his adventures, albeit tamed and at home. In a revealing
query to a friend, he writes, "Does the thought ever strike you, when
looking at pictures in a house, that you are to run and jump at one, and
go right through it into some behind-scene world on the other side?"
(1:295). To FitzGerald, the otherworld was safely intriguing when it lay
on the other side of one's room. Thus this definitive armchair traveler

went to work on the *Rubáiyát,* packaging the Orient for all the world's homebodies, for, as we shall see, the *Rubáiyát* is about home more than anything else.

FitzGerald's literary activities were also those of a collector. Apparently less motivated by the greatness awarded to originality than by the power derived from acts of ordering, clarification, and transmission, he aspired to be an exhibitor of words. One of his earliest productions, *Polonius: A Collection of Wise Saws and Modern Instances* (1852), was a compilation of contemporary adages. He kept many scrapbooks, some devoted to recording the lives and deaths of Newgate criminals and others to cataloging English sea words and the vocabularies of rustic dialects. FitzGerald recorded the many hours he spent in the British Museum in a commonplace book called "Museum Book," a collection of extracts from English authors and sketches of sixteenth- and seventeenth-century costume. Less interested in his own status as an author, FitzGerald busied himself collecting other authors. Besides Khayyám, he translated Sophocles, Aeschylus, the Persian Jámi, and Calderón; other authors he hoped to present anew in improved, often abbreviated editions. He wished to publish a collection of John Dryden's best prefaces. His admiration of Madame de Sévigné's letters manifested itself in a dictionary of her dramatis personae. And he condensed Charles Lamb's life into a calendar of significant dates and events. *Clarissa* he longed to cut.

Cutting, or "tesselation," as he called it, was often an integral, if odd, part of FitzGerald's acquisitions. His literary adaptations, abbreviations, and translations were cuttings, in effect, because he usually wished to condense first and compile later. And he frequently cut the pictures he purchased: "I have been playing wonderful Tricks with the Pictures I have: have cut the Magi in two—making two very good Pictures, I assure you; and cutting off the dark corners of other Pictures with *Gold Ovals*—a shape I like within a Square, and doing away with much Black background" (2:459). This voice that delights in its own impudence is familiar to readers of FitzGerald's correspondence. Elsewhere he defies his friends' displeasure with his tessellations, claiming "considerable Pleasure" with his own "handywork": "I dare say you won't like all my Cuttings down of Pictures—covering up the dark sides with golden Spandrils, etc. But I am sure these Pictures are so much darker than when painted: and I prefer Gold to Blackness. Besides, Encrease of Frame, if it may hide and huddle part of a Picture, makes the rest look more precious" (2:460). One biographer uncritically refers to FitzGerald's proclivity to rip out pages from books he collected.[10] Such visions of the collector, however, are disturbing in their implication that, for FitzGerald, possession does not mandate the obligation to preserve but rather promises a delightful awareness of prerogative. And it was to this man, at home among his collections, hard at work collecting words and acquiring things exotic, that Khayyám's rubaiyat came in 1856—yet another possession that FitzGerald would claim to have "ingeniously tesselated."

Edward Cowell, FitzGerald's friend and a professional orientalist, had first encouraged FitzGerald in his Persian grammar lessons and later introduced him to the poetry of Omar Khayyám, a Persian astronomer and mathematician who lived from 1048 to 1131. Cowell discovered Khayyám's rubaiyat, or quatrains, in the Ouseley manuscript in the Bodleian Library, transcribed the 158 quatrains, and, ultimately, sent his transcription to FitzGerald. The ruba'i was a verse form popular among Persian academics and laymen. Believed to have originated in the ninth or tenth century, the ruba'i established a highly conventionalized, oral tradition that showcased a poet's skill and versatility. Usually extemporaneous, the ruba'i commemorated an occasion or articulated a passing idea. The oral nature of the verse obscures its original purpose; however, some scholars conjecture that Persian teachers composed rubaiyat as entertaining interludes to long lectures. Many maintain that such is the origin of the rubaiyat of Khayyám, who rarely committed his thoughts, poetic or academic, to paper. It was rather his followers and their followers who compiled his verse into collections. And it was FitzGerald, armed with his "Moving Finger [that] writes," who inscribed Khayyám most indelibly on the page. While Cowell published a scholarly essay on Khayyám, FitzGerald went to work on the translation that Alfred, Lord Tennyson would extol as a "golden Eastern lay" and James Merrill would later praise as "Omar's honeyed pages"—an adaptation of the Persian rubaiyat that would become "one of the world's most popular books." [11]

Scholars such as Edward Heron-Allen at the turn of the century and Arthur Arberry in the twentieth century have detailed FitzGerald's many alterations of Khayyám. Arberry conveniently summarizes Heron-Allen's findings: "49 of the stanzas are more or less faithful renderings of single quatrains, or parts of them; 44 are contaminations of more than one quatrain; several belong to other poets; and 3 cannot be traced to any known original." FitzGerald's most extensive renovation involved reconstituting what he considered Khayyám's fragments into a westernized whole. To FitzGerald the discursiveness of the Eastern manuscript was initially enchanting and yet ultimately aggravating. About his Persian original Fitz-Gerald boasted, "It has amused me however to reduce the Mass into something of an Artistic Shape" (2:260). Under the guise of salvaging Khayyám, FitzGerald discarded his pyrotechnic versatility in order to construct what he called "a sort of Epicurean Eclogue in a Persian Garden." At the expense of a variety that struck him as disorder, he insisted on highlighting an epicurean theme that was consistent with what Edward Said has identified as "the free-floating mythology of the Orient" central to nineteenth-century orientalism. To the Victorian audience, Said writes, "an Oriental lives in the Orient, he lives a life of Oriental ease, in a state of Oriental despotism and sensuality, imbued with a feeling of Oriental fatalism." [12] Such prescriptions underscore the accommodated, cliché-ridden nature of FitzGerald's confinement of Khayyám to beautiful sadness and blissful languor.

Unity through the theme of epicureanism alone, however, did not satisfy FitzGerald. Sensing the rubaiyat's lack of shape, he transformed Khayyám's self-contained quatrains into a narrative complete with beginning, transitions, and closure: "It is an amusement to me to take what liberties I like with these Persians, who (as I think) are not Poets to frighten one from such excursions, and who really do want a little Art to shape them." [13] FitzGerald reconceived Khayyám's fragments as the story of a soul despairing and submitting during the course of a day that opens with dawn, "Wake! For the Sun," and closes with night, "Yon rising Moon." [14] By contrast, Khayyám interspersed his quatrains with numerous aubades, refusing to be restricted to any one day. FitzGerald's transitional words map out the linearity of the verses: by beginning quatrains with "Indeed," "And," "But," "So," and "Then," he establishes their interconnectedness and indicates that the poem's sum is, indeed, greater than its parts. FitzGerald's *Rubáiyát* even boasts an inset tale, the narrative of the pots in stanzas 82 through 90. Having imposed plot on the epigrammatic rubaiyat, FitzGerald transformed the verse into a linear, written text, thereby altering the nature of one's reading experience of Khayyám. In effect, FitzGerald's Khayyám became something much more familiar to Victorian audiences, who favored collections of narrativized lyric like Tennyson's *In Memoriam A. H. H.* and Dante Gabriel Rossetti's *The House of Life*.[15]

FitzGerald also liberally censored Khayyám, achieving unity by homogenizing Khayyám's tone and excising his bawdiness. According to FitzGerald's stereotyping, an Oriental languishes rather than laughs; thus Khayyám's humor seemed inappropriate to FitzGerald. For example, FitzGerald omitted the following ruba'i, which Arberry in his 1952 literal translation thus transcribed:

> *Henceforth I'll strut before my home,*
> *A wine-jug on my topmost lock;*
> *And if they take me for a cock,*
> *Why, they can make a saw my comb.*

(101)[16]

Khayyám's pose as a braggadocio is too carnivalesque for FitzGerald's rarefied Eastern meditation. FitzGerald repeatedly prettified and thus softened the agon with mortality central to the Persian original. For example, Khayyám's voice is at times urgent:

> *I pressed my lip against the bowl*
> *In an extremity of greed,*
> *Seeking to snatch my ardent need,*
> *Long life for my too fleeting soul.*

(127)

Undoing the "ardent need," FitzGerald by contrast demurs, "Then to the Lip of this poor earthen Urn / I lean'd, the Secret of my Life to learn" (35). While Khayyám presses and seeks, FitzGerald leans. FitzGerald also modulated Khayyám's Dionysiac abandon. For Khayyám the theophanic moment comes in inebriation:

> *Last evening, drunken with good sack,*
> *I passed the tavern open wide*
> *And there a bearded elder spied*
> *Drunk, and a wine-jug on his back.*

(107)

But for FitzGerald revelation occurs in sobriety, and the drunken old man turns into an "Angel Shape":

And lately, by the Tavern Door agape,
(58)   *Came shining through the Dusk an Angel Shape*
Bearing a Vessel on his Shoulder.

FitzGerald's Persian-garden setting westernizes or, more accurately, anglicizes Khayyám's bleaker setting in "this desert place" (233). While Khayyám speaks of mountains, meadows, and the surge, FitzGerald alludes to multiple "garden-sides." FitzGerald's setting is a domestic landscape, more logically an English than a Persian garden. His lovers are protected "underneath the Bough" of a British tree in the translation's most famous quatrain, 12. Moreover, FitzGerald omits all references to Khayyám's young boy lover, which would have been deemed unacceptable in Victorian verse.[17] For Khayyám the presence of the boy's body serves as the vehicle for the playfulness and liveliness of his rubaiyat. The "lucky-footed lad" is the primary reason for Khayyám's exuberance: "With shining lads in boyhood's bloom / Drink wine, where shining roses glow" (221). Khayyám's invocation to the boy, "The dawn is in the sky; rise up, / My simple, silly, pretty boy," disappears from FitzGerald's translation (99). Whereas Khayyám apostrophizes the "soft down . . . / of buried beauty" (125), thus praising synecdochically boy love, FitzGerald ungenders the line into "once lovely Lip" (20).

The paradox of the collectible remains: boy love is part of the East's allure, part of its otherness, for FitzGerald and other Western writers like Sir Richard Burton working within the conventions of Victorian orientalist poetry. Yet FitzGerald must ultimately suppress the homoerotic as well as de-emphasize the orgiastically heteroerotic elements of his original, for Khayyám also confesses an appetite for a plurality of maidens: "Tis better to be drinking all / The day, and pretty maids to love" (194). In short, the home culture must triumph; the heterosexual monogamy of FitzGerald's "Beloved" and "I" must prevail. FitzGerald, in fact, censors Khayyám's general fascination with the body. While Khayyám repeatedly refers to his own aging body as a grotesquerie—"my rounded paunch will gape," "my hairs are hoary white," "my old brow's weary frown," and "my shrunk and weary thighs" (110, 117, 118)—FitzGerald's meditation on mortality oddly omits the body. The physicality of FitzGerald's *Rubáiyát* is minimal, at most aestheticized into murmuring lips and moving fingers.

Revisions such as these, one might argue, are a necessary part of any translation. One writer on translation, Reuben Brower, condones such activity: "We translate the less familiar by putting the more familiar in its place."[18] All learning, he concludes, is translation of sorts: we assimilate the unknown by familiarizing it. But FitzGerald's *Rubáiyát* is a special, and especially problematic, case. This becomes clear in the light of recent work in translation studies that exposes the political, often combative nature of translation as the confrontation of one culture with another.[19] One translation theorist quotes Victor Hugo: "When you offer a translation to a nation, that nation will almost always look on the translation as an act of violence against itself. . . . There is . . . a violation of frontiers." A claim such as Nietzsche's about ancient Rome—"at that time translation meant to conquer"—prompts us to make distinctions among translations based on the significance of translation at a given time or the social and historical contexts that inform each act of translation.[20] One must also consider the translatability of a language at any given time, for, although translation is always executed by those who know for those who do not, the status of Persian in the nineteenth century would make it more remote, and thus more vulnerable, than German, for example. And one must examine the translator's motives and attitude toward a source text. Of the two models for translation, authority over or fidelity and responsibility to the text, FitzGerald seems to fit the former.[21] A member of what translation theorists label the hegemonic language and culture, FitzGerald assumes a paternalistic pose as the civilizer or improver of the dominated language and culture, Khayyám's Persian.

Although critics have construed FitzGerald's revisions as mistranslations, errors attributable to his inadequate knowledge of Persian, FitzGerald, as we have seen, freely co-opts his acquisitions. His numerous bold assertions concerning his translations bear witness to his sense of triumph. Even about his restoration of Calderón, who would have enjoyed greater status at the time than Khayyám, FitzGerald writes, "Scarce a Plank remains of the original . . . all done to conciliate English, or modern, Sympathy."[22] He repeatedly condemns oriental languages as "obscure," "unreadable," and "sadly defective." After completing his translation of Khayyám, FitzGerald boasts to Cowell: "It seemed to me that I really had brought in nearly all worth remembering and had really condensed the whole into a much compacter Image than the original.

This is what I think I can do, with such discursive things, such as all the Oriental things I have seen are."[23] His repeated use of the possessive in discussing Khayyám—"But in truth I take old Omar rather more as my property"[24]—and his discourse of rape—"having done my Will for the present with the *Mantic*" (2:264)—are politically charged. An incident FitzGerald confesses to Barton is especially revealing: "I have had a sneaking desire to keep the picture [a Gainsborough] by me, and not to lose it from my eyes just yet. I am in love with it. I washed it myself very carefully with only sweet salad oil . . . and that, with the new lining and the varnishing, has at least made the difference between a dirty and a clean beauty. . . . I believe I should like it all the better for its being a little fatherless bastard which I have picked up in the streets, and made clean and comfortable" (1:292). Sporting a patronage that has turned all too quickly patronizing, perhaps FitzGerald conceived of his Khayyám in similar fashion, as a "little fatherless bastard," as a dirty beauty that, peripheral to the hearth, needed the cleansing of domestication. FitzGerald's paternalism grows all the more disturbing when juxtaposed to his other guises as lover, violator, and prettifier.[25] His choice of language, such as the phrase "pretty impudence" to describe a translation or the words "Tricks," "Frippery," and "sneaking desire" to characterize his revisions, exposes the kinship for FitzGerald among aesthetics, aggression, and transgression.[26]

These improvements partake in a cultural imperialism intimately linked to Victorian imperialism. A member of an imagined community, FitzGerald reconstitutes Khayyám's fragments in a fashion parallel to the way Victorian Britain constructed India or Nigeria.[27] As Said maintains, "Nearly every nineteenth-century writer . . . was extraordinarily well aware of the fact of empire."[28] It is no surprise that Burton was an early admirer of the *Rubáiyát* or that he encouraged the founding of the Omar Khayyám Club of America.[29] Nor is it surprising that the text Cowell gave to FitzGerald was based on a manuscript found by Sir Gore Ouseley while on political duty as ambassador to Persia under King George III. An instance of what we call popular imperialism, FitzGerald's transfiguration of Khayyám demonstrates how the enterprise of empire building thrived in the home culture. The collection and preservation of the *Rubáiyát* demonstrate one culture's hegemony over another. And the *Ru-*

báiyát was besieged twice, through two acts of collecting. First, FitzGerald claimed Khayyám's verse as his own through translation. Then, his transfigured Khayyám was discovered and collected by a populace equally desirous of unusual acquisitions.

In 1859 the publisher Bernard Quaritch printed 250 copies of Fitz-Gerald's *Rubáiyát*. Unable to sell them at a shilling a copy, however, he was forced after a year to reduce his price and consign the *Rubáiyát* to his penny remainder box. It was here that in 1861 the Celtic scholar Whitley Stokes discovered the anonymous, obscure poem and gave it to Rossetti, who read it with delight and recommended it to Algernon Charles Swinburne, John Ruskin, and William Morris. When Rossetti went back the next day to buy more copies, Quaritch had shrewdly raised his price. Thus a phenomenon one could call the Fitz-Omar craze had begun. During FitzGerald's lifetime the poem went through two more editions (1872, 1879), largely to satisfy American demand, for his fame had become transatlantic. After the turn of the century Heron-Allen was able to gloat in his introduction to the 1910 Dodge edition of the *Rubáiyát*, "A copy of this first edition was sold at auction on the 10th of February 1898, to Mr. Quaritch for £21, and I have received an offer from America for £45 for a copy." In 1901 a Massachusetts publisher sold twenty-two copies of a twelve-volume set of FitzGerald's complete works for twelve thousand dollars a set.[30]

The sheer number of editions of the *Rubáiyát* that line library shelves today dramatically attests to the poem's cult following in the nineteenth and early twentieth centuries. Everyone seemed to own a copy of the *Rubáiyát;* it had become a household name and Fitz-Omar, a household god. As Arberry claims, "There can scarcely be a household in all Britain which has not at some time possessed a copy in some shape or form." His paean continues, "British soldiers have taken it with them into action in two world wars." A bibliography compiled in 1929 cites 586 editions of the *Rubáiyát* worldwide.[31] From 1880 to 1923 Houghton Mifflin sold 43,112 copies of the *Rubáiyát* in six editions. In advertising its selection of editions—the folio, gilt top for $25.00; the smaller quarto, gilt top for $12.50; the 16mo, uncut for $1.50; and the Red-Line Edition for $1.00—the publisher acknowledged the poem's wide-ranging readership. The many inscriptions inside the books' covers attest to the poem's status as a gift book among family and friends. Elaborately designed gilt covers (sometimes encrusted with stones and protected by miniature locks, both simulated and real) and ornamental title pages indicate the poem's status as treasure book. The tables of contents display the variety of apparatuses that embellish the poem—biographical prefaces; FitzGerald's preface on Khayyám's life; critical introductions and notes; rich color illustrations; descriptions and sketches of Khayyám's grave; comparative inquiries into FitzGerald's revisions; encomiums to Fitz-Omar composed by appreciative reader-converts—all evidence of the poem's status as a compelling curiosity.[32]

The poem's remarkable reception continued in the founding of Omar Khayyám Clubs in both England (1892) and America (1900); the presence of such learned societies proved that Khayyám had become the object of systematic accumulation. Members included such eminent figures as Arthur Wing Pinero, George Meredith, Thomas Hardy, Arthur Conan Doyle, Lawrence Alma-Tadema, and Edmund Gosse—a club president. At meetings the members attended Persian dinners and displayed their collected Eastern exotica as well as their bejeweled, miniature copies of the *Rubáiyát*. The academy, too, became interested in the *Rubáiyát*. In the wake of FitzGerald's publication, newly discovered manuscripts purported to be authentic Khayyámic verse multiplied. This Khayyámic furor elicited both intense enthusiasm and grave mistrust among orientalists, historians, and theologians. A long, embattled critical tradition continuing until the 1970s ensued over the legitimacy of FitzGerald's translation and those of his supposed correctors.[33] Meanwhile, the *Rubáiyát* inspired other artistic creations: choreography by Isadora Duncan, song cycles, a parody by Rudyard Kipling, and poems by T. S. Eliot.

The *Rubáiyát*'s critical reception repeats the pattern of its popular consumption, perhaps most evident in the self-satisfied body of Western criticism the *Rubáiyát* has generated and sustained. The most frequent image critics use to discuss the *Rubáiyát,* the gem—whether it be "a jewel," "a Persian pearl," or "a ruby in a ring of gold"—encapsulates the poem's problematic status in a museum culture.[34] Although this metaphor of the gem connotes the poem's talismanic value, its small dimensions delineate what Susan Stewart calls "collapsed significance."[35] Susceptible to a miniaturizing that is consistent with the popular miniature packaging of the *Rubáiyát,* this poem's value becomes inseparable from its pretty, crafted, possessable diminutiveness. Khayyám's verse remains entrenched in the categorically Oriental, in the land of seers and Eastern serenity; it persists, a bit of wisdom literature that one can hold in one's hand. Other critics have appropriated the *Rubáiyát* by de-emphasizing its otherness and focusing instead on the familiarity, even the topicality and novelty, of FitzGerald's translation.[36] In 1869, in the first American review of the *Rubáiyát,* for example, Charles Eliot Norton claimed that "in its English dress it reads like the latest and freshest expression of the perplexity and of the doubt of the generation to which we ourselves belong." In 1921 the scholar Hugh Walker called the *Rubáiyát* "a 'criticism of life,' not in some far-off country and among unfamiliar men, but here and now."[37] And John Hay, speaking to the Omar Khayyám Club in 1897, asserted that between the two poets there was "no longer any comparison": "Omar sang to a half barbarous province; FitzGerald to the world."[38] Thus, the question of territoriality, so central to translation, has been resolved: Khayyám has crossed the border; the alien tongue has become the domestic word; the Persian import has yielded one of Britain's greatest exports to the world.[39]

The implications of the *Rubáiyát's* reception are as revealing as those of its translation: Khayyám's rubaiyat became thoroughly objectified—on the one hand, the idol of a cultic popular enthusiasm and, on the other, the grounds for many a specialist's expertise. The poem's reception history indicates that possessing the text was as important as reading it, if not more so. The thrill involved in possession is consistent with the rhetoric of conquest that characterizes this text's existence in the West. Its reception as treasure book and curio suggests that readers shore up copies not for their ruin but against their ruin. And of this particular use or purpose the *Rubáiyát* itself is strangely proleptic. The translation's most familiar lines recommend collecting the book:

> *A Book of Verses underneath the Bough,*
> *A Jug of Wine, a Loaf of Bread—and Thou*
>   *Beside me singing in the Wilderness—*
> *Oh, Wilderness were Paradise enow!*

In Arberry's translation, Khayyám's ruba'i is simpler and earthier:

Then simple things if they be mine—
  A loaf the purest heart of wheat,
  A thigh of lamb to be my meat,
For thirst a flagon of good wine:
And if, to cheer my wilderness,
  A maid refusing not my kiss,
  That were a life of perfect bliss
No sceptred sultan can possess.

(161)

FitzGerald's most fascinating refinement has again prettified the lines, omitting the reference to the flesh (the thigh of lamb) and offering in its stead a book of verses. Moreover, in FitzGerald's first and second versions of this quatrain, he placed the book of verses in the third position in the lines' opening list. His revisions make the book's presence increasingly dominant. Self-conscious not only about its bookishness but also about its reception, the poem commands to be taken along on picnics and read under boughs. While itself meditating on mortality, the poem as a phenomenon narrates a tale of endurance. The poem overtly endorses "infinite resignation" yet covertly recommends taking the book, reading it in polite company, and surviving long enough to pass it on to others. In effect, the brevity of life jars with the longevity of the text: the poem's nihilistic message clashes with its empowering use.

Walter Benjamin's articulation of the collector's "bliss" in his essay "Unpacking My Library" helps illuminate the triumph behind the seemingly pensive lines of the *Rubáiyát*.[40] Assuring his reader that the collector's mood is "certainly not an elegiac mood but, rather, one of anticipation," Benjamin ascribes to the collector—who lives through his objects—"enchantment," "inspiration," "thrill," and "renewal." He speaks of collecting as a conquest both exotically and erotically charged. In a telling trope that recalls us to Burton's work as a translator, Benjamin compares the purchase of a marketplace item to "the way the prince bought a beautiful slave girl in *The Arabian Nights*": the collector is the dispenser of freedom and captivity alike.[41] Benjamin's fantastic collector embodies "the ardent desire to hold on to it forever" essential to FitzGerald's original appropriation of Khayyám and the subsequent consumption of the translated Khayyám. But far greater than possession of a collectible is its transmissibility, which Benjamin calls a collection's "most distinguished trait." As the transmission of the *Rubáiyát* confirms, the collectible allows everyman the distinction of the legatee, as heir to the remote past or, better yet, to an understanding of that remote past. The heightened intimacy of Benjamin's essay only underscores this point; the setting of a private home, which Benjamin foregrounds at the end, reminds us that here Benjamin is fundamentally concerned with a "dwelling," with the domestic uses for a collection. To envision the *Rubáiyát* in the home, as a drawing-room collectible, shows it at its most powerful. Although in "Fugitive Articulation" Schenker expresses dismay over the *Rubáiyát's* fall from "exotic prophesy to Victorian gimcrack," it is precisely its status as gimcrack, as reproducible and transmissible collectible, that is most significant.

It is, in fact, Schenker's vision of the *Rubáiyát* at home that gives us a most accurate sense of the poem's appeal: "The besieged master or mistress of the house may guiltlessly indulge himself or herself in a momentary escape into [the *Rubáiyát's*] amoral world without husbands or wives or fathers or children or even Englishmen (and yet how English!)." FitzGerald customized Khayyám for home use, or—having relied on Robert B. M. Binning's *Travels in Persia* (1857) for his source on things Persian—he "Orientalized" the Oriental, to use Said's phrase. In other words, the poem's orientalism and fatalism seem necessarily simulated, its Persian airs at best self-conscious. In certain ways, FitzGerald was determined to give an oriental flavor to his *Rubáiyát,* evident in his inclusion of an erudite footnote early in the text, in his use of Persian names in stanza 10 for evocative effect rather than substantive meaning, and in his overwriting of Khayyám's "roof-top of the world" as "The Sultan's Turret." The overly specular presence of the sultan is perpetuated in the illustrations that accompany many editions of the *Rubáiyát.* As Jorge Luis Borges has suggestively claimed, "FitzGerald interpolated, refined, and invented, but his *Rubáiyát* seem to demand that we read them as Persian and ancient."[42] Norton's assertion that the *Rubáiyát* "in its English dress . . . reads like the latest and freshest expression of . . . perplexity" offers a sartorial metaphor that perfectly captures FitzGerald's masquerade; however, it seems more accurate to see FitzGerald's accomplishment as more elaborate: dressing the Englishman in Persian costume or, in minstrel-show fashion, first dressing the Persian in English guise and then demanding a Persian "impersonation." The *Rubáiyát* cannot, in short, divest itself of its oriental drag; its very preciousness is linked to its preciosity. It began its life as kitsch—as recyclable, reproducible exoticism or, as some would claim, "Persianism." Kermode summarizes this point well: "Having left Persian poetry out, FitzGerald was putting English poetry in, and his changes obscurely touch the heart of a people which rarely reads verses and rarely drinks wine. He is exotic without being foreign." Non-English yet so English, not foreign yet so exotic, the *Rubáiyát* becomes what George Steiner has called "instant exotica." [43]

In his 1898 biographical preface to *Rubáiyát of Omar Khayyám,* Michael Kerney wrote about FitzGerald, "the magic of his genius has successfully transplanted into the garden of English poetry exotics that bloom like native flowers." This image of the flower captures the tenuous position of the collectible in a museum culture. Kerney's paradox, this possibility of native exotics, is a striking assertion of the Victorian will to domesticate the exotic. But it is also more than metaphor: while Persia gave to FitzGerald a collector's item in verse, it also relinquished an acquisition equally treasured to the Royal Gardens—rose hips from Khayyám's grave. In 1884 William Simpson, an "artist-traveller" for the *Illustrated London News,* wrote to Mr. Quaritch of his travels and spoils: "In front of Omar Khayyám's tomb I found some rose bushes; it was too late in the season for roses, but a few hips were still remaining, and one or two of these I secured, as well as the leaves,—some of which are here enclosed for you; I hope you will be able to grow them in England; they will have an interest." [44] After grafting at the Royal Gardens, Khayyám's roses were planted on FitzGerald's grave by the Omar Khayyám Club of England on 7 October 1893. Verse commemorated the ceremony:

> *Here, on Fitz-Gerald's grave from Omar's tomb*
> *To lay fit tribute, pilgrim singers flock:*
> *Long with a double fragrance let it bloom,*
> *The rose of Iran on an English stock.* [45]

> *Reign here, triumphant rose from Omar's grave,*
> *Borne by a fakir o'er the Persian wave;*
>   *Reign with fresh pride, since here a heart is sleeping*
> *That double glory to your master gave.*

Hither let many a pilgrim step be bent
To greet the rose re-risen in banishment;
    Here richer crimsons may its cup be keeping
That brimmed it ere from Naishápúr it went.[46]

The *Nation* covered the event, praising Kew Gardens' success as "the English answer to Omar's line, 'The flower that once has blown for ever dies.'" Again, the odd transposition characteristic of Khayyám's fate is evident: Western ingenuity had defied Eastern fatalism, for in response to Omar's line the English answer rings with imperial indomitability. As James Clifford has argued about collecting, "For all its love of the past, [it] gathers futures."[47] Thus the English future is built on the Persian past, its victorious wholeness reconstituted on Persian fragments, whether they be quatrains or rose hips. It is then that the "English answer" articulates the eerie promises of "richer crimsons," "double fragrance," "double glory," and resurrection in banishment that lie behind FitzGerald's *Rubáiyát,* explaining its success and its "Reign here, triumphant."

The deictic force of this final phrase helps to close my argument. Read in light of the interlocking practices of empire building and collecting in order to display, the *Rubáiyát*—in its various stages of translation, consumption, and reception—is a triumphant text, giddy with its own success. Collected and possessed, the *Rubáiyát* was an empowering and powerful text for an entire community, in particular that closer community or mass elite that formed the core, the "club," of appreciative readers. The *Rubáiyát* was fashioned at home and used in the home, its most important milieu. Transported from another world, this domesticated exotic could even construct for its reader a sense of home away from home by confirming the value of the homeland and making all the world an English garden. But it is also in this moment of its greatest force that the *Rubáiyát,* read in the context of Victorian museum culture, seems most sad. Examined for its full cultural progress, the *Rubáiyát* permits a reading against the grain that reveals it to be a far sadder poem than we suspected, giving new meaning to FitzGerald's claim that his translation was "saddest perhaps when most ostentatiously merry."[48] As the epigraphs from Pound and Rushdie that open this chapter suggest, FitzGerald's *Rubáiyát* is a text without a home, a country; "borne across," it is a migrant text, displaced onto the borders, an example of what Homi

Bhabha, borrowing from Freud, calls an "unhomely text" that ultimately rejects the idea of home as specious.[49] Even FitzGerald, in a curious hedge, seems to acknowledge Khayyám's dispossession: "As to old
Omar—I think he has done well, considering that he began his English
Life as an 'Enfant Trouvé'—or rather 'perdu' in Castle Street 15 years
ago."[50] FitzGerald himself is uncertain whether he has found or lost
Khayyám; or perhaps for FitzGerald, Khayyám is refashionable: he is old,
he is "Enfant"; he is "Trouvé" and also "perdu." To adapt in turn Fitz-
Gerald's words to the purpose at hand, the *Rubáiyát* offers the "fugitive
articulation" of an "all-[but]-obliterated tongue." It is for its ghostly presence, for its fleeting and exilic eloquence, that the *Rubáiyát* becomes articulate for us once again. It underscores the political and cultural workings of here and there, of insider and outsider, of inclusion and exclusion
that are central to the act of translation, the making of collections, the
building of museums, the constructing of cultures. For the tale of possession and dispossession it narrates, FitzGerald's *Rubáiyát of Omar Khayyám*
is, once again, a curious piece.

III

Acquired Taste: The Museum Enterprise Comes Home

To this end London established its great School of Design and Decoration. There to have gravitated the fragments of a Past that has crumbled. . . . Her call has gone round the world, and temples and palaces deliver up their treasures that they may gather in London, there to teach the millions how they may beautify the latter-day temple, which is the Home, and refine the latter-day King, which is Man.

—Moncure
Conway,
*Travels
in South
Kensington*

IN 1833 SIR JOHN SOANE, most notable as the architect of the Bank of England, enlisted the aid of Parliament in order to establish his house-museum at Lincoln's Inn Fields as a permanent, public institution. Four years before his death in 1837, Soane succeeded in preserving his private collection as a national trust, thereby benefiting his country while ensuring his own fame as a collector. His house-museum was the culmination of more than thirty years of fervent collecting and continued expanding. His original residence and architectural office were housed in 12 Lincoln's Inn Fields; in 1808 he built an extension behind 13 on the east side and in 1811 transplanted the family domicile to 13. Later, in 1823, Soane executed plans to extend behind 14. Such growing parameters were necessary to hold his diverse and expanding collection. He needed space for the Shakespeare and Tivoli recesses; for the cat, rat, and human skeletons; for the ruins of a monastery as well as the instruments of torture; for the Seti I sarcophagus he purchased from Giovanni Belzoni as well as the exhibit of Napoleona. An overview of the contents of Soane's collection attests to his acquisitiveness:

  313 Greek and Roman marbles
   76 architectural fragments from Renaissance and after
  442 plaster casts from classical and Renaissance originals
   34 models of antique buildings
   50 medieval architectural and decorative fragments
     more than 50 pieces of classical statuary
   38 Egyptian and Graeco-Egyptian items
   31 antique and 24 Renaissance bronzes
   55 works in plaster by sculptor John Flaxman
     gem and medal collections
    6 miscellaneous medieval works
   12 Peruvian pots
   42 Chinese ceramics
    1 volume of Indian miniatures
   30 natural curiosities.[1]

Such an inventory gives some sense of Soane's eccentricity. And yet Soane, I will argue, is representative of a cultural phenomenon that emerged in the early nineteenth century—the dual craze for collecting and exhibiting. Moreover, his life span, 1753–1837, makes him a significant cusp figure, in part continuous with what came before. Moving through his house-museum, through the Monk's Parlour to the Crypt and the Sepulchral Chamber that overlook the Monument Court, one thinks of older aesthetic traditions such as the Gothic and the folly. The sheer variety of the house's contents suggests Soane was a virtuoso or an enthusiast, a descendant of the eighteenth century and Thomas Shadwell's Sir Nicholas Gimcrack. Some might argue that Soane's house-museum is the legacy of an even older tradition: what Mark Girouard calls the "power-houses" of the Renaissance, the *villa-museo,* or the curiosity cabinets enshrined in the manors of nobility. But it is more accurately Pitzhanger Manor, Soane's residence prior to moving to Lincoln's Inn Fields, that can be described as a power house or *villa-museo.* Here Soane functioned as the curator of a familial curiosity cabinet, a purely private collection nestled in the countryside. Here he hoped to found an architectural dynasty, comprising himself and his faithful sons. His dismay over his sons' refusal to become architects compelled him to leave and finally sell Pitzhanger. In effect, when the power to bequeath failed Soane, he turned urban and public simultaneously by moving to Lincoln's Inn Fields.[2] Here he erected a museum, opening it as a school for architectural students unable to study abroad. Here in one house in one city he assembled, both through fragment and in whole through cork and plaster models, the best of the Western world, the gems of Venice, Rome, and ancient Athens (fig. 7). As a distinctly urban and civic site that mixes the public with the private, as a space of not only collection but exhibition, Soane's house-museum, despite its affinities with that which comes before, is characteristically nineteenth-century.

Although elements of Soane's presentation, such as his fanciful juxtapositions and delightful use of mirrors and lighting, suggest a romantic aesthetic concerned with atmosphere and effect, his writings reveal other motives for the construction and arrangement of his collection. In 1830, 1832, and 1835–36 at his own expense Soane published a catalogic guided tour of his house called *Description of the House and Museum*. Changes among the three versions indicate his increasing awareness of audience as well as his growing duty to and ambition for them. Even seemingly minor word variations, such as when Soane changes the 1830 description of the final resting place of the Seti I sarcophagus from "the most *secure* part of my *House*" to, in 1835–36, "a *conspicuous* part of my *Museum*," attest to his developing sense of the curator's educative mission to exhibit rather than to hoard. Soane's other revisions often underscore the key roles ego and nation play in collecting, how in the house-museum the curator and the community he serves and the ideal he honors become central. Soane's nationalism is evident in the 1832 edition's dedication to the duke of Sussex as well as in an addition to his introductory list of motives: "And, lastly, to evince the desire of the Possessor of the Collection to promote, to the utmost of his power, the interests of British Artists." The 1835–36 edition more explicitly honors Soane's achievement, opening with a bust of him as its first plate and closing with a copy of his act transforming the house-museum into a civic institution. Soane's most telling addition in 1835–36, however, is the testimony of his friend Barbara Hofland, whom he identifies simply as "a lady" and whose express purpose is to render "the following pages more pleasing and attractive to young minds." Not only is the inclusion of her commentary evidence of Soane's growing awareness of a wider ranging audience; her "pictorial and poetical remarks" serve as interpretative gloss to

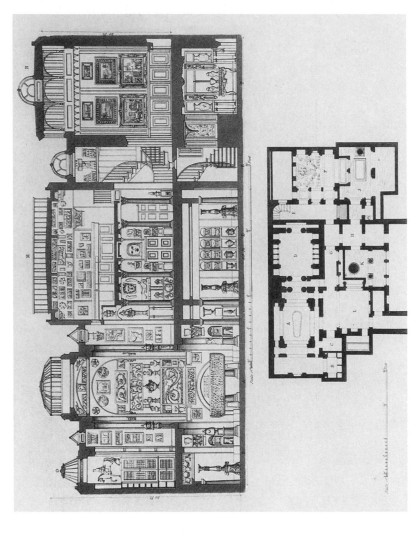

Fig. 7. "Section through the Museum," 1827, from John Britton's *The Union of Architecture, Sculpture, and Painting*. (Courtesy of the Trustees of Sir John Soane's Museum)

Soane's dispassionate, catalogic prose, effusing over his tasteful acquisitions in a way that the curator himself could not.

In his house-museum, Soane was engaged in the parallel tasks of self-construction and boosterism. Anxious about his lineage and uncertain about his posterity, this collector, whom everyone knew to be the "son of a humble bricklayer," used his collections to construct a new identity and a better future for himself. He was a self-made man in a society awakening to the dreams of self-help and social mobility. Wordplay in an article from the *Penny Magazine* in 1837 captures the fairy tale at the heart of the Soane house-museum: "He was the 'architect' of his own fortune: for though, by his marriage, he eventually inherited a considerable property, still he was one of those men who 'make themselves.'" Often praised by his public for managing so "much in little space," Soane impressed the *Penny Magazine* as combating not only the close quarters of an urban dwelling but also the smallness of means and circumstance. To the many Victorians who would later visit his house-museum, Soane was an emblem of the museum enterprise come home. By example, he proved the importance of acquired taste, of tasteful acquisitions in the home and, in his words, championed the ameliorative effect of domestic collecting: "From the general spirit of improvement in every part of the United Kingdom, our houses, with their plaster outsides, will be converted into grand hotels, with facades of solid stone, worthy the metropolis of this mighty empire."[3]

This utopian impulse to turn every house into a museum rather than a castle is the final realization of the ever expanding nineteenth-century dissemination of aristocratic and church art. Just as royal cabinets had relinquished their holdings to museums, civic museums yielded to the homes of the populace. Richard Owen, the curator of the Natural History Museum, was not alone in his hope that museum visitors were themselves collectors and that "the local collector . . . expects or hopes to find, and ought to find, the help and information for which he visits the galleries of a Public Museum." In 1888 Thomas Greenwood included among his "Useful Rules to Keep in Mind on Visiting a Museum" the imperative "Make a private collection of *something*." Several of Greenwood's other memorandums (there are twelve in all) suggest ways of taking the museum home: "5.—Have a note-book with you and record your impressions, so that on a succeeding visit you may pick up your information where you left off on the previous visit. 6.—Introduce in conversation your impressions of what you see in Museums."[4] Evident in such counsel is Greenwood's earnest faith in the museum's promise of civility. Collecting became one of the democratized luxuries the middle class could now afford due to the French Revolution and the industrial revolution. As John Steegman argues in *Victorian Taste: A Study of the Arts and Architecture from 1830 to 1870,* although other ages had collected, the nineteenth century publicized in unprecedented fashion the charms and benefits of collecting. Selling electrotypes, plaster casts, and photographs of everything from Wedgwood to silver to lace, Victorian museums from their inception encouraged the public to take part of the museum home with them. The South Kensington's selection of art for sale was outstanding: "For three or four pounds any museum or private collector may obtain perfect copies of ancient shields, salt-cellars, tankards, tazzas. . . . Franchi's copper-bronze copies at £30 are nearly as good as the originals, which were considered cheap at the £300 paid by the museum." Museum guidebooks were filled with advertisements that described the goods of various importers, thus intensifying the public's desire to own replicas of what they had just seen in the museum. Consider the importer Nosotti's boast of "Gilt *Objets d'art.* Most Extensive collection in the kingdom" or Liberty and Company's advertisement for "aesthetic and eastern art fabrics in characteristic eastern design" or Phillips and Company's claim to be "importers of the finest Teas, Coffees, Cocoas, colonial and continental produce, also of The Faience and Art Manufactures of Japan, China, and India."[5] This alliance of museum, department store, and factory—bolstered by the grand tour's evolution into tourism— made possible the dream Henry Cole cherished in making the Crystal Palace a permanent edifice: to enable "the many to have what the few always have."[6]

Popular styles in home decor, particularly eclecticism and the picturesque, helped to encourage the formation of Victorian house-museums. In *The Art of Decoration* (1881), Mary Haweis offers a lavish list of the requisite objets d'art, recommending a domestic world gone international, a home that is the summa of the world's finest: "Thus a modern eclectic room may admit modern Oriental objects in sufficiently small quantities, Indian, Chinese, African, and the like, modern German,

Swiss, and Russian carving and casts, Italian mosaics, Doulton ware, Minton's china and tiles, and all the best efforts of the nineteenth century." In 1868 Charles Eastlake, the principal apostle of the picturesque or house-beautiful movement, published *Hints on Household Taste,* a manual that counseled on the importance of art in the home. Collecting art at home, argued Eastlake, refines the entire household: "The smallest example of rare old porcelain, of ivory carving, of ancient metalwork, of enamels, of Venetian glass, of anything which illustrates good design and skilful workmanship, should be acquired whenever possible, and treasured with greatest care. It is impossible to overrate the influence which such objects may have in educating the eye to appreciate what really constitutes good art. An Indian ginger-jar, a Flemish beer-jug, a Japanese fan, may each become in turn a valuable lesson in decorative form and colour." Although Eastlake considered himself an opponent of eclecticism and a champion of the simplicity in design that would fuel art nouveau and the Arts and Crafts movement of William Morris, his list above suggests his collector's penchant: he too delighted in the beauty of assembled things. Indeed, later he explicitly recommends assembling a domestic museum: "A little museum may thus be formed, and remain a source of lasting pleasure to its possessors, seeing that 'a thing of beauty is a joy for ever.'" Clarence Cook, whose treatise *The House Beautiful* (1878) packaged Eastlake's directives for an American audience, also invited the world to come home; his frontispiece identifies the precise pleasure found in the cosmopolitan home—what contemporary reaction praised Soane for time and again: the resourcefulness of getting "much in little space," of contracting the whole world to fit under one roof (fig. 8). Such a packed corner, with sufficient room left for the dutiful repose of a domestic angel, suggests that in their attempts to locate the center of the Victorian home at the hearth, the mantel, the upholstered chair, the piano, scholars have overlooked a likely spot—what Victorians themselves would have called the art corner, which Cook here describes:

> *Such a "hanging" cabinet might be made a museum for the preservation of all the curiosities and pretty things gathered in the family walks and travels. The bubble-bottle of old Roman glass stirred in walking by one's own foot in the ruined palace of the Caesars, and not bought in a shop; the Dutch drinking-glass, with the crest of William the Orange;*

Fig. 8. "Much in Little Space," 1980, from Clarence Cook's *The House Beautiful*. (Courtesy of Dover Publications)

the trilobites found in a Newburgh stone-wall, or the box of Indian arrow-heads, jaspar, and feldspar, and quartz, picked up in a Westchester County field; bits of nature's craft and man's, gathered in one of these pendant museums, may make a collection of what were else scattered and lost.[7]

The moral and educative agenda behind such aesthetic counsel becomes more apparent in W. J. Loftie's *Plea for Art in the House* (1876). In his opening plea Loftie targets the concerns of his middle-class audience—respectability, industriousness, profit, and tamed and productive children: "Art is therefore pleaded for on such grounds as the manifest prudence of making collections, the civilizing effects of taste upon young persons, the pleasure of pursuing an object, and, generally, the economical value of art training both to the individual, the family, and the nation at large."[8] Loftie's confessed pleasure with the pursuit as well as his confidence that diligent home life leads to a prosperous nation suggests that, for him, to collect is to endorse the shibboleths of Victorian bourgeois culture, commodity fetishism and nationalism. Hoping to entice his readers to form house-museums of their own, Loftie turns to the favorite rhetorical stratagem of self-help books, the case in point, to offer exempla of collectors and their financial and moral successes. His conversation with a Mr. Smith, concerning a prudent investment in ancestral portraiture, is emblematic of the successful middle-class appropriation of patrician privilege:

> *I cannot help wondering how Smith comes to have a Reynolds worth, say, 250 £.*
> *"An ancestor?" I repeat.*
> *"Not at all," he replies. "My illustrious ancestors . . . never could have afforded to sit to [sic] Reynolds. He would have asked a long price for such a portrait as that; and it's worth more now. I bought it." (26)*

In narrating how the determined collecting of a certain Mr. Gillott of Birmingham leaves his family comfortable at his death, Loftie underscores how the house-museum enshrines the delayed gratification and perpetual industry of the Protestant work ethic. Initially a denial, collecting shores one's self and one's children against later ruin, promising that most important of all afterlives, prosperity here on earth.[9] Loftie offers another case in point: "A wise father . . . told me that he encouraged each of [his children] from the first to 'make a collection.' . . . In after life all these young men and women found themselves in the possession of at least a portion of the pocketmoney they had received in youth, and found . . . a love for something which could serve as an amusement and relaxation for leisure hours" (97). Loftie pleads most urgently for collecting: "Yet a little reflection may perhaps convince us, not only that it may be a moral but even a religious duty" (89).[10]

Loftie's earnest arguments place the vogue of homes beautiful and house-museums in a larger context, the housing reform movement of 1840 to 1890. Wishing to beautify homes for the purposes of moral and social edification, activists such as Octavia Hill argued in *Homes of the London Poor* (1875) that no one could expect the poor to be respectable when their homes were not respectable, that the poor needed beauty in their lives to uplift. Thus, there are many records of middle-class observers relieved to see evidence of the will to collect in working-class homes; for the ubiquity of ornament, knickknacks, and kitsch heralded an improved lot for England's most desperate.[11] Such is the pleasure of Henry Mayhew, who, with the acute and thorough particularity of the collector's eye, praises the house of a "thriving costermonger": "The wall over the fire-place was patched up to the ceiling with little square pictures of saints, and on the mantelpiece, between a row of bright tumblers and wine glasses filled with odds and ends, stood glazed crockeryware images of Prince Albert and M. Jullien." Concerning the positive social effects of the Bethnal Green Museum, a journalist from the *Eastern Argus* asked the following rhetorical question: "What home is there without its engravings, its home-made drawings, photographs, water-colours or oil paintings? From the Queen in her state apartments at Windsor Castle, to the labourer in the mean and tidy cottage, the same decoration of the walls is found!"[12] If industrial work challenged one's dignity, domestic collecting could reaffirm human will after work hours. Moreover, collecting appeared to promise the acclimatization of society's most dangerous elements. Certainly, the house-museum is striking evidence of the Victorian grand investment in the value of the home. As the home became more clearly connected to respectability, the importance of the best room or the front room—the standard spaces for collection and exhibition—intensified.[13] With its moral, aesthetic, and cultural defenses, the Victorian house-museum upheld Victoria and Albert's national campaign to improve the taste, and lives, of their public.

The representation of house-museums in Victorian narrative is as multivalent as was their real-life utility.[14] Many houses of Victorian fiction are richly drawn with museumlike spaces: aviaries, menageries, conservatories or winter gardens, grand-entrance or exhibition halls, small but densely packed spaces of whatnots, curio cabinets, and keepsake albums. For certain novelists, such spaces help to sensationalize the essential drama. Charlotte Yonge's *Heartsease* (1854), for example, opens with Violet's marveling over Lord Martindale's "museum of wonders"—an interior that represents a grand world against which the vulnerability of Yonge's ingenue is heightened. But such a place can also be utopia, as when Norman in Yonge's *Daisy Chain* (1856) describes Dr. May's new conservatory entrance as "a fairy land, where no care, or grief, or weariness could come." In *Little Dorrit* (1855–57), Charles Dickens characterizes the Meagleses, that "new sort of practical people," through their house-museum, claiming it to be "just what the residence of the Meagles family ought to be":

> There were antiquities from Central Italy, made by the best modern houses in that department of industry; bits of mummy from Egypt (and perhaps Birmingham); model gondolas from Venice; model villages from Switzerland; morsels of tessellated pavement from Herculaneum and Pompeii, like petrified minced veal; ashes out of tombs, and lava out of Vesuvius; Spanish fans, Spezzian straw hats, Moorish slippers, Tuscan hair-pins, Carrara sculpture, Trastaverini scarves, Genoese velvets and filagree, Neapolitan coral, Roman cameos, Geneva jewellery, Arab lanterns, rosaries blest all round by the Pope himself, and an infinite variety of lumber. There were views, like and unlike, of a multitude of places; and there was one little picture-room devoted to a few of the regular sticky old Saints.[15]

A parodic Sir John Soane, Mr. Meagles on tour and in his house not only provides much of the novel's humor but also serves Dickens's realistic portrait of an empowered middle class. Yet the Meagles house of souvenirs invites us to confront the novel's central menace as well. Mr. Meagles's spoils partake in an internationalism that leads all the traveling characters in the novel astray and detaches them from their native goodness—a pernicious *Geist* embodied by the cosmopolite, the "picturesque" Rigaud. Moreover, Mr. Meagles's acquisitiveness bears some resemblance to the hoarding, or vulgar materialism, that resides in the financier Merdle's bosom; and his appropriation of the world, that which compels him to turn Harriet Beadle into the exotic Tattycoram only then to domesticate her, results in the kind of imbalance of power that infects the Clennams. Later in the century, this ethics of collecting that the Meagleses first invite us to ponder generates deep ambivalence in Henry James's *The Spoils of Poynton* (1897), a tale of possession in which the house-museum is the central character and in which every other character—from the Vetches at penny bazaars to the philistine Brigstocks who ransack novelty magazines to Mrs. Gereth, the curator of Poynton—collects. One of James's working titles, "The House Beautiful," indicates his debt to Clarence Cook; another, "The Old Things," exposes his true passion for the donnée of his novella. Nevertheless, James understands that collecting can turn transgressive, that, in the campaign waged in the house of culture, Mrs. Gereth's curatorial acts—particularly her desire to own Fleda—are emblematic of her will to power. As the politics of collecting unfolds, possession reveals its sinister side and Mrs. Gereth's spoliation necessitates that Poynton, however exquisite, must burn.[16]

What follows is a closer examination of three house-museums from Victorian narrative. First, Charlotte Brontë's *Jane Eyre* (1847) and Edmund Gosse's *Father and Son* (1907) uncover the dark ramifications of the house-museum's imperative, "much in little space." In the filled space of house-museums, Brontë and Gosse depict childhoods that are painful, claustrophobic; at the site of education and indoctrination, oppression lurks and rebellion erupts. For these authors the house-museum is a house of horror; its close ties to the much feared figure of the father uncover a struggle between power and freedom that ultimately unleashes the menace of transgression. These house-museums disprove sentimental notions of Victorian domesticity, showing that the Victorians themselves broke down firm distinctions between the domestic and political realms. In inviting the empire home, house-museums made the home neither easily woman's sphere nor child's haven. However, the third narrative, Dickens's *Our Mutual Friend* (1864–65), redeems the museum enterprise by exploring the connections between collecting and the city, between remembering and meaning. Home among his collections, Mr. Venus proves the necessary and beneficial force of the collector's power: the museum reenchants the world as Mr. Venus "articulates" the possibility of rescue from the novel's pervasive anomie. These three narratives, bildungsroman, autobiography, and urban novel, respectively, demonstrate a wide range of responses to domestic collecting in the nineteenth century, and the progression of the discussion will, as we shall see, ultimately take us back to Lincoln's Inn Fields and John Soane.

Jane Eyre presents a series of homes for its protagonist, repeatedly revising the kind of ending appropriate for Jane as well as reconceiving the suitable space for her passionate, female self. Where can she thrive, the novel asks—Gateshead, Lowood, Thornfield, Marsh End, Morton Cottage, Marsh End altered, or Ferndean? This preoccupation with houses owes much to the traditions of both the bildungsroman and, with its interest in mysterious rooms and dark psyches, the gothic novel. Yet this "spatially articulate" novel is drawn to a particular kind of house, the collector's house, for the most charged scenes concerning what will emerge as the novel's political subtext.[17] The red-room at Gateshead, the backdrop for the novel's most extreme depiction of suffering and one of its most resonant moments (for here the motif of imprisonment first appears), is a museumlike space. It possesses immensity—"it was one of the largest and stateliest chambers in the mansion"—untouchability, and permanence: "This room was chill, because it seldom had a fire; it was silent, because remote from the nursery and kitchens; solemn, because it was known to be so seldom entered."[18] As the seat of the patriarch—"it was in this chamber he breathed his last; here he lay in state . . . and, since that day, a sense of dreary consecration had guarded it" (46)—it guards well its contents, insisting on a visitor's reverent observation of certain rites: "Mrs. Reed herself, at far intervals, visited it to review the contents of a certain secret drawer in the wardrobe, where were stored divers parchments, her jewel-casket, and a miniature of her deceased husband; and in those last words lies the secret of the red-room" (46). That the site of possession functions as the site of Jane's containment, holding both her present and her future, is key to the rest of the novel: as the site of the rebellious Jane's imprisonment, the red-room prefigures such issues as masculine power and possession, the feeling of displacement in exotic residences, and female suffering. Thus in order to convey the "violent tyrannies" of the surrogate patriarch John Reed (46), Brontë positions him in the conservatory, describing how he "stripped the hothouse vines of their fruit, and broke the buds off the choicest plants in the conservatory" (47). Symbolically, Jane remains trapped in the horticultural collection during her schooling at Lowood, the institution that intends to break her and that Brocklehurst boasts is the "nursery of chosen plants" (67).

When Jane enters Thornfield, the doors open on the novel's most

elaborately drawn house-museum. Like the red-room, Thornfield possesses an immensity that subdues Jane: "A very chill and vault-like air
pervaded the stairs and the gallery, suggesting cheerless ideas of space"
(129). The house's monumentality is confirmed when Jane views its
facade; the words "stately," "imposing," "a gentleman's manor-house"
help form her description. Jane's tour of Thornfield's rooms and their
contents, "the beautiful books and ornaments on the consoles and chif-
fonnieres" (153), leads her to the house's third floor—the scene of
the novel's eventual unraveling—which Brontë most directly likens to a
museum:

> *The furniture once appropriated to the lower apartments had from time
> to time been removed here, as fashions changed: and the imperfect light
> entering by their narrow casements showed bedsteads of a hundred years
> old; chests in oak or walnut, looking, with their strange carvings of palm
> branches and cherubs' heads, like types of the Hebrew ark; rows of ven-
> erable chairs, high-backed and narrow; stools still more antiquated, on
> whose cushioned tops were yet apparent traces of half-effaced embroider-
> ies, wrought by fingers that for two generations had been coffin-dust.
> All these relics gave to the third story of Thornfield Hall the aspect of
> a home of the past: a shrine of memory. (137)*

Below, the dining and drawing rooms yield exotic treasures: the "Tur-
key carpet," the "Tyrian dyed curtain," "crimson couches and otto-
mans," the "pale Parian mantelpiece," the "sparkling Bohemian glass,
ruby red" (135). Later decorated with "vases of exotics" and "a large
marble basin, . . . an ornament of the conservatory—where it usually
stood, surrounded by exotics, and tenanted by gold fish"—these rooms
will become the suitable setting for the evening of charades at Thornfield
(195, 212). Replete with such alien and mysterious beauties, this "fairy
place" leaves Jane with a feeling more akin to pain than to delight, caus-
ing her to find greater comfort initially in the familiar, feminine space of
Mrs. Fairfax's "snug, small room" (127).

Brontë introduces the reader to the master of Thornfield through
the things his house contains. This detailed exotic decor draws attention
to Rochester's exotic connections, a cosmopolitanism that confronts Jane
on her arrival at Thornfield. The continental Adele is certain proof of
his worldly ventures, but Jane also learns early of his facility in French

and, through Mrs. Fairfax, of his worldwide travels, an accomplishment Rochester subsequently acknowledges: "I have battled through a varied experience with many men of many nations, and roamed over half the globe" (165). Rochester's mastery over the exotic gives him the power to play many parts: to impersonate the fortune-telling sibyl and to mimic well in the charades, where he "look[s] the very model of an Eastern emir," "costumed in shawls, with a turban on his head. . . . His dark eyes and swarthy skin and Paynim features suited the costume exactly" (212).[19] Such a command of the exotic is confirmed not only by his acting and actions but also, throughout the novel, by his use of language. In conversations with Jane, Rochester unintentionally reveals his associations with the East by relying on an unusual body of information, whether it be likening himself to an Eastern slave purchaser, calling himself as enigmatic as a sphinx, or making references to the "pyramids of Egypt" and to hieroglyphs (297).

For Jane, Rochester's exotic connections are painful; she confesses, "The Eastern allusion bit me again" (297). Before any character or reader can fully understand, Jane feels that Rochester's travels mark his transgression—hence, her fear when she discovers his West Indies connection: "I knew Mr. Rochester had been a traveller: Mrs. Fairfax had said so; but I thought the continent of Europe had bounded his wanderings; till now I had never heard a hint given of visits to more distant shores" (220). Eventually exposed as his crime, Rochester's trespass on the distant shores of the West Indies is the barrier of which Jane dreams but cannot name: "I continued also the wish to be with you, and experienced a strange, regretful consciousness of some barrier dividing us" (309). The novel's colonial subtext—first glimpsed in the allusive web of Rochester's speech—exposes his exoticism to be symptomatic of that which he denies, complicity with the actions of his father. Here again, Rochester's skill at charades bears some significance: he must play the roles and hide the secret the house contains. Wishing to relate to Jane a tale of his victimization at the hands of his father and the Masons, Rochester exposes his own power to victimize—through both deed and speech. In short, he reveals that he took Bertha Mason as his wife in order to ensure his own fortune. When discussing his courtship and marriage, Rochester admits both an attraction to and a scorn for native otherness. He confesses his overwhelming disgust with Bertha's "pigmy intellect," savage face, wild darkness, gross animality, and untamable femaleness; she was a "true daughter of an infamous mother" (334). Acknowledging his superiority, "I was of a good race," Rochester scorns what he mockingly calls his prize and recounts his explorer's gambit across Europe to collect many women of many nations. It is appropriate that Thornfield's third floor, which as a "shrine of memory" is the home of Rochester's past, contains behind the "grim design" of its pictorial cabinet and its tapestried walls his costliest collectible, a colonialist's mad wife. Monumental and memorial, Thornfield stands a different sort of haunted house; possessed of the political crimes of the past, it does not let Rochester forget.[20]

In *The Madwoman in the Attic* Sandra Gilbert and Susan Gubar have famously claimed Jane and Bertha to be the novel's most vital character cluster and their encounter "the book's central confrontation."[21] However, Gilbert and Gubar's psychosexual reading of feminine rage privileges a subjectivity that runs counter to Brontë's own preface, which targets custom and convention. Their focus softens the politicized gender critique located at the novel's center in the interstices between husband and wife, collector and collected, and colonialist and colonized. Bertha is significant for her ability to shed light on what ails Rochester; she is testimony to the fact that, however much Rochester as the second son has ironized his father's actions, he, too, is guilty. Such taint infects his marriage proposal to Jane—his choice of words, his curious disclaimer, his twisting of the marriage vow: "When once I have fairly seized you, to have and to hold, I'll just—figuratively speaking—attach you to a chain like this (touching his watch-guard). Yes, bonny wee thing, I'll wear you in my bosom, lest my jewel I should tyne" (299). Thornfield's secret collection houses the mystery from which Jane is excluded; it suggests the sinister possibility that Rochester still wields the collector's prerogative, which again informs his love talk to Jane:

> "I would not exchange this one little English girl for the Grand Turk's whole seraglio—gazelle-eyes, houri forms, and all!"
>
> "I'll not stand you an inch in the stead of a seraglio," I said; "so don't consider me an equivalent for one. If you have a fancy for anything in that line, away with you, sir, to the bazaars of Stamboul, without delay, and lay out in extensive slave-purchases some of that spare cash you seem at a loss to spend satisfactorily here."

*"And what will you do, Janet, while I am bargaining for so many
tons of flesh and such an assortment of black eyes?"*
    *"I'll be preparing myself to go out as a missionary to preach lib-
erty to them that are enslaved. . . . I'll stir up mutiny." (297–98)*

In this exchange Jane embraces the cause she has championed throughout
her life, liberty and liberation, while Rochester unwittingly attests once
more to the despotism of his desire, the kind of injustice Jane abhors.
When Rochester later wishes to ornament her with the family jewels and
new, extravagant dresses, Jane learns the painful lesson that the collector's prerogative includes the right to display as well as to contain his
possession.

As the repository for the Rochester men's colonial acquisitions,
Thornfield must fall. Jane's dream foretells it; and Brontë's preface, in an
appropriate architectural analogy, promises such demolition: the world
"may hate him who dares to scrutinize and expose, to raise the gilding
and show base metal under it, to penetrate the sepulchre and reveal charnel relics" (36). Although Gilbert and Gubar call Thornfield "the house
of Jane's life, its floors and walls the architecture of her experience" (347),
Thornfield is the indisputable house of Rochester's life; it is the museum
of the past he cannot disinherit.[22] It is Brontë's depiction of the great
house of the English countryside, as well as the power structure based
on property both home and abroad it represents, in dereliction.[23] Razing
the patriarchal house-museum makes way for Jane's house, for the space
of feminine desire—Ferndean. Lying beyond society's conventions, this
anomalous residence can tell no stories of despotism. Unlike the house-
museum that sought to control the natural, Ferndean is in harmony with
nature, allowing the green world to subsume its walls: "The house—
scarce, by this dim light, distinguishable from the trees; so dank and green
were its decaying walls" (455). Here, Jane is pleased to see no assertions
of order: "There were no flowers, no garden-beds" (455). The change
in residence signals the necessary subduing of Rochester, and his "long,
strong arm" and "rounded, muscular, and vigorous hand"—emblems of
his collector's privilege—must remain disabled, for now the collector
submits. Thus the novel purges the potential for tyranny, and Jane can
enjoy the mutuality for which she has longed but which the hierarchical
relationship of collectible to collector made impossible. A novel about

power in all its perfidious imbalances, *Jane Eyre* finds the tale of colonialism hidden within a house's collections. It punishes despotism and rectifies female exclusion from the tale of possession, thus, finally, making room for Jane.[24]

Like *Jane Eyre,* Edmund Gosse's *Father and Son* is a book about power, the potential submission to it and the eventual liberation from it. The "tragedy essential," as Gosse calls it, or the "struggle" and final "disruption," centers on a son's rebellion against a father's pietism. Yet the "struggle between two temperaments" erupts also as a conflict between a father's scientism and a son's romanticism, between a father's commitment to museums and the mind and a son's devotion to nature and the soul. Although published in 1907, *Father and Son* recounts Gosse's childhood in high-Victorian culture nearly sixty years earlier. Two facts we learn about Gosse's father are significant: he is a participant in "the wide revival of Conscience" and "a zoologist, . . . a writer of books on natural history."[25] Readers too often privilege the first fact at the expense of the second, as does the Penguin Modern Classics edition, which calls the autobiography a "well-documented chronicle of religious fanaticism." It is, rather, the father's involvement in the enterprise of collecting that most thoroughly challenges the son's dreams to be a poet. Therefore, Gosse depicts his upbringing against the background of a museum culture, referring to Wyld's great globe, the British Museum, the Sculpture Gallery at the Crystal Palace, and "the newly-invented marine aquarium [that] was the fashionable toy of the moment" (55).[26] Two childhood house-museums filled with a father's collections and natural science experiments, the immediate scene of the text, register Gosse's pathos-rich ambivalence toward his father—his respect, "sad indulgence," and hostility.[27]

With piquant focus, Gosse writes, "As I look back upon this faraway time, I am surprised at the absence in it of any figures but our own. He and I together, now in the study among the sea-anemones and starfishes . . . now under the lamp at the maps we both loved so much, this is what I see: no third presence is ever with us" (67–68). This spot of time is the autobiography's representative scene: father and son in a house filled with collections of sea life, circumscribed by the small, illuminated space of a lamp's light. Even the presence of a mother cannot diffuse the oppressive intensity of the scene. *Father and Son* portrays a child haunted if not thwarted by the dialectic of power and servitude that sustains the father's acquisitions. Collecting is for Gosse not only a chilling actuality of his childhood but also a powerful metaphor for the father's will to possess and control living things that come under his influence, especially his son. Gosse's childhood homes are the site of such patriarchal power; they are houses of horror and confinement monitored by what he calls a father's "police-inspection" (221).[28] Details of the houses' collections paint the scene. Gosse portrays himself against a backdrop of "two, and sometimes three aquaria in the [study], tanks of sea-water, with glass sides, inside which all sorts of creatures crawled and swam" (81); the "glass case of tropical insects" in the sitting-room (60); "the framework of a greenhouse" (79); and the hothouse of orchids.[29] The overdetermined fullness generated by Gosse's effective use of space captures the "much in little space" of house-museums. Here he can enjoy little liberty; even his occupancy in such a (pre)occupied world is doubtful. Yet amid the father's translated scientific brochures and illustrated manuals of flora and fauna, Gosse, "the child of a naturalist," must survive.

The primary sensation for readers of *Father and Son* is claustrophobia. In recalling so effectively the confines of the small, packed space, Gosse never allows the reader to forget the presence of "the indomitable four walls." The "intellectual cell" of the family, "bounded at its sides by the walls of their own house," vicariously binds the reader just as it directly binds Gosse (16). The narrative never relents in retracing the boundaries: "I became keenly attentive to the limited circle of interests open to me" (25). Even the house's horsehair sofa is "small, coffin-like" (171), and Gosse's retreat is appropriately named the "Box-room," where he claims to be "most carefully withdrawn, like Princess Blanchefleur in her marble fortress" (27). The spot of time that marks Gosse's culminating crisis finds its appropriate mise-en-scène in the orchid hothouse, where the father's overblown exotica choke Gosse. Here he breaks out, opting for the cold grass over the gaudy orchids: "There was a morning, in the hot-house at home, among the gorgeous waxen orchids which reminded my Father of the tropics in his youth, when my forbearance or my timidity gave way. The enervated air, soaked with the intoxicating perfumes of all those voluptuous flowers, may have been partly responsible for my outburst. . . . I broke from the odorous furnace of the conservatory, and buried my face in the cold grass" (221).

For the child Gosse the household space is always the arena of his co-opted and regulated existence. We never forget his smallness: "I knelt, feeling very small, by the immense bulk of my Father" (171). In the narrative's dialectic of space and dimension, the inside or small predominates, yet the desire for the outside or immense never subsides. Likening his soul to Fatimah held prisoner in a tower by her captor, Gosse longs for the liberated perspective of an open window. The father's myopia, however, always constricts the son's desire for what he calls the "Pisgah-view." It is as if the "son of a man who looked through a microscope" (118), of a man who "saw everything through a lens, nothing in the immensity of nature" (95), longs for the telescope and all that it as metaphor promises: "The daring chapters of Michael Scott's picaresque romance of the tropics were that telescope and that window" (144). As a child, Gosse haunts the window, the threshold between inside and outside: "My childhood was long, long with interminable hours, hours with the pale cheek pressed against the window-pane" (57).[30]

This heightened state of inwardness, characteristic of Gosse's childhood, creates a fishbowl effect that depletes his subjectivity. The glass pane of the window and the glass case of the collections become mirrors in which he sees himself as object: "But clear enough is the picture I hold of myself" (81). We watch as he watches himself watching: "Those pools were our mirrors, in which, reflected in the dark hyaline and framed by the sleek and shining fronds of oar-weed there used to appear the shapes of a middle-aged man and a funny little boy" (96). In both senses of the word, the *discipline* of the father has so utterly stifled the imagination of his son that Gosse can only objectify himself. Gosse has become pure objectivity, and the romantic subject—that freedom of expression and self for which Gosse long yearns but can only later through an acquaintance with literature identify—is disabled. He repeatedly envisions his childhood self to be one of his father's collected, captured, and showcased objects. He writes, "I felt like a small and solitary bird, caught and hung out hopelessly and endlessly in a great glittering cage" (139). And later, "I compared my lot with that of one of the speckled soldier-crabs that roamed about in my Father's aquarium, dragging after them great whorl-shells" (202).

Gosse's portrait presents a child incapable of childlike exuberance. He mimics his father's museal discourse well:

A lady—when I was just four—rather injudiciously showed me a large print of a human skeleton, saying, "There! you don't know what that is, do you?" Upon which, immediately and very archly, I replied, "Isn't it a man with the meat off?" . . . If I venture to repeat this trifle, it is only to point out that the system on which I was being educated deprived all things, human life among the rest, of their mystery. The "bare-grinning skeleton of death" was to me merely a prepared speci-men of that featherless plantigrade vertebrate, "homo sapiens." (23)

In similar fashion, the young Gosse views a canvas by Holman Hunt as a "brilliant natural specimen," claiming "I was pleased to have seen it, as I was pleased to have seen the comet, and the whale which was brought to our front door on a truck. It was a prominent addition to my experience" (164–65).[31] Both anecdotes, even as they convey some of the humor Gosse promises to deliver in his account, strike a certain plangency, mourning the loss of wonder in a disenchanted world characterized by the bleak, solitary option—and here the word *addition* is key—of accu-mulating information. Because he must, Gosse is able to impersonate the sensibility as well as the discourse of his collector father, a mimicry so perfect that it eventually reveals the limitations of this sensibility. Here he records the recording of the nonevent of his birth: "The event was thus recorded in my Father's diary: E. delivered of a son. Received green swallow from Jamaica. . . . What the wording exemplifies is my Father's extreme punctilio. The green swallow arrived later in the day than the son, and the earlier visitor was therefore recorded first; my Father was scrupulous in every species of arrangement" (10). Gosse's impersonation inevitably veers toward parody, as he confesses elsewhere about his copies of his father's illustrations: "They were, moreover, parodies . . . of his writings, for I invented new species, with sapphire spots and crimson tentacles and amber bands" (119). At other times, he is direct in his re-buke, as when he acknowledges that his father's very greatness rests on excessive sacrifice and extreme limitations: "As a collector of facts and marshaller of observations, he had not a rival in that age; his very absence of imagination aided him in this work. But he was more an attorney than philosopher," and "again I repeat, he was not a philosopher; he was incapable . . . of forming broad generalizations and of escaping in a vast survey from the troublesome pettiness of detail" (85, 95). Through such condemnation, Gosse praises the spirit that his childhood "copies" in all their wild departures embody and reaffirms as well the central values of his autobiography—the heart, the soul, and the imagination.

Mimicry and parody, the competing activities of Gosse's child-hood, collide in the most intense passage of *Father and Son,* the carmine nightmare in chapter 7. In a highly deflected way, this scene reveals his attachment both to his father and to museum culture. Gosse's desire in the dream to reach his "goal" of the "ruby-coloured point" labeled CARMINE demonstrates his wish to usurp the father's privilege and handle the rare ink drawn from the beetle. In essence, this dream ex-presses a longing for the museum label, for the juice of the very beetle that frightens Gosse, for the position of the father that terrifies him. Yet the dream yields a counterreading too. One could argue that, in trans-forming the preserved bug and its label into the intense ruby color its crushed body produces, Gosse's dream turns a collector's tools in trade into the visual symphony of an aesthete's delight. Either interpretation could explain his mixed emotions about this dream, "the attainment of which alone could save us from destruction" but which he also finds to be "distressing," "agitating," cause for "inexpressible distress" and "fren-zied despair." [32]

The acute, narrow mind of the father co-opts the son's existence, leaving little room for imagination and soul. Thus the polar terms of the narrative's conflict come into focus: science and romanticism, museum and imagination, fact and fancy. Gosse's delineations rest on such binaries: "I was told about missionaries, but never about pirates, I was familiar with humming-birds, but I had never heard of fairies. Jack the Giant-Killer, Rumpelstiltskin and Robin Hood were not of my acquaintance, and though I understood about wolves, Little Red Ridinghood was a stranger even by name" (22). The terms of the conflict point to the double-voiced discourse of the narrative: Gosse can speak the father's tongue, the taxo-nomic language of museums and scientific collecting, yet he can also explode subversively into romantic lyricism. Inspiring Gosse to rebel against his father and his discipline, Wordsworth emerges in the narrative as the alternative guardian figure, promising to restore Gosse's enervated subjectivity. At times, Gosse directly discusses the work of Wordsworth, as when he begins chapter 5 with a synopsis of *The Prelude.* Elsewhere, however, the influence of Wordsworth is subtle; his centrality most indisputable when Gosse's lack of self-consciousness is most evident. For example, Gosse's description of his carmine nightmare and the frenzy of his racing and roaring, the light and noise above and about him in what seemed a "monstrous vortex," rings with language borrowed from the stolen-pinnace and cliff-hanging scenes of book 1 of *The Prelude*. When Gosse recalls the place he loves best, the wildly sublime rock pools at Oddicombe, we see that he has internalized the credo of Wordsworthian romanticism, what he calls "nature-romance":

> *No road, save the merest goat-path, led down its concave wilderness, in which loose furze-bushes and untrimmed brambles wantoned into the likeness of trees, each draped in audacious tissue of wild clematis. Through this fantastic maze the traveller wound his way, led by little other clue than by the instinct of descent. For me, as a child, it meant the labour of a long, an endless morning, to descend to the snow-white pebbles, to sport at the edge of the cold, sharp sea, and then to climb up home again . . . clutching at the smooth boughs of the wild ash, toiling, toiling upwards into flat land out of that hollow world of rocks. (72)*

Father and Son is not only Gosse's portrait of two temperaments but also a study of two epochs. Here he offers a gloss on the past and present, lamenting the crimes the passage of time has permitted. Having acknowledged that his account is in part a tale of tears, Gosse mourns the changes to Oddicombe: "When last I saw the place, thus smartened and secured, with its hair in curl-papers and its feet in patent-leathers, I turned from it in anger and disgust, and could almost have wept. . . . What man could do to make wild beauty ineffectual, tame and empty, has amply been performed at Oddicombe" (72). Even his recollection of the former Oddicombe is shattered: "These rock-basins, fringed by corallines, filled with still water almost as pellucid as the upper air itself, thronged with beautiful sensitive forms of life,—they exist no longer, they are all profaned, and emptied, and vulgarized. An army of 'collectors' has passed over them" (97). Desacralized by the rage that collecting has become, the rock pools of Devonshire, where "there is nothing, now, where in our days there was so much," mark the site of Gosse's harshest attack on his father (96). Holding his father implicated in if not accountable for the pillage, Gosse bemoans the impoverishment of the earth: the "fairy paradise has been violated." Indeed, the elder Gosse's acquisition of natural spoils evokes Satan's original trespass into Eden: "Father, in spite of his scientific requirements, used not seldom to pause before he began to rifle [the flower beds], ejaculating that it was indeed a pity to disturb such congregated beauty. . . . We burst in, he used to say, where no one had ever thought of intruding before; and if the Garden of Eden had been situate in Devonshire, Adam and Eve . . . would have seen the identical sights that we now saw" (97). Despite the father's claim to see with the eyes of prelapsarian man, it is clear that Gosse identifies his father's collecting as an intruder's unholy act. Gosse's final outrage reminds us that the graceful prose of *Father and Son* has been punctuated by the depiction of violent acts, that this seemingly quiet book has been all along a narrative about violation in which the desacralized earth is inhospitable to a son's reverie. In effect, Gosse's struggle is to be a child in the age of Darwin, to be Wordsworthian after the advent of Victorian science has founded the Victorian museum enterprise. In a nature that has been collected, categorized, and illustrated, Gosse's attempts to locate the sublime are futile. To such futility the house-museum of his childhood is, finally, memorial.

Taken together, the nightmarish gothic vision of the stuffed house in *Jane Eyre* and the lament over a bleak life of accumulation in *Father and Son* expose two enterprises that fueled the work of museums: empire and science. In *Our Mutual Friend* Dickens explores a third, the city. But the power that must be purged from *Jane Eyre* and punished in *Father and Son* emerges an indispensable social force in *Our Mutual Friend*. Nevertheless, Dickens first launches what appears to be an exploration of the dark underbelly of Victorian museum culture, presenting a series of menacing images of the collected, the accrued, and the aggregated—from the "accumulated scum of humanity [that] seemed to be washed from higher grounds, like so much moral sewage," to "that mysterious paper currency which circulates in London when the wind blows, gyrated here and there and everywhere."[33] Dickens then asks, "Whence can it come, whither can it go?" (191), giving a sinister spin to the central question of this study, What does one do with all the things of the world? *Our Mutual Friend* depicts what we today know all too well to be the effect of overproduction and consumption: waste. Here, in the infernal world order that ensues, garbage itself turns into industry, and money, dirt, and death are intimates. Heaping becomes the novel's essential occupation as well as its disturbing preoccupation, from Silas Wegg's "grim little heap" to the novel's primary space, the London dustheap: "Between Battle Bridge and that part of the Holloway district in which he dwelt, was a tract of suburban Sahara, where tiles and bricks were burnt, bones were boiled, carpets were beat, rubbish was shot, dogs were fought, and dust was heaped by contractors" (76). The "whole metropolis" is, in fact, one gigantic "heap of vapour charged with muffled sound of wheels and enfolding a gigantic catarrh" (479). The many heaps of *Our Mutual Friend,* where hoarding and sifting are undertaken in desperate anticipation, expose a citizenry in dark mimicry of the collecting and rearticulating central to the museum's enterprise.

Here the museum's work is taken up outside the museum's walls, on the streets, sustaining a sometimes prosperous, oftentimes desperate street life. The many heaps of *Our Mutual Friend* are house-museums of a sort where characters—making much out of little—make their livelihoods and their homes. Jenny Wren fashions doll costumes from fabric scraps, Miss Pleasant Riderhood recycles goods in her leaving shop, Hexam and his mud-larking, river-dredging cohorts pilfer the Thames, and Boffin profits as the Golden Dustman. Boffin's heaps loom in his own backyard and make Silas Wegg dissatisfied with his own "grim little heap." It is fitting that Boffin, at the nadir of his "corruption," and Wegg, at the height of his avarice for heaping, read from R. S. Kirby's *Wonderful and Scientific Museum,* chosen from the aptly titled "pile of wollumes" that collects the tales of hoarders.[34] From this "museum" Wegg narrates the lives of collectors and their house-museums, discovering "the miser's secret hoards" in jackets, bowls, crevices of walls, under cushions and chair covers, behind the backs of drawers, and up chimneys. Indeed, the appropriately excessive description of "the house, or rather the heap of ruins, in which Mr. Dancer lived," which was "very rich in the interior," overwhelms Wegg with desire (543, 544). Furthermore, the tales of the misers underscore the distinction between hoarding and collecting, for, although the heaps of *Our Mutual Friend* are the site of both accumulation and sifting, time and again accumulation persists unrelieved by order. In the infernal world order where dirt is business, chaos rules and life devolves—to use Dickens's phrase—into "the jumble."

Out of the cluttered world of the novel, however, emerges a distinctive character, the sallow-faced, weak-eyed, dusty-reddish-haired articulator, Mr. Venus. Mr. Venus's shop, known also as "Mr. Venus's museum" and "Home, Sweet Home," turns out to be the novel's most important interior of collecting complemented by sorting (851, 562). "Stuck so full of black shelves and brackets and nooks and corners" (123), Mr. Venus's shop possesses the much in little space of house-museums, as his quick inventory suggests: "A Wice. Tools. Bones, warious. Skulls, warious. Preserved Indian baby. African ditto. Bottled preparations, warious. Everything within reach of your hand, in good preservation. The mouldy ones a-top. What's in those hampers over them again, I don't quite remember. Say, human warious. Cats. Articulated English baby. Dogs. Ducks. Glass eyes, warious. Mummied bird. Dried cuticle, warious" (126). Mr. Venus's shop is home to the eclectic, or what he delights to call the "miscellaneous," well represented by the cosmopolitan human skeletons that are his masterpieces: "I have just sent home a Beauty—a perfect Beauty—to a school of art. One leg Belgian, one leg English, and the pickings of eight other people in it" (124). Here Mr. Venus rules as a master of the museum underworld, exposing the museum's connections to the nefarious realm of the riverside when he confesses, "I was down at the water-side, looking for parrots" (562–63). We learn that he often works for museums, "looking for a nice pair of rattlesnakes, to articulate for a Museum" (563). Although Mr. Venus's affiliation with the museum world proper implicates the museum in the nefarious world of river dredgers, dealing sailors, and resurrection men, his house of horrors eventually proves home to the animating force of the novel. Hard at work in his Clerkenwell shop, Mr. Venus possesses powers that mark him as the novel's guiding spirit, link him to the central plot of Boffin's fall, and ultimately elevate him as the novel's unlikely hope.

Yet scholars have frequently underestimated the importance of Mr. Venus.[35] Although he was a late and hasty addition to the novel, Mr. Venus facilitates what both Dickens and many readers have acknowledged to be the genuine surprise of the novel—not Rokesmith's true identity but Boffin's feigned fall. It is Mr. Venus who first plants the idea of Harmony Jail's hidden wealth in Silas Wegg's head. He then keeps Wegg in a tantalizing state of suspension and suspense by holding on to the will, which allows Wegg's greed to fester but keeps him harmless to Boffin. Eventually, Mr. Venus exposes Wegg to Boffin, denouncing "Weggery" and all that it entails, vagary and villainy foremost in his mind. Alongside John Harmon, Mr. Venus presides over the undoing of Wegg in his final trial. Such usefulness to the plot ties Mr. Venus to key themes of the novel as well. His alliance with Wegg deepens the novel's meditation on dangerous partnership, the kind of bond based on avarice that potentially links the young Bella and Harmon and inextricably ties such pairs as the Lammles and Gaffer Hexam and Rogue Riderhood together. Thus exposed, these false friendships give way to the resurrection of the true mutual friend, and, once again, Mr. Venus is present—this time, to restore Boffin and John Harmon to their authentic identities.

Even Wegg can enumerate the sources of Mr. Venus's power: "patient habits and delicate manipulation . . . skill in piecing little things together . . . knowledge of various tissues and textures . . . the likelihood of small indications leading him on to the discovery of great concealments" (357). Nothing escapes this detail man; he is the appropriate nemesis to the obfuscating, misarticulating, and lying Wegg. He also provides the appropriate contrast to Podsnappery, the worldview that files down "everything in the universe" to fit into its totalizing categories (175). From Mr. Venus's attentiveness to minutiae will come that great discovery, the truth. Asserting to Boffin that he will "articulate the details," Mr. Venus "entered on the history of the friendly move, and truly recounted it" (641). Repeatedly, Wegg and Mr. Venus hold discussions concerning inspection, inspection of Boffin and, unknown to Wegg, of Wegg himself. Playing the role of inspector to Wegg's inspected situates Mr. Venus in the company of Dickens's detective heroes like the character named Inspector in *Our Mutual Friend* and, most famously, Bucket in *Bleak House*. What the detective and the collector share, marked by Mr. Venus's "over-tried" eyes, is the ability to cut through the cant, and the complex "tissues and textures," of life.

Like his client the museum, Mr. Venus pursues a profession based on parts and wholes. As the articulator, he can construct whole bodies out of skeletal parts, but he can also threaten someone like Wegg with dispersal. Such power has always been Mr. Venus's weapon; it is why Wegg first goes to his shop. Wegg explains, "I tell you openly I should *not* like . . . to be what I may call dispersed, a part of me here, and a part of me there, but should wish to collect myself like a genteel person" (127). Later, Venus threatens the unruly Wegg: "I don't just now want any more trophies of my art. But I like my art, and I know how to exercise my art" (558). As an articulator of bones, Mr. Venus oversees both dismembering and assembling. While he can disperse Wegg, he also promises to collect

him or "hold [him] over" (127). Thus, like the museum, his shop becomes the site of both dispersal and collection, miscellany and panorama.
In his own words, Mr. Venus's collection of "human warious" adds up to
the "general panoramic view" (126). Dismemberment and metonymy
yield rearticulation and organic wholes. Venus's vision is synecdochic: he
"looks round for 'that French gentleman,' whom he at length descries to
be represented . . . by his ribs only" (125). Venus knows Wegg by means
of his severed leg: "You're somewhere in the back shop across the yard"
(126). This deformed leg, whose bone is as twisted as its former owner,
first prepares Mr. Venus to articulate Wegg's villainy. Clearly, Mr. Venus's
skills lie not only in dismembering but also in remembering—an important service rendered in a world too long neglected.

Mr. Venus's profession, which the novel repeatedly calls an artistry,
takes the unarticulated or heaped and gives it pattern and order.[36] Our
first vision of Mr. Venus's shop is suggestive: from the poorer shops of
small retail traders in commodities to eat and drink and keep folks warm,
Italian frame makers, barbers, brokers, and dealers in dogs and singing
birds, "Mr. Wegg selects one dark shop-window . . . surrounded by a
muddle of objects vaguely resembling pieces of leather and dry stick, but
among which nothing is resolvable into anything distinct, save the candle
itself . . . and two preserved frogs fighting in a small-sword duel" (122).
The description of Clerkenwell depends on the indistinct and aggregate;
however, from such obfuscation emerge the light of Mr. Venus's candle
and the illumination derived from his carefully delineated art preserved
in the mummified amphibian grotesquerie. Thus, the heap that can be
ordered becomes a possibility, and Mr. Venus can boast: "Mr. Wegg, if
you was brought here loose in a bag to be articulated, I'd name your
smallest bones blindfold equally with your largest, as fast as I could pick
'em out, and I'd sort 'em all, and sort your wertebrae, in a manner that
would equally surprise and charm you" (128). The leitmotiv of the
dueling frogs confers order on the structure of the novel's plot and recalls us to the constancy of Mr. Venus's effort even as it reminds us of
his other practice, taxidermy. His animated collection awes visitors to his
shop. Wegg watches as "the babies—Hindoo, African, and British—the
'human warious,' the French gentleman, the green glass-eyed cats, the
dogs, the ducks, and all the rest of the collection, show for an instant as
if paralytically animated" (130). Later, when Mr. Boffin visits the shop,

"the whole stock seemed to be winking and blinking with both eyes" (640). As professional and symbolic animator in Boffin's restoration, Mr. Venus is, again, linked to the novel's key theme of resurrection, repairing the social body in the process of breathing life into the dead.

Both articulator and animator, Mr. Venus holds province over the novel's most vexed site, the body. He makes his living by dealing with the body, in death, which immerses him in the novel's dirtiest but most rewarding work, that of death and life. In the world of *Our Mutual Friend* too many characters—like Fascination Fledgeby, friend to both the Lammles and the Podsnaps—live to die. But a few find that in death is life, that renunciating worldly pursuits and identity leads to spiritual renovation. Such is the logic behind Jenny Wren's call to Fledgeby, "Come back and be dead," a call Fledgeby cannot answer (334). It sustains the many characters who die in order to live—Harmon and Wrayburn key among them, but Betty Higden is also so moved in her ascension through death. Mr. Venus's comedic ability to wrest life from death is compatible with his role as the diligent lover, foregrounded in his name.[37] But Venus the lover is also Venus the scientist, as the most coded of possible allusions in Mr. Venus's name suggests: is it possible that Dickens had some knowledge of *The Archidoxes of Magic,* where Paracelsus identifies the scientist Venus as the "repairer of wounds," he who "preserveth wounds in such manner, so that no accident can invade them, nor the Air or water hurt them?"[38] Resolving the confusion over identity and restoring characters to their proper homes, Mr. Venus embodies the counterforce to the social disintegration that threatens the world of *Our Mutual Friend.* Otherwise, the dustheaps as well as the excesses and vanities they symbolize might have buried London alive. Much like Jenny Wren, who out of fabric scraps and fragmentary visions of real life spins the fancy for her dolls, and much like the circumspect John Harmon, Mr. Venus can construct meaning out of the sadness. All three—figures of the artist, figures of Dickens—possess the same mien, well-worn with the care and carefulness essential to their tasks.

The power of Mr. Venus might best be understood in the light of a commentary by Dickens on a contemporary museum. In an article titled "Owen's Museum" Dickens expresses his great pleasure in having visited London's Natural History Museum. Using language that might as readily apply to Mr. Venus's work as to his own novelistic art, Dickens praises the organic wholes and smooth-running narratives essential to a museum's exhibits. "I walked in," he narrates, "to follow in the track of those fine progressive steps which have led up from the rude beginnings of all things, to the highest development yet known to humanity." As Dickens describes this neatly ordered Darwinian plot ("I wondered at the links which make a rat the ancestor of the ape"), "next," "then," and "and" are his favorite words: "The next series," "The next step," "Then came," "Then, there was," "And then, following," "And then I turned." The profusion excites him, while the ordering of it pleases him: "nothing has been left out"; "this museum has a beautiful specimen of each, set in its proper surroundings, not all huddled together in one case." This harmonious vision valorizes the museum's restorative powers, which fight against the fracture of existence in an urban, industrial, and globalized world.

Dickens's faith in the museum as an antidote to anomie recalls Sir John Soane's great hope for Lincoln's Inn Fields and all that it contained. The ingenious "folding shutters" Soane designed for his Picture-Room in order to quadruple the wall space for mounting art are evidence of what Barbara Hofland in her notes to the 1835–36 *Description of the House and Museum* called "the extraordinary power of contrivance exhibited in containing space as it were out of nothing." Soane's Model Room, a trove replicating the architectural best of Western civilization, boasts all the world within; without, its two southern windows afford what Soane called "a panoramic effect of some of the magnificent structures of the Metropolis."[39] This double perspective of the old world, under one roof, and the new world, expansive but immediately at hand, reveals a dialectic of coziness and grandeur, miniature and monumental, at play. Elsewhere in the house, Soane displayed fragments rescued from buildings demolished in his own time, seemingly collected in the spirit of salvage or repair, that also help to carry on the work of harmony within the house. By commingling the past with the present, Soane's collections erect one great, continuous tradition—one perfect world—in which the past becomes accessible or available and the present becomes as grand as the past. To stand in the midst of Soane's collections is to sense strongly that preserving the past can be akin to revising it and that ordering the past, giving it coherence, can be nothing more—and certainly nothing less— than the consummation of a wish. And that wish is often for home: to belong instead of to long.

Joseph Gandy's 1818 painting of Soane among his designs and buildings plays tricks with perspective by fantastically including all of Soane's
own designs as well as his acquired visual and architectural constructions
under one roof, situating a small Soane within their midst (fig. 9). This
vision of a world well designed places the collector at the appropriate
spot, at the center of his collections—a vision echoed by such arrangements within the house as Soane's portrait in the dining room, the first
image one sees in the tour route Soane recommended, or Soane's bust
nestled in the middle of the Dome Room, attended to by four walls of
antiquities, authentic and replicated. In effect, the copia of collection
promises the collector a situated life or, even more powerfully, an extended life. By activating the subtle interplay between self and objects and
thus living on through one's collection, one achieves a collector's immortality: "He that communeth with [the dead], doth obtain / A partial conquest over time." [40] With epitaphic solemnity, Soane's words confirm the
triumph: "He went on from a pure love to promote the interest of art
until at last he had raised a nest of wasps about him to sting the strongest
man to death." [41]

This curious choice of the conceit of a wasps' nest, with its double-
edged suggestion of comfort and aggression, implies how collection was
for Soane his most valiant fight against his own dispersal. It takes us back,
too, to those darker underpinnings of the Victorian museum enterprise
explored by Dickens in *Our Mutual Friend* where lurks the invidious
meaninglessness inherent in discontinuity. Loss motivates collecting, acquiring, and hoarding. Disorder and randomness prompt organizing and
cataloging—all of which Soane acknowledges most movingly in the unusual piece from which the trope of the wasps' nest comes, *Crude Hints,
Towards an History of My House* (1812). Soane's one attempt at fiction is
a futuristic tale narrated by "an Antiquary" who discovers the ruins of
Soane's house-museum and conjectures about its use: "What an admirable lesson is this work to show the vanity of all human expectations—
the man who founded this place piously imagined that from the fruits of
his honest industry and the rewards of his professional application he had
laid the foundation of a family of artists and that the *filii filiorum* of his
Loins might smitten with [*sic*] the love of Art and anxious to show their
gratitude for the benefits and ease and comfort they derived from it dwell
in the place from generation to generation—that a race of artists would
have been raised." [42] This passage churns with a disturbing fusion of fancy

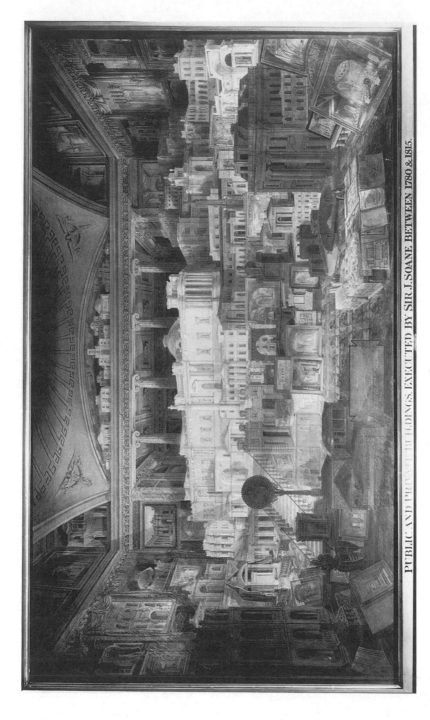

Fig. 9. Perspective of various designs for public and private buildings executed by John Soane between 1780 and 1815, 1818, pen and water-color by Joseph Gandy. (Courtesy of the Trustees of Sir John Soane's Museum)

and anxiety characteristic of the entire tale; for the archaeologically minded Soane, the image of his house in ruins is both a clever conceit and a painful reminder of the cycle of forgetting and neglect that cancels out a collector's care. Such phrases as "family of artists," "the *filii filiorum* of his Loins," and "race of artists" point to Soane's deep concern about his history and lineage. Longing for the permanence promised to those who dwell "from generation to generation," Soane is haunted by generational anxiety. What can his loins engender; what is his past, and what is his future? As we have seen, only when Soane realized that community, family, and race were no longer dependent on dynasty or blood did he become a self-fashioner of community, an educator, a founder of a museum. In effect, then, the educative ambitions realized in Soane's house-museum are founded on anxiety. Perhaps in similar yet larger measure, Victorian culture became interested in museums in order to erect pasts and ensure futures to fill some ontological void even as the copia of collection threatened to fall back into the miscellany of debris. Thus, as this final fiction on collection—housed within a collector's museum— proves, this chapter ends where chapter 2 concluded, with the collector at home and the specter of homelessness ever pressing on us.

IV

A Gallery of Readings:
Rendezvous in the Museum

The Museum was notoriously a place where eventually you met everyone you knew.

—David Lodge, *The British Museum Is Falling Down*

ON 4 APRIL 1837—three months after its founder's death—Sir John Soane's house-museum at Lincoln's Inn Fields admitted the public, averaging sixty-four visitors a day. In 1851, the year of the Great Exhibition, the small Soane Museum was open for a total of 108 days and attracted, on average, seventy-seven visitors a day. Initially, the museum observed an exacting admission policy that made people desirous of visiting: "Apply either to a Trustee, by letter to the Curator, or personally at the Museum a day or two before" the planned visit.[1] However, later curators, particularly George Birch (curator from 1894 to 1904), who came in on his own time so that the museum would be open on Saturday afternoons, worked to make the museum more accessible. By 1890 every cheap printed guidebook to the South Kensington included the Soane Museum, along with the British Museum and the National Gallery, as one of the nation's great collections. Its hours were listed, and directions to Lincoln's Inn Fields were posted. Finally, Soane's great ambition appeared to be realized: his museum had become a public institution accessible to the masses, living up to an earlier claim in the *Mirror* that it was "indeed a boon to the public of much value."[2]

This transformation of private house into public museum provides a sequel of sorts to the preceding chapter. While chapter 3 focused on how the work of the museum came home, this chapter will move in the opposite direction to follow the people out into the public sphere and into the museum to examine what became a national pastime in the nineteenth century, the museum visit (fig. 10). Two of the age's most public figures, Queen Victoria and the duke of Wellington, were avid museum goers; indeed, the duke had attended the Crystal Palace on almost every one of its 164 days. And people followed suit, as curators grew more accommodating and museums became increasingly receptive to larger audiences. The number of days on which no admission was charged multiplied, weekend and evening hours expanded, admission restrictions relaxed, and cheap guidebooks proliferated. In the 1868 *Guide to the South Kensington Museum* the National Gallery advertised free days on Mondays, Tuesdays, Wednesdays, and Saturdays. Even the British Museum, which most doggedly resisted public access, announced in the 1879 *Guide to the South Kensington Museum* that Saturdays would become free days. In the 1890 guide the British Museum boasted that every day except holy days would be free and that the museum would be open until eight in the evening during the early summer months. In the 1894 guide the British Museum advertised that portions of its collections would stay open until ten, for it had installed electric light, one of the first public buildings in London to do so. In 1896 the museum stayed open on Sundays.

Such late evening hours for museums were the inspiration of Henry Cole in his South Kensington Museum. As is evident from his writings, Cole considered relaxed museum admissions his greatest achievement: "For the first time in this or any other country working men or the weekly wages class have been enabled equally with the richer classes visiting in the day time to use a Public Museum without sacrificing their daily earnings."[3] On this accomplishment, Cole unceasingly contrasted his museum with the British Museum: "These objects would afford instruction and pleasure to thousands rather than to hundreds only in Bloomsbury." And "double the number of persons frequent the Art Library than attend the Print Room of the British Museum." Cole believed his museum to be a new type of institution, "unlike any other similar public Institution." The installment of gas lighting in the museum was a necessary, vital innovation: "In 1858 the Gas cost £780 in 1864 £3632.19.6. This expense indicates an amount of work carried on beyond the hours of daylight which is only equalled by arrangements for lighting the House of Parliament."[4] The house of the people now rivaled

Fig. 10. "Sketches in Berlin: Sunday at the Museum," 1873. (Courtesy of the Illustrated London News Picture Library)

the House of Lords. The 1865 *Guide to the South Kensington Museum* posted a liberal admission policy: "Admission Free on Monday, Tues., Sat., 10–10 Admission Sixpence on Wed., Thurs., Fri. 10–4,5,6 according to season." Moreover, the museum's art schools were open until nine, enabling working-class artisans to work for wages by day and study for improvement by night.

Today, such late-night hours seem remarkable, yet the figures for attendance are even more extraordinary. In the first year of opening, Cole writes, "The visitors to the Museum in nine months have been three fold the numbers at Marble House. They have exceeded 330,000." Again, Cole characteristically defends his museum at the expense of the older, exclusionist British Museum: "The average annual number at Marlborough House were 98,336. In 1858 at South Kensington there have been 456,288 persons. It was not until 1841 after 70 years from its foundation and an expenditure of about a million of pounds sterling that the annual visitors at the British Museum reached even 319,374 persons a year."[5] Cole had ample reason to be proud of his numbers. In its first year the South Kensington attracted 268,291 visitors. In 1862, an exhibition year, the museum drew crowds of 1,241,369. (For the sake of comparison: the museum registered 916,477 people in 1987.) Until the century's close, except for the years 1864, 1865, and 1867, attendance figures did not drop below 830,000. A special exhibition in 1876, *Scientific Apparatus*, attracted 275,813 people; and in 1881 an exhibition of Spanish art treasures brought in 1,022,000 visitors.[6] Cole had done all he could to make his museum easy to visit. Because he worried that the suburban site of the South Kensington made access difficult, he listed in his guides train schedules and taxi fares from various metropolitan stops to the museum. From the museum's inception Cole insisted on a library and artisan school, and his boldest innovation was the museum's great refreshment halls, the first museum restaurant in the world. A trip to his museum was to be a day's excursion.

The prominence of the South Kensington's refreshment halls most clearly demonstrates Cole's aspirations. When people entered the original front entrance, they first encountered the refreshment halls, resplendently decorated by the museum's art teachers and students and visible through large arched doors and glass walls. Immediately to the entrance's left rose the staircase leading to the art school; here students, teachers, and visitors could mingle. Thus greeted, visitors were treated to sensations of pleasure, conviviality, and entertainment before they witnessed collections of art. In light of such hospitality, the museum became an ideal place to rendezvous. Yet anxiety over the reality of museum crowds intensified as museum going grew in popularity. Newspapers published crowd reports, much like air-quality reports of today. The use of police to monitor the crowds was always an expense in Cole's annual budget; he was even pleased when the police cost rose from £3,110 in 1858 to £6,800 in 1864, an indication, he thought, of the museum's expanding work.[7] Museum officials were continually worried that classical sculpture would incite lewd behavior in both the male and female student copyists or invite the advances of excited sailors on visiting dock girls in the museum-going crowds. Officials were equally concerned about the potentially threatening presence of lunatics, derelicts, and suffragettes. Contemporary accounts, however, usually commended visitors for their good behavior. "These crowds . . . never make the rooms seem crowded; their decorum is equal to that which is preserved in the best drawing-rooms; there have been only two cases in the history of the [South Kensington] museum where persons have been ejected (the fault being tipsiness)."[8] Even when the crowd was as diverse as that described in the *Report from the Select Committee on the National Gallery* (1850), control was maintained: "The Gallery is frequently crowded by large masses of people, consisting not merely of those who come for the purpose of seeing the pictures, but also of persons having obviously for their object the use of the rooms for wholly different purposes; either for shelter in case of bad weather, or as a place in which children of all ages may recreate and play and not unfrequently as one where food and refreshments may conveniently be taken."[9]

Although Victorian museums aimed to serve a large audience, they were equally committed to stratagems of crowd management. Museums aspired not only to display art to the public but also to teach that public how to receive art.[10] Museums invested in monitoring devices—police, guards (Cole liked to choose retired military for the post), guidebooks that instructed museum goers on proper behavior (the South Kensington published a popular sixpence guide as well as a more opulent one-shilling book with color plates), casings, cordons, special lighting, and labels— to ensure the "ordering of the experience" for their public.[11] From the

Popular Handbook to the National Gallery (1888), for example, one learned not only about art but also about the status of art: the price of acquisitions, the thrilling tale of collecting, and the ranking of the gallery. The handbook was also interspersed with quotations from the best British poets: the age's own Browning, Tennyson, and D. G. Rossetti, as well as Shakespeare, Milton, Spenser, Dryden, and Pope. Its greatest feature, however, was choice excerpts from Ruskin's art criticism so that the masses could be tutored by the age's supreme art critic. First and foremost, the museum was an agent of decorum, a dispenser of etiquette. The museum taught the crowds not to touch art, what not to bring to a museum, where not to go next in the perfectly laid-out, unfolding ordering of art. The museum instructed the public on how to behave, disciplining and regulating its thoughts. The museum demanded surveillance: as people surveyed the collections before them, they in turn were watched.

As the symbolic space of nationalism, museums not only foster community in the tamest sense of that word; they also work to build something more directly, societally instrumental—something more akin to commonalty or consensuality.[12] In their commitment to edification, to the production of knowledge, museums construct a community, or collectivity, of the tasteful. As Thomas Richards has argued in *The Imperial Archive*, "whether undertaken by the museum, the university, or the geographical bureau, the project of amassing knowledge has usually presupposed not only an invisible interconnectedness among forms of knowledge but also a cultural cohesiveness among communities of knowers."[13] In effect, museums—one of the age's "invented traditions"—participate in what scholars have called social imperialism by challenging, in their transmission of culture, an individual's autonomy and agency and reasserting in turn duty and obligation.[14] This architectonics of tradition and heritage, this cultural authority turned political authority, informs the grammar of visuality and spatiality that Ruskin delineates for museums in "Picture Galleries: Their Functions and Formation" (1880). Not only the age's supreme art critic but also its most impassioned museologist, Ruskin speaks with utopian fervor about the perfect museum: "The first function of a Museum . . . is to give example of perfect order and perfect elegance, in the true sense of that test word, to the disorderly and rude populace. Everything in its *own* place, everything looking its best because it is there, nothing crowded, nothing unnecessary, nothing puzzling." The ideals of culture and acculturation and the desirability of distinction(s) prompt Ruskin to praise museums for their canon-forming powers in terms that are as readily social as they are aesthetic: "Nothing should be let inside the doors that isn't good of its sort. . . . The absolute best in each art, so far as attainable by the communal pocket, should be authoritatively exhibited, with simple statement that it *is* good, and reason why it is good. . . . The museum is only for what is eternally right." [15]

Serving to civilize new or savage elements, museums gave a culture a way to know its own boundaries. As an article from the *Times* claimed, the museum is "to be as a mirror held up before the knowledge of the age." [16] The museum became the idol of a citizen's honorable duty, as evident from the London travels of Thomas Sopwith, a mining engineer and railway surveyor. Even just a brief excerpt from his itinerary highlights his dutifulness: "Went through the museum of the Zoological Gardens in Bruton Street, and a very admirable museum it is. I next spent an hour at the Western Bazaar, and saw Haydon's pictures of Eucles and Punch, with which I was much pleased. . . . I then visited the beautiful and extensive exhibition of paintings . . . at the galleries of the Society of British Artists . . . went to the Royal Menangerie [*sic*] at Charing Cross." [17] Sopwith's careful recording of details and his attention to his aesthetic judgments suggest a pride in his visits. The London travels of Henry Mayhew's protagonist Cursty Sandboys in *1851: or, the Adventures of Mr. and Mrs. Cursty Sandboys* also teach a lesson, for beneath the sheer playfulness of this madcap tale lies Mayhew's endorsement of an education that goes beyond reading and writing, an education in standards for industrial art. Mayhew describes the exhibition site itself as something to behold: "The consequence is, that the groups within the building have already assumed a very picturesque appearance. To those who have watched the character of the visitors since the opening—the change in the dresses, manners, and objects of the sight-seers has been most marked and peculiar." *Punch* had to agree when it recommended that "a real exposition of Industry would require that the INDUSTRIOUS themselves should be exhibited as well as their productions. In a glass hive we ought to show the bees at work." [18] As the arena of the new middle class and the diligent working classes, the museum solicited not only attendance but employment as well. Such an opening up of opportunity made the museum the realm of new possibilities for self-improvement and upward mobility.

Yet the complexity and vitality of the nineteenth-century museum scene often go unrecognized in twentieth-century accounts. Too frequently, today's museologists feel the need to decry, or caricature, nineteenth-century museums in order to claim innovations as their own: "The typical nineteenth-century museum with its emphasis on objects and specimens was sometimes a static and even forbidding place for the general public. It was dead quiet and could be musty; visitors felt constrained to talk in hushed tones there." [19] Ivan Karp and Steven Lavine begin their anthology *Exhibiting Cultures: The Poetics and Politics of Museum Display* with the historical distinction between museum as "temple" and museum as "forum," arguing that only now have museums become "contested terrain." In her highly acclaimed study *Towards a New Museum,* Victoria Newhouse construes the early public museums as mausoleums and today's museums as "vehicles of entertainment," in spite of her later acknowledgment that the Pompidou's architectural precursor is London's Crystal Palace.[20] And theorists of postmodernism, although interested in the institutionality of the museum, sometimes undervalue the nineteenth-century museum so that they can erect the concept of the correct and corrective museum. In her essay on the Musée d'Orsay, for example, Patricia Mainardi states that only in postmodern architecture is "the resolutely inert, non-multi-media quality of nineteenth-century art . . . subsumed by the highly dramatic 'amazing space.'" [21] She goes on to insist that the "museum-as-spectacle" is a twentieth-century phenomenon, apparently overlooking how devoted a spectacle-loving populace Victorian museum crowds were. One need only visit Richard Owen's Natural History Museum to witness the Victorian use of "amazing space." Owen loved the vaulted hall and the long gallery; he pursued the great space and the immense specimen, insisting on bewildering dimensions wherever he could, in order to dazzle his gazers. Indeed, his move to South Kensington was prompted by his desire for more space, and he was willing to sacrifice the public access afforded by Bloomsbury for it. In many ways the master of spectacle, Owen understood the power he wielded. By promising visions on a grand scale, he courted public devotion: "Birds, shells, minerals, are, however, to be seen in any museum; but the hugest, strangest, rarest specimens of the highest class of animals can only be studied in the galleries of a national one." In addition to this superlative sense of his own mission, Owen's plans for the Index Museum, where at late hours the masses could view all the kingdoms of nature in one room, and his request for a new large lecture theater, then an uncommon feature of museums, indicate his sense of entitlement regarding the natural world surpassed only by an uncanny sense of the crowd. On the museum's opening day, 18 April 1888, the *Times* proclaimed, "This is a great day with the young people of the metropolis, and will be an epoch in many lives."[22] That day, sixteen thousand people visited Owen's museum.

Not surprisingly, museums came to serve as the great arena for the crowd not only in Victorian life but also in Victorian fiction. In Henry James's *A London Life* (1888), the Soane Museum provides the setting for the novella's climactic scene in chapter 8. In part James utilizes the backdrop of the museum to impart to his reader the urban landscape, to vivify "a London life." An integral part of James's realism, the museum also serves his international theme as the site of education for the American. The museum is thus an expression of both urban and urbane existence— a cherished "source of knowledge" and privilege for James's American protagonist, Laura.[23] Laura spends much of her time in museums, cultivating her mind and thereby divorcing herself from her sister Selina's coarseness. It is the "poor girl's notions," James writes, that make Laura believe that in museums she finds "occasions for detachment, an escape from worrying thoughts" (75). To Lincoln's Inn Fields, then, Laura escapes with Mr. Wendover on a sight-seeing excursion. At the Soane Museum she hopes to forget her sister's transgressions and "qualify" herself; however, the museum turns out to be the site of Laura's humiliation. In the basement of the museum she and Wendover encounter Selina and her lover, Crispin, on a clandestine rendezvous. Here for the first and only time Laura witnesses her sister's otherwise rumored infidelity with Captain Crispin. In the Soane Museum, Laura's naïveté is undone.

Details ranging from mummies to pagodas portray the Soane Museum as a romantic interior, initially presenting the suitable backdrop for Wendover's courtship of Laura. James elaborates on the sense of wonder and pleasurable fear Laura feels observing the "strange vague things" of Soane's collection. Laura and Wendover take it all in properly: feeling young in the midst of age, applauding Soane's "prudent virtue of keeping," admiring the Hogarths, and taking note of the "sarcophagi, the mummies, the idols, pagodas, the artless old maps and medals" (80). This tidy scene of connoisseurship, enhanced with some romance and an equal measure of romanticism, remains within the confines of a comedy of manners. As Laura and Wendover descend to Soane's basement, which Laura calls a "cave of idols," however, the tone darkens. James's use of the pathetic fallacy in the fitful flashes of lightning and the "great deal of thunder" transforms the collectibles into "ambiguous[ly] sinister" objects and the social comedy into an exposé of public life. At the heart of Soane's collection, in the room of the Seti I sarcophagus (what Soane once called the "most conspicuous place in [his] museum"), Laura must face her greatest fear, scandal. As it turns out, the retreat takes Laura to the house of culture, where she must acknowledge the pains of being a cultural outsider. The backdrop of the museum highlights her illegitimacy and subsequent susceptibility to the newspaper's probe. In the novella's most charged scene Laura's expectations for the museum fail, pointing to James's ambivalence about bourgeois museum culture.

Although Laura remains surprised by "the strange accident of their meeting" in "one of the least known" spots in London (82, 79), according to attendance figures and fulfilling curators' ambitions, everyone was going to the museum. It is thus not surprising that Victorian novelists often turned to the museum as a rich scene for action. Time and again, novelists express an affinity with the museum enterprise: in true triple-decker fashion, the museum presents a wide canvas, complete with an abundance of things and characters ordered with a multiplot's mastery. Even a domestic novelist like Jane Austen described the particular appeal of her visits to museums in an 18 April 1811 letter to her sister Cassandra: "Mary and I, after disposing of her Father and Mother, went to the Liverpool Museum, and the British Gallery, and I had some amusement at each, tho' my preference for Men and Women, always inclines me to attend more to the company than the sight."[24] In short, the museum satisfies Austen's writer's eye not in the objects it houses but in the crowd it attracts—providing ample material and models for "Men and Women," that is, characters and relationships. As we shall see in Charlotte Brontë's *Villette* (1853) and George Eliot's *Middlemarch* (1871–72), the marriage plot and museums, where characters fall in and out of love, often intersect. Exhibited objects become the gauge for sensibility and for the matching of sensibilities; thus the gaze becomes incisive and amorous simultaneously. Moreover, the museum insists on the presence of society, forcing love and culture to collide, and Lucy Snowe and Dorothea

Brooke will wrestle against the museum in order to affirm their private passions. In E. M. Forster's novel *Maurice* (written 1913–14) the panic of the cultural outsider becomes inevitable as desire's battle against the demands of convention and community ends in climactic departure from the British Museum. A tale of cultural estrangement, if not dispossession, *Maurice* gives added resonance to James Boon's plangent utterance, "Any museum, any museum at all, makes me sad." [25] For Brontë, Eliot, and Forster, love in the museum challenges the normative by prompting an interrogation of cultural constructions of gender and sexuality—for the museum, as a cultural construct that poses as the temple of essentialism, is the necessary site, whether it be for affiliation or resistance. What follows, then, is a gallery of closer readings of these fictionalized rendezvous in museums, scenes that are often overlooked even though the novels in which they appear are frequently taught, analyzed, and discussed. This chapter is, in effect, an exposition of expositions prompted, in part, by a more general curiosity about the affinities between museums and novels and the connections between collecting and narrative. As Mieke Bal persuasively argues in "Telling Objects," "collecting is an essential human feature that originates in the need to tell stories. . . . Collecting is a story, and everyone needs to tell it." [26] The master pattern of the museum may have much to reveal about the master narratives of the century. And so a tour of readings through a gallery of museum fictions begins.

Gallery A: The Museum under Revision

In chapter 19 of *Villette* Lucy Snowe ventures out of the home in order to visit a Villette picture gallery. Such migrations from the domestic to the public sphere recur throughout the novel, with the effect of exposing the imbalance of cultural enfranchisement between men and women. Understandably, then, the trip initially fills Lucy with great trepidation: the public space, the impersonal interior of the museum gallery, represents for her the space of the cultural, the other or nonself, the masculine. At first she marvels at Dr. Bretton's "insider's information": "I often felt amazed at his perfect knowledge of Villette; a knowledge not merely confined to its open streets, but penetrating to all its galleries, salles, and cabinets: of every door which shut in an object worth seeing, of every museum, of every hall, sacred to art or science, he seemed to possess the 'Open! Sesame.'"[27] Later, in the gallery, M. Paul directs Lucy's gaze, forbidding certain sights to her, and de Hamal takes pleasure denied Lucy in viewing the forbidden *Cleopatra*. Yet Lucy's fear has clear limits: she admits up front that she likes to visit picture galleries but "dearly" prefers to be left there alone. Her eagerness to go and observe coupled later with the intricate discernments of her art criticism and her maneuverings through the crowd during the visit make the scenes of chapter 19, titled "The Cleopatra," some of the novel's most interesting and revealing. Here in the museum Lucy's strengths and Brontë's pressing interest in interpretation—developed through Lucy's narrative method and explored within the thematics of the novel and of this scene—become apparent.

As many readers have claimed, *Villette* depicts numerous scenes of education and examination that Lucy must endure; only with time and growth will she be able to conduct in addition to submit to both. These scenes of education and examination, moreover, often fall to and are executed by "the shared assumptions" of society.[28] One such scene of instruction unfolds in the Villette gallery, which presents a test for Lucy in the canon; it is an ordeal that she both endures and triumphs over, for, as Janet Gezari argues, Lucy resembles most of Brontë's characters, who "define themselves in terms of their accommodation and resistance to hostile circumstances." In the hostile sphere of the gallery we watch Lucy perform as Joseph Boone so accurately describes: "Continually swerving out of our grasp just when we think we 'have' her, Lucy paradoxically creates a space both within and outside her text that allows her to become an autonomous self, one who escapes traditional female choices and confinement within traditional categories of the Victorian heroine."[29] Swerving away from pure accommodation and escaping through resistance, standing simultaneously within and outside the gallery space, Lucy proceeds to recount her own art criticism. She is most defiant before the resplendent *Cleopatra*. As "the queen of the collection," this showpiece demands special treatment: "set up in the best light, having a cordon of protection stretched before it, and a cushioned bench duly set in front for the accommodation of worshipping connoisseurs" (180). Yet Lucy refuses to be accommodated or to worship; rather, she embarks on a willful rereading of the painting before her. Her demystification of the masterpiece exposes the vases and goblets on the canvas to be mere pots and pans and the painting's lavish ornamentation to be "wretched untidiness": "A perfect rubbish of flowers was mixed amongst them, and an absurd and disorderly mass of curtain upholstery smothered the couch and cumbered the floor" (180). Lucy grows impatient with the artist's and model's indulgences: "She ought to have been standing. . . . She had no business to lounge. . . . She ought likewise to have worn decent garments. . . . There could be no excuse" (180). In debunking the Cleopatra's sensuality as "very much butcher's meat," Lucy expresses her most radical disenchantment with the masterpiece: representations of woman as flesh dehumanize woman, even making her complicit in her own commodification. The Cleopatra's body—this "*commodity* of bulk," "that *wealth* of muscle, that *affluence* of flesh"—becomes the site of consumption, and the patriarchal archive has appropriated the body of woman (180, emphasis mine).

The Cleopatra is not, however, the only specularized woman Lucy confronts in the museum. With equal repulsion, at M. Paul's request, she observes *La Vie d'une femme,* a narrative painting that also objectifies woman, casting her into the determined roles and poses of maiden, wife, mother, and widow. The two masterpieces form a revealing diptych, one representing the exotic, sensual female that man desires and the other the domestic, dutiful female of Victorian sentimental narrative that man expects. Neither image elicits Lucy's approval. Her assessment of the narrative painting is even more vitriolic than her mischievous revision of *Cleopatra.* Lucy must resort to such language as "most villainous," "she-hypocrite," "most exasperating," "cold and vapid," "bloodless, brainless non-entities" (182). The reasons for Lucy's investment in such art criticism become clear when she must ultimately confront herself as specularized woman, for the museum setting prompts M. Paul's condemnation of her inability to play both nurse and nun (Sister of Mercy) to Marie Broc the cretin. "Women who are worthy the name," argues M. Paul, take naturally to nurturing. But Lucy resists the gendered argument, "Could Monsieur do it himself?" (184). After rejecting the many "master"-pieces of piecemeal Victorian mistresses, Lucy turns to "some exquisite little pictures of still life." In these representations of life that stand outside gender and ego, Lucy finds a taste and a truth all her own. She is able to rescue for herself "fragments of truth here and there which satisfied the conscience" (179).

In the museum Lucy forms discriminations that aid her in remapping representations that initially leave her little space. She finds space for herself, for her private self, in the public space of the museum. Only after offering her interpretation of *Cleopatra* does Lucy check her catalog for the "official" description of the "notable production," but the catalog cannot restrain her from dismissing the masterpiece in the end as "an enormous piece of claptrap" (180). And M. Paul cannot insist that Lucy continue to study *La Vie d'une femme* when she chooses to gaze at *Cleopatra:* "But I have looked at her a great many times while Monsieur has been talking: I can see her quite well from this corner" (184). Her defiance comes, however, only as the fruit of a fierce battle between what Lucy calls Will and Power: "The former faculty exacted approbation of that which it was considered orthodox to admire; the latter groaned forth its utter inability to pay the tax; it was then self-sneered at, spurred up, goaded on to refine its taste, and whet its zest. The more it was chidden, however, the more it wouldn't praise" (179). Here Lucy makes explicit the revisionist tendency of her iconoclastic tastes. Her Will does not win the battle, even though it is capable of weakening her Power, which is synonymous with passion. In fact, her Power becomes more resistant and defiant for the struggle. Finally, the heterodox emerges triumphant, and Lucy is able to blaspheme in the temple of culture: "Nor did I, in the end, tremble to say to myself, standing before certain chefs d'oeuvre bearing great names, 'These are not a whit like nature'" (179).

Lucy's bold reinterpretations are the work of her revisionary gaze within the museum, her actions on and interactions with her environment. Among the many specular females and observing males, Lucy watches—"I remained quiet; yet another minute I would watch" (185). She claims early that her visit to the museum is not for pure pleasure or passive reception: "Meantime, I was happy; happy, not always in admiring, but in examining, questioning, and forming conclusions" (179). With a gaze that is inquisitive, even inquisitorial, Lucy demonstrates what Joseph Litvak identifies as her "contestatory energies" and what Rachel Brownstein calls her "strange new energies that can transform conventional signs."[30] Here, in the Villette museum, the conventional sign turns out to be the overdetermined sign of woman. The countermoves of Lucy's art criticism typify her strengths of intellect and imagination evident throughout the novel; it is such energy, which often directs the

novel's own narrative method, that much recent scholarship identifies as
Brontë's true interest and innovation in *Villette*. What Litvak subsumes
under the term "theatricality," what Gezari identifies as "defensiveness,"
what Judith Lowder Newton describes as the "revision of scripts" are all
functioning within the space of the gallery.[31] Like the figure of the Vashti
that appears later in the novel, the focus of much recent criticism, the
gallery's *Cleopatra* foregrounds the novel's central issues of role-playing,
enactment, observer, and observed. But the museum goes beyond the
theater in examining image and assessment and, through representation
and then evaluation, defending "the right to speech."[32] Lucy's contest
within and her contestation against the museum do not raze it but rather
challenge the coherence and completeness of the collection, leaving the
museum under revision or, better yet, under (re)construction.

Gallery B: Resisting Rome

Dorothea Brooke enters a museum only to yearn to escape its walls, staying only long enough to redirect her love to a worthy object. In *Middlemarch* Eliot sends Dorothea and Casaubon to Rome for their wedding
journey. The Roman action takes place predominantly in the Vatican
Museum, where the novel's central love conflict ensues. Here the reader
is first apprised of Dorothea's disillusionment with married life: five
weeks into her honeymoon, she doubts her love and respect for Casaubon. The Vatican Museum is thus the site of a pivotal scene—what one
critic calls "one of the most dazzling moments in *Middlemarch*" and another identifies as "the most striking scene of aesthetic response depicted
in George Eliot's *Middlemarch*."[33] Eliot's purposes in choosing such a setting are manifold. As Dorothea moves through the carefully drawn space
of the museum, she reflects and is in turn observed and reflected on by
Naumann, Will, the narrator, and reader alike. The tableau of Dorothea
among the marbles forms an intensely visual, perspectival scene. We are
asked to watch Will and Naumann watch Dorothea; and we are asked to
watch twice, for in the next chapter the scene is replayed from an omni-
scient point of view. This scene of spectatorship parallels the novel's larger
themes of what we know and how we know what we know. More point-
edly, however, Eliot's comparisons of Dorothea with an art object within
the collection, the Cleopatra/Ariadne statue, establishes an image with at

least a triple valence. Like Lucy, Dorothea stands before a Cleopatra, in a similar "confrontation with the conventionalized and prescriptive aesthetic ideals of femininity." Unlike Lucy, though, Dorothea echoes, indeed intensifies and surpasses, the sexuality of the figure in the collection, this Cleopatra that Abigail Rischin calls "the quintessential object of male desire and the embodiment of the desiring female subject."[34] Descriptive details foreground Dorothea's sensuality: her "long cloak" "thrown backward," the "one beautiful ungloved hand [that] pillowed her cheek," and the luminous "white beaver bonnet."[35] Yet Eliot is quick to clarify that the statue depicts not Cleopatra but Ariadne and has suffered, during the early years of the nineteenth century, from the misprision of spectatorship. Eliot indicates to future readers of her novel that she and her readers of the 1870s would have been aware of this misidentification that when corrected turns the sexualized woman into the mythic woman abandoned by Theseus, as Dorothea will be by Casaubon. Additionally, Dorothea's museum trip subjects her to the pain of "measuring her ordinary woman's life against the conflicting images of heroic womanhood."[36] Whatever the significance of the sculpture—whether it be erotic, tragic, or heroic—Dorothea will prove, as we shall see below, the museum's resistant visitor.

Most immediately, the museum confirms the incompatibility of Dorothea and Casaubon. As its title indicates, book 2 of *Middlemarch* explores the old and young; thus the Vatican Museum appropriately reveals a young Dorothea visiting, at her husband's recommendation, an old world of sculpted Meleagers and Ariadnes. Contrasting Dorothea's charm with the "voluptuousness" of "the reclining marble," Naumann draws the distinction: "What do you think of that for a fine bit of antithesis? . . . There lies antique beauty . . . and here stands beauty in its breathing life" (140). Casaubon and Dorothea embody such an antithesis. His pursuit of the antique is suitable to the museum and museumlike Rome. Accordingly, Eliot often describes Casaubon's work through museal metaphors, likening his notes to "shattered mummies," "fragments," "crushed ruins," or "the surplus stock of false antiquities" (351, 152). Indeed, Dorothea's first impressions of Casaubon set the analogy in motion: "Almost everything he had said seemed like a specimen from a mine, or the inscription on the door of a museum which might open on the treasures of past ages" (24). Casaubon's hunt for the "key to all mythologies" and his endless collecting and classifying are archaeological, museal activities that identify him with the historicity of the antique world. Often he speaks in the idiom of a museum catalog or Baedeker guide. In response to Dorothea's desire to know about the frescoes in the Villa Farnesina, "But do you care about them?" Casaubon can only reply, "They are, I believe, highly esteemed. Some of them represent the fable of Cupid and Psyche, which is probably the romantic invention of a literary period, and cannot, I think, be reckoned as a genuine mythical product. But if you like these wall-paintings we can easily drive thither; and you will then, I think, have seen the chief works of Raphael, any of which it were a pity to omit in a visit to Rome. . . . Such at least I have gathered to be the opinion of conoscenti" (146). Casaubon's ambition to be one of the "conoscenti," to know what is held to be edifying or striking, leaves him unmoved by the mythic erotic pair, thereby alienating the passionate Dorothea, who yearns for the romantic inventiveness Casaubon condemns. Her lack of interest in the museum—she "went on through the Museum out of mere listlessness as to what was around her" (150)—is antithetical to Casaubon's commitment to scholarly accumulation, an acquisitiveness that dooms him in a novel preoccupied with "the hoarding of information and the limitation of what can be known." [37]

When Casaubon recommends the frescoes to Dorothea, Eliot describes the "measured official tone" of his speech (146). This official quality of the museum goer or art connoisseur generates Eliot's critique of a sphere that she, in her own life, found congenial yet that for Dorothea includes the potentially oppressive, always powerful realms of knowledge, history, and society. Dorothea's trip to the museum "does not bridge the gap between . . . art and her own sense of purpose. As the novel progresses, Ladislaw becomes less the aesthete, but Dorothea does not become more the connoiseuse." [38] In a novel that will praise "unhistoric acts," this move beyond the cultural knowledge contained within the archive is imperative. For Dorothea the museum visit is one in a series of oppressions she suffers not only at the hands of her husband but also at the hands of society. The museum becomes for her a site of great pain as she must confront her alienation in an unknowable world, her marginality and dispensability in the official world that leaves her with what Raymond Williams has called a "divided consciousness of belonging and not belonging." [39] Thus Rome's collections haunt Dorothea:

Ruins and basilicas, palaces and colossi, set in the midst of a sordid present, where all that was living and warm-blooded seemed sunk in the deep degeneracy of a superstition divorced from reverence; the dimmer but yet eager Titanic life gazing and struggling on walls and ceilings; the long vistas of white forms whose marble eyes seemed to hold the monotonous light of an alien world: all this vast wreck of ambitious ideals, sensuous and spiritual, mixed confusedly with the signs of breathing forgetfulness and degradation. (143–44)

This bristling passage is unforgettable as the vision it describes "jars" and "shocks" Dorothea, who, the narrator tells us, will never forget these images of surreal Rome. This "city of visible history, where the past of a whole hemisphere seems moving in funeral procession with strange ancestral images and trophies gathered from afar," heightens "the dream-like strangeness of [Dorothea's] bridal life" (143). The museum emerges as one of the many weblike images the novel invokes to convey the constraints under which individual life must struggle. By highlighting character in setting, the museum is emblematic of the novel's central philosophical debate about the individual's struggles within and often against community. Dorothea searches in her life for a living tradition continuous with the present but fails to find it, and her museum visit highlights the failure of this quest. In short, Eliot, like Brontë, is skeptical of the shared assumptions of intellectual inheritance; thus the museum becomes a receptacle for the novel's pessimism about collective life.

The scene in the Vatican Museum readdresses the issues articulated in Eliot's prelude: how can man or woman achieve nobility of action and character in a world, history, or society hostile and foreboding? But in the novel's devaluing of collective and collected life, its championing of the individual emerges, and thus the scene in the museum is as much one of promise as of menace. Dorothea's suffering in and ultimate resistance to the museum highlight dichotomies important to the novel such as knowledge and ardor, reason and feeling, community and individual. Debunking the taxonomic reason housed within the public space of the museum, the novel finds private space for generosity and passion. As Gillian Beer acknowledges, "This emphasis on plurality, rather than upon singleness, is crucial to the developing argument of *Middlemarch* which, with all its overtly taxonomic ordering, has as its particular deep counter-enterprise the establishment of individual diversity."[40] Indeed, Will and Dorothea rendezvous, or at least encounter each other, in the museum. But their indifference to their surroundings is significant. When we first see Will, the narrator tells us he "had just turned his back on the Belvedere Torso in the Vatican and was looking out on the magnificent view of the mountains from the adjoining round vestibule" (140). And Dorothea seems equally uninterested in art: "Her large eyes were fixed dreamily on a streak of sunlight which fell across the floor" (140). Later we learn that it is not even the sun but the very interior of her soul that consumes her energies. Dorothea prefers the drive out into the Campagna, "where she could feel alone with the earth and sky," over the "best galleries," "chief points of view," "grandest ruins," and "most glorious churches" (143). She later exclaims, "There were so many things which are more wanted in the world than pictures" (153). Dorothea and Will meet in the museum only to escape its walls.

The novel's romanticism is thus able to flourish. The chance for sublimity lies outside society, outside its institutions, outside a museum's walls. The novel condemns most involvements in the world as acquisitiveness—Bulstrode, Rosamond, even Lydgate are tainted—and privileges instead a Wordsworthian native generosity, perpetually unrealizable, unmanifested, and therefore untainted. Dorothea's pain within the museum marks her eventual glory. To Will she relates, "When I begin to examine the pictures one by one, the life goes out of them, or else is something violent and strange to me. . . . It is painful to be told that anything is very fine and not be able to feel that it is fine" (153). Dorothea confesses throughout the novel her inability to understand art; yet this deficiency is a sign of her transcendence. When she admits she cannot produce a poem, Will accordingly says she is a poem. Similarly, Dorothea's status as pure image and essence makes her an unsuitable museum goer. She needs to stand outside society, outside the novel's panoramic realism, and exist within the novel's lyrical, romantic core. She also must stand outside class, distanced from the self-estrangement of middle-class materialism. Knowledge of museum art is too much a thing, too much an accomplishment or acquisition, too much a part of the bourgeois world embodied by the Vincys. Indeed, Eliot hints at a class critique when she writes, "The weight of unintelligible Rome might lie easily on bright nymphs to whom it formed a background for the brilliant picnic of Anglo-foreign society; but Dorothea had no such defense" (143). Touring the museum world is the corrupting vice of the bourgeois elite. As Dorothea later laments, the art of Rome "adorn[s] life for us who are well off" (395). Accordingly, Casaubon's work seems all the more odiously leisured, and the fixed tradition of a museum's canonicity becomes his suitable symbol: He "'lives too much with the dead' and in so doing manages to deaden his responses to the existential needs of the living." In short, he "studies history; he does not contribute to its making." His temperamental opposite, Dorothea is antimuseal. As D. A. Miller has argued, with words unwittingly suited for a discussion of the museum, "All the protagonists of *Middlemarch* want 'something else': something not yet possessed or even available in their community. In a full sense of the word, they *desire*." [41]

Gallery C: Blackmail in the British Museum

Maurice goes to the British Museum to confirm his homosexuality, wielding the revisionism of Lucy and the resistance of Dorothea. Here Maurice learns that he and Alec must live outside class but that with such marginalization comes immense freedom: all England is theirs. This rendezvous in the museum is *Maurice*'s climax; it is the chapter that Forster insisted "had to be extended," and critics have usually acknowledged the resonance of the scene.[42] Lytton Strachey called it the scene of the "fatal sentence . . . 'he loved Alec.'" In a 1971 review in the *New Statesman*, V. S. Pritchett claimed, "The blackmailing scene in the British Museum, with its lies, its collapse and abrupt reconciliation, is excellent." And Claude Summers called the "meeting of Alec and Maurice in the British Museum . . . one of the novel's most delightful scenes."[43] But critics have tended not to explore the reasons for that very excellence and delightfulness. Why in part 4 does Forster choose the British Museum for Alec and Maurice's rendezvous? Why in response to Alec's request "say where in London" does Maurice write, "A. S. Yes. Meet me Tuesday 5.0 p.m. entrance of British Museum. B. M. a large building. Anyone will tell you which. M. C. H." (217)? Why in the museum does the threat of blackmail loom and the promise of union occur?

It is initially clear that Maurice wishes to meet in the British Museum because it appears to be neutral territory and neutrality makes for the best battleground. Maurice is prepared to meet Alec and face his blackmailer's charge. Having once feared arrest, he is now invigorated by an athleticism that is ethical, and he acts out of the decency fundamental to a gentleman's fighting code: "He did feel fit, anxious to play the game, and, as an Englishman should, hoped that his opponent felt fit too. He wanted to be decent, he wasn't afraid" (220). Providing the common ground of a public-access site, the museum neutralizes the opponents' class difference. As Maurice says, the museum is the place "anyone will tell you which." The degree to which the diversity of its collections and its audiences makes the museum transsocial ultimately transforms it into asocial space; thus the museum also fits Maurice's vision of Alec and himself as outcasts struggling "without benefit of society" (217). One enters the museum anonymously, "without name." (Thus it is appropriate that Maurice later loses his name when he says to Ducie, "No, my name's Scudder.")

Yet the site of the British Museum offers Maurice the indisputable advantage of being a home field. Having sunk below his class in the act of soliciting a lower-class youth, Maurice finds a place that will soothe "his suburban soul" (58); he returns to the niche that England had prepared sometime ago for his youthful self, the "solid young citizen" of the prosperous bourgeoisie (154, 55). As the chapter of the rendezvous opens, the scene is intensely urban: "The rain was coming down in its old fashion, tapping on a million roofs and occasionally effecting an entry. It beat down the smoke, and caused the fumes of petrol and the smell of wet clothes to linger mixed on the streets of London. In the great forecourt of the Museum it could fall uninterruptedly, plumb onto the draggled doves and the helmets of the police" (219). For such a setting, Alec, the "untamed son of the woods," is sorely unprepared. His arrival at the museum shows him in his most unprepossessing and dispossessed state. The museum tests him, exposing his enervation (the echoing sneezes and debilitating chill), his ignorance ("What's all this place?"), and his menial, base desires for blackmail, which Forster likens to a "hunger": "The roar echoed down vestibules, and his face, convulsed and distorted, took a sudden appearance of hunger" (220). Submitting him to such trenchant discomfiture, the museum transforms Alec into a grotesque. The man who longed to make his way in the world and better himself, whether through emigration or blackmail, now stands admonished for his presumption. (In the next chapter Forster writes of Alec, "He wasn't deferential any more. The British Museum had cured that" [228]. As we shall see, the natural man Alec eventually triumphs over culture.)

When Maurice sets the British Museum as the scene of the rendezvous, he smiles, and his face becomes "mischievous and happy" (217). Again, his mischievous intent is to end the brutal dance of near blackmail, in which one exchanges knowledge for money and/or power, precisely at the site that exposes his potential blackmailer's ignorance.[44] In the museum, that class-encoded repository of knowledge, Alec relinquishes the damning bit of evidence, Maurice's letter to him. Yet Maurice's pleasure in confirming the appointment opens even more widely on the novel's more serious purpose: it enables Forster to culminate the radical critique of culture that has been necessary to prepare the way for homosexual desire, to draw into question the rule of the normative and pave the way for an embrace of difference. Throughout, *Maurice* criticizes institutional culture through the methodical debunking of school, religion, science and medicine, and ultimately the museum. Maurice's planned blasphemy, to meet his lover in the "poor," "solemn and chaste" British Museum, is sufficient reason for his smile. To Alec, Maurice irreverently defines the museum as "old things belonging to the nation" (220). It is appropriate that Maurice meets Ducie, who in the novel's opening scene prompts him to review the lessons of his preparatory school education—to be like father and never shame your mother—who teaches the young Maurice about the "mystery of [heterosexual] sex," and who, we learn in the second paragraph of the novel, is "orthodox," in the museum (13, 9). The educator and institutional figurehead Ducie significantly misunderstands the purpose of Alec and Maurice's meeting: "He addressed the silent pair on the subject of the British Museum—not merely a collection of relics but a place round which one could take—er—the less fortunate, quite so—a stimulating place—it raised questions even in the minds of boys" (224). This scene highlights the inability of society and its institutions to understand the passions and struggles of individuals; it then advances Maurice in the "rediscovery of the personal self below the social self."[45] In effect, this rendezvous reminds Maurice and Alec who their true foes are. As they become increasingly aware of their alienation, Maurice and

Alec draw closer. And we watch: "They kept wandering from room to room as if in search of something. They would peer at a goddess or vase, then move at a single impulse" (223). It is appropriate that Ducie views the museum as the catechizer of schoolboys into the joys of British solidarity, while for Maurice and Alec the museum only signals their marginal status.

As the threat of blackmail gives way to the avowal of love, Maurice abjures regimented existence for the freed body and its pleasures. Appropriately, the museum fades and daylight breaks on the lovers in a "strange hotel, a casual refuge"; eventually, the cancellation of the social realism emblematized by the museum makes room for the symbolic idealism of Forster's greenwood narrative closure. The twice-mentioned detail of the police within the museum—the patrols in the museum's forecourt and Maurice's threat of police action against Alec—is not coincidental. Like the novel's other institutions, and perhaps even more dramatically, the museum represents the regulated life. In his address "Art for Art's Sake" (1949) Forster condemns society's intrusions on individuals' lives: statesmen and politicians "tend, however, to confuse order with orders, just as they confuse creation with regulations. Order, I suggest, is something evolved from within, not something imposed from without; it is an internal stability, a vital harmony."[46] In his essay "For the Museum's Sake," written only three years after he completed *Maurice,* Forster explicitly condemns the museum as a debased enterprise, complicit in national hubris and international competitiveness: "After the Treaty of Vienna every progressive government felt it a duty to amass old objects, and to exhibit a fraction of them in a building called a Museum, which was occasionally open free. 'National possessions' they were now called, and it was important that they should outnumber the objects possessed by other nations. . . . As far as Museums breed anything it is a glib familiarity with labels." By the end of the essay Forster confesses a "determination to rob the British Museum," which, in its reduction of the museum's stature, *Maurice* has already accomplished.[47]

This broader social critique runs parallel with another, more intimate battle that Forster wages in *Maurice* in order to resolve for himself, and his characters, the Uranian debate. In the museum Maurice learns "that even the Clive of Cambridge had lost sanctity" (221). Here Maurice lets go of the nonphysical, Greek homosexuality that Clive idealized in their school days. The hellenizing mission that Clive and the museum share reminds us of Clive's exit from the text; he has become the ill traveler in a dead Greece, languishing in the dead theater of Dionysus in chapter 22. Wandering through the museum's Hellenic collections leaves Maurice and Alec dispassionate (Alec is literally chilled). At first sight the museum is likened to a "tomb, miraculously illuminated by spirits of the dead" (219). When espied by Ducie, Maurice is suitably "bending over a model of the Acropolis," a monument to Western culture and enlightenment (223). In this epiphanic moment Maurice chants three times "I see," for here he pierces through the hollowness of Oxbridge Hellenism, freeing himself from Clive and awakening yet again—this time to a countereducation in physical love. Even Alec notices the difference between their love and the Greco-Roman collections: "He looked back, his colouring stood out against the heroes, perfect but bloodless, who had never known bewilderment or infamy" (224). Transgressing the orders of both contemporary society and Clive's Hellenism, Maurice's confession of love for Alec shakes Western culture: "The rows of old statues tottered" (225). Maurice and Alec prefer instead the winged Assyrian bulls, which mark the first glimpse of a lovers' rapprochement. Maurice and Alec find them alluring because of their masculinity, virility (each notices that his bull has a fifth leg), and deviance or monstrosity . "standing each by his monster, they looked at each other, and smiled" (222). This pornographic gloss in the house of official culture stands in contrast to the censored lessons of Ducie; it suggests the bulls are an objective correlative for Maurice's renunciation of Western rationalism in favor of a sensuality that is Eastern and heterodox. Maurice has forsaken Christ, God, and Clive and is prepared to take Alec as his true comrade. Alec and Maurice escape the electric light of the museum: "They left the enormous and overheated building, they passed the library, supposed catholic, seeking darkness and rain" (225).

The rendezvous in the museum is the necessary penultimate phase, the expurgation, that prepares Maurice for the winged flight out into nature at the novel's conclusion. And the abrupt replacement of this meeting with a climactic departure underscores Forster's exploration, under the influence of Edward Carpenter and Walt Whitman, of the "opposition between nature and the products of an industrial society."[48] In the museum erotics and class come together; the museum has permitted

Forster to examine what many critics consider the greatest project in-
forming his corpus: fostering the rich possibilities of kinship between
democracy and homosexuality. In the museum Forster takes what Alan
Wilde calls "the more difficult step," a "reorientation of [his own] ideas
about class."[49] When Maurice claims his name is Scudder, his immediate
intent is to defuse Alec's blackmail ruse. Yet this renaming also registers
his alliance with his lower-class lover within the hallowed hallways of the
palace of high art. It is a counterpledge, a willful, whimsical, and wistful
mislabeling that shakes the official culture of the museum. Indeed, Maurice refuses to acknowledge any prior acquaintance with Ducie; he insists
they are strangers. In rejecting the established canon symbolized by the
space of the museum, Maurice becomes the vehicle for what Robert K.
Martin has persuasively identified as the leading mission of Forster's later
writings—to construct a homosexual tradition. Although such a mission
leads in this novel to an otherworld at best vaguely imagined, the very
movement beyond language and visualization at the end reminds us that
Maurice, and Forster, have entered the museum only to leave its eternal
verities and prosaic realism forever behind.

Gallery D: "Museum Quality," or Moving Up in the Louvre

Rendezvous in museums were part of the urban realism of nineteenth-
century fiction, produced in an age proud to record the hourly arrival of
visitors on free days to the South Kensington's Animal Division: 11:00,
10; 12:00, 34; 1:00, 82; 2:00, 92; 3:00, 185; 3:30, 213; 7:30, 185; 8:00,
47; 8:30, 441; 9:00, 414.[50] But rendezvous in museums also provided
nineteenth-century novelists with an essential tableau. Through scenes
played out within a museum's walls, novelists explore how culture defines
individual desires and how those desires can, in turn, defy society. In
the museum, moreover, political wisdom is often gained; characters frequently obtain a deeper understanding of the machinations of power as
they affect daily lives. For—because museums represent to a society an
efflorescence of its own civilization; because their imposing facades, their
cathedral-like ceilings, their massive dimensions embody an architecture
of consensus—museums cannot be understood divorced from the problematics of power. Again, Henry James provides a summary of and, here,
a conclusion to my argument. In the opening scene of *The American*

(1879) the protagonist Christopher Newman studies Murillo's Madonna as he reclines on an ottoman in the center of the Louvre's central gallery, the Salon Carré. Despite his definitively American naïveté, signaled by a fastidious observance of his Baedeker and museum guides as well as the extreme case of museum fatigue he must endure, Newman has, in this scene of siege, "occupied" and "taken serene possession" of the world of high art. This New World Christopher Columbus, this American "new man," has journeyed to Europe in search of a wife and a culture. Having arrived in Paris only three days earlier, Newman is already at the Louvre, where he can satisfy what he calls "a mighty hankering, a desire to stretch out and haul in." [51] Newman sees all of European culture ripe for "taking in," "made for him," purchasable like bazaar goods (73, 103). Accordingly, he first becomes "conscious of the germ of the mania of the 'collector'" when he buys his first copy of great art. Moreover, here, in front of a Paolo Veronese, Newman meets his old acquaintance, Tristram, who later introduces him both to the world of Old Europe's Bellegardes and, more particularly, to Madame de Cintré, who will prove to be Newman's greatest, if elusive, possession. In short, the opening scene in the museum serves up James's international theme, as it provides visual shorthand for his conviction that "Americans in Europe are *outsiders*." [52]

Yet the Louvre also provides the common meeting ground for Newman and Noémie, the lower-class copyist in the Louvre, who, with her father, haunts the galleries for her own purposes. Her broadcast in the Louvre that "everything I have is for sale" most unabashedly exposes the mass cultural milieu of the museum, suggesting that it is the cultural traveler Newman and the social aspirer Noémie who are most at home in the Louvre (199). Her transactions, which initially appear in stark contrast to her rarefied workplace, uncover the hidden agenda, what James calls "a great deal of by-play," of many museum goers (36). Like Newman, Noémie believes that the museum is the best place to "launch herself" (200). Indeed, Valentin falls in love with her in the smaller apartment devoted to Italian masters, for in the Louvre the parvenue Noémie can encounter the patrician Valentin. And Newman, driven by his "democratic instincts" to extend his life beyond the years devoted solely to business, frequents the museum, where crowds promise diversity and classes mix and thus the socially ambitious can circulate successfully. As it turns out, the museum in *The American* is less the shrine of

Old World forms and more the mart of New World energies. Thus James's premise of American dispossession yields to the novel's reversal of power: as the mise-en-scène for James's melodrama of aggression and near revenge, the Louvre grants the new man final moral superiority. Although Newman may feel at home in his museum more readily than do Lucy, Dorothea, and Maurice, in both his desires and success he best exemplifies Daniel Sherman's astute observation, which articulates the premise of all four novels discussed in this chapter: "We recognize museums above all as places, places where people come into contact with the visible manifestations of culture, with the various instruments and symbols of power and status, and with each other." [53]

If one characterizes the novel's defining focus as the individual in the crowd, then the affinities between the novel and the museum become clear. One scholar has made the kinship explicit: "The museum is one of the most brilliant and powerful genres of modern fiction, sharing with other forms of ideological practice—religion, science, entertainment, the academic disciplines—a variety of methods for the production and factualization of knowledge and its sociopolitical consequences." Indeed, like museums, novels often center on acts of intellection and representation, on knowledge—particularly the pleasure of naming and identifying—on searches for origins and relations, that is, provenance. Like museums, novels explore a certain sense of the past and the self; both depend on circumstantial evidence, on physical description of a material world constituted of many subjects and many more objects. Both then order this profusion, committed as they are to visuality and visualizing, to inviting the reader or visitor to visualize a world and comprehend the ties between community and vision. To see and belong capture Mikhail Bakhtin's description of the novel, a description that articulates the work of museums as well: "It is necessary to constitute this great world on a new basis, to render it familiar, to humanize it. It is necessary to find a new relationship to nature, not to the little nature of one's own corner of the world but to the big nature of the great world, to all the phenomena of the solar system, to the wealth excavated from the earth's core, to a variety of geographical locations and continents. . . . A man must educate or re-educate himself for life in a world that is, from his point of view, enormous and foreign; he must make it his own, domesticate it." [54]

V

"The Works on the Wall Must Take Their Chance": A Poetics of Acquisition

In our Museum galleries
To-day I lingered.

—D. G.
Rossetti,
"The Burden
of Nineveh"

IN THE FINAL stanzas of Tennyson's "The Palace of Art" (1832), the soul sickens of her remote "high palace" and escapes to "a cottage in the vale":

So when four years were wholly finished,
  She threw her royal robes away.
"Make me a cottage in the vale," she said,
  "Where I may mourn and pray." [1]

The soul's progress is often interpreted as an allegory for Tennyson's poetic development. The two abodes, the palace and the cottage, house Tennyson's conflicting poetic impulses toward romantic subjectivity and Victorian objectivity, respectively. The soul's retreat from the palace thus signifies Tennyson's abjuration of Keatsian bower lyrics in favor of Victorian community narratives. Indeed, after renouncing the art of pure beauty for an art of morality and domesticity, Tennyson assembled "The English Idyls." Here he privileged "the sense that handles daily life" ("Walking to the Mail"), shunning the sensibility of earlier works such as "Mariana," "The Lady of Shalott," and "The Hesperides." Much like his created soul, Tennyson recoiled from the isolated, imaginative life in order to construct laureate, collective mythoi.

Too many readers, however, overlook the third dwelling offered in

the poem's end, the palace of art gone public. The soul, even as she retreats to her rural abode, does not order the palace demolished:

> *Yet pull not down my palace towers, that are*
>   *So lightly, beautifully built;*
> *Perchance I may return with others there*
>   *When I have purged my guilt.*[2]

The cottage turns out to be only the penultimate dwelling place, a pur-
gatorial cleansing ground for the infernal delights of private art connoisseurship in the palace. The soul, representative of Tennyson the artist,
finds ultimate satisfaction and reward in visiting the palace of art with
others. The turning outward of the private gaze disarms art of its dangers.
Consequently, the discourse of transgression—"What is it that will take
away my sin, / And save me lest I die?"—is purged from the poem. By
the conclusion the "lordly pleasure-house," described exhaustively, lav-
ishly, even lovingly and possessively, becomes public property.

   A parable of personal artistic metamorphosis, "The Palace of Art"
reflects a wider transformation central to the political and cultural milieu
of post-Napoleonic Europe, for the French Revolution and the Bona-
partist regime democratized certain privileges, including the privilege of
owning and/or observing art. In short, Tennyson's poem can be read as
an allegory for the birth of the nineteenth-century museum: the aristocrat's mansion unlocked becomes the people's exhibition hall. Napoleon's
dissemination of cabinet collections for public consumption affected
British culture in numerous ways. The British were able in unparalleled
measure and number to enjoy works of art newly displayed in European
museums. The Louvre was particularly popular, and William Hazlitt was
its best British publicist. About his first visit to the Louvre, he wrote,
"There was her [art's] treasure, and there the inventory of all she had.
There she had gathered together her pomp, and there was her shrine,
and there her votaries came and worshipped as in a temple. The crown
she wore was brighter than that of kings. Where the struggles for human
liberty had been, there were the triumphs of human genius. For there, in
the Louvre, were the precious monuments of art."[3] Hazlitt identifies the
causal connection between the Revolution and the museum. The battleground lays the foundation for museum walls; art usurps the throne and
crown of kings, ushering in a new, modern epoch.

The Revolution also enabled Britain to acquire works of the European masters. Now that the heirloom was a commodity, Britain could stock its newly planned museums. The revolutionary spirit reached Britain's shores, instituting programs of politically charged cultural renovation. British aristocrats were encouraged, at times pressured, to commit their collections to public view. Hazlitt's *Sketches of the Principal Picture-Galleries in England* begins with a telling advertisement: "It may not be improper to mention here that Mr. Angerstein's pictures have been lately purchased for the commencement of a National Gallery, but are still to be seen in their old places on the walls of his house" (6:16). It was the nationalization of private collections like Mr. Angerstein's that made public handbooks and guides like Hazlitt's necessary. The museum had become an industry. And the industrial revolution, with its advances in modes of mechanical production and reproduction, furthered this democratization of luxury. Through purchase, tour, or copy, an unprecedented number of British people in the nineteenth century felt the pleasure of having, for, although collecting was popular in the eighteenth century, it was a privilege of the few; and the few rarely exhibited. By calling the Louvre a "tenantless mansion of godlike magnificence" (8:14), Hazlitt highlights the new democratizing program implicit in the nineteenth century or civic museum: owned by no one, the "mansion" is now owned by all.

The final tableau of Tennyson's poem—the poet's returning with others to the "museum"—is a scene that became increasingly important to nineteenth-century poets. As museums emerged the great civic project of Victorian society, poems wrestling with the museum grew more common. Not only did these museum poems mimetically capture the poets' experiences in the galleries; they also afforded poets the opportunity to explore an issue relevant to their own enterprise: the survival of art in the marketplace. As the facilitator, or facility, of the popularization of art, the museum—less a shrine or temple than the center of the commercialized art trade—exposed art to a more diversified public than ever before, permitting art to be displayed, gazed at, photographed, copied, commodified, and in all manners consumed. By combining thwarted romantic lyrics and Victorian narratives (the two main subdivisions of Victorian poetry), museum poems erect a new phenomenological construct: the poetic consciousness is placed within the civic sphere. Here the artist confronts other artists (through art objects) as well as his public and also wrestles with the exigencies the commodification of art entails: reception, proprietorship, commission, and transmission. Here he may face the burden of previous artistic generations. Here he may meditate on art's relationship to empire and imperialism, on culture's connection to power.

Before turning to the poems themselves, however, I must explain how a look at nineteenth-century poetry and museums leads to certain theoretical reconsiderations. These poems skew in significant ways the *ut pictura poesis* tradition. Although museum poems endorse the sisterhood of the arts by making analogies between verse and visual art, they supersede the concerns of pictorialism. Museum poems do not, for example, belong to the centuries-old fashion in which the single and singular painting or sculpture inspires the poet to compose an occasional poem. Thus D. G. Rossetti's "The Blessed Damozel" is not a museum poem, despite its intensely visual orientation and despite the Pre-Raphaelites' perfect embodiment of *ut pictura poesis*. Pure pictorialism, simple picturesque, Simonides's talking pictures and visual poems construe art only as the still beautiful form. Comparing a poet's activity to a collection of works of art rather than to an isolated masterpiece uncovers radically divergent issues. By acknowledging the work of art as one of many, the museum demystifies art and focuses on what some would call extraartistic issues. It places art in context—in the context of history, culture, politics, and economics.

Many of the pioneering studies of *ut pictura poesis,* such as Rensselaer Lee's *Ut Pictura Poesis: The Humanistic Theory of Painting,* Jean Hagstrum's *The Sister Arts,* and Lawrence Lipking's *The Ordering of the Arts in Eighteenth-Century England,* tend to elide such contexts. Even more recent interart scholarship like Wendy Steiner's *The Colors of Rhetoric* and W. J. T. Mitchell's *Iconology: Image, Text, Ideology*—work that is more sensitive to historical and cultural difference—does not sufficiently address the issues raised by poems about museums and by artists for whom certain idealisms are problematic.[4] Hagstrum writes, "The pictorial in a verbal medium necessarily involves the reduction of motion to stasis."[5] Pictorialist studies often aim for art as stasis, as perfected beauty, while the museum poem explores art in the vortex.[6] The museum poem is, to borrow Robert Langbaum's time-honored phrase, yet another kind of poetry of experience. While the museum poem exposes the disorder and clutter of existence, pictorialism aims for the idyll and ideal of order. It is a kind of utopianism: the ordering of the arts "had revived a dream: the dream of a unified culture in which all great works of art could be securely ranked and placed within one great idea of art."[7] As we shall see, the museum poem often engages in a critique of culture, shattering this very dream of cultural unity. Murray Krieger's essay "The Ekphrastic Principle and the Still Movement of Poetry; or *Laokoön* Revisited" best illustrates the failure of pictorialism to address the complexities of museum poems. Krieger begins discussing a specific kind of poem, then claims midway through his argument that all poetry is necessarily ekphrastic, and finally concludes (and this is his most disturbing point) that the best poetry is ekphrastic: "But I would give the special liberating license to our best poetry, insisting on its ekphrastic completeness that allows us to transfer the human conquest of time from the murky subjective caverns of phenomenology to the well-wrought, well-lighted place of aesthetics." By concentrating on Krieger's terms, we come to understand the spirit antithetical to the museum poem's program. Krieger praises the timeless in art—the "permanent form," the "artifice of eternity," "self-sufficiency," and "circularity." For him space becomes the anodyne for man's dwelling in time. By "a transformation of earth into art" and into a "frozen sort of aesthetic time" (that thus becomes atemporal timelessness or timefulness), all poetry transcends "the linear chronology of life's transience." In the tradition of Cleanth Brooks, Krieger claims the urn as the emblem for poetry. And, of course, he affirms Keats's "Ode on a Grecian Urn" as the great icon of ekphrasis. Krieger sees in this poem a turning away from the empirical in favor of the archetypal: "These [the unanswered factual questions of the poem] have guaranteed the poet's exasperation at . . . the inadequacy of fact before artifact. The final two lines confer universal absolution in that they absolve in absolute terms . . . the poet's need to ask such merely informational questions."[8] What happens, however, to ekphrastic principles when poets and readers ask "merely informational questions," such as who discovered the urn, which country owns it, and which culture produced it? Nineteenth-century poems about museums are interested in precisely these kinds of political and economic questions. The following pages explore what I call the poetics of acquisition articulated by poets who lived in an acquisitive age. The nineteenth-century museum—and the culture it erected—is the important, often neglected context that gives the following poems their texture.

Ian Jack's *Keats and the Mirror of Art,* although in some ways superseded by more recent critical trends that politicize the romantic poets, nevertheless contextualizes Keats's poetics in interesting ways. One of the book's central discoveries is that the museum was important to Keats and his friends. Their letters, essays, and memoirs reveal that Keats, Joseph Severn, Benjamin Robert Haydon, and Hazlitt frequented the museums and loved to collect. In March 1819 Keats wrote to his brother and sister-in-law George and Georgianna Keats, "In the morning Severn and I took a turn about the Museum—there is a Sphinx there of a giant size, and most voluptuous expression, I had not seen it before."[9] Haydon's autobiography assiduously records the days and hours spent at exhibits, especially the Elgin Marbles. About an exhibition of Italian masters, Hazlitt marvels, "I was staggered when I saw the works there collected, and looked at them with wondering and with longing eyes. A mist passed away from my sight: the scales fell off. . . . From that time I lived in a world of pictures." Hazlitt's "world of pictures" is by no means fantastic. Jack's study uncovers the literalness of the phrase: British society at the time was a world of pictures, pulsing with "the remarkable circulation and celebrity of many of the world's greatest pictures."[10] Keats wrote in such a world, finding sources in the museums for his visionary poetry.

Jack also discusses the significance of copies and copying in Keats's circle. The print shop, an institutional by-product of the museum, was an equally popular site for Keats and his friends—for both buying and making prints. Hazlitt explains how the original work of art becomes copy and copy becomes print. He takes his Raphael copy to "London, as this is frequently done," to "get prints taken." Hazlitt is, in fact, an enterprising copyist: "I have begun to copy one of Titian's portraits. . . . I made a very complete sketch of the head in about three hours, and have been working upon it longer this morning. . . . I intend to occupy the vacant days of the week in making duplicates of the copies which I do here, and in doing a picture of myself, in the same view as that of the Hippolito de Medici."[11] And Haydon's awe of the Elgin Marbles spurred him on to copy: "I drew at the marbles ten, fourteen, and fifteen hours at a time; staying often till twelve at night, holding a candle and my board in one hand and drawing with the other; and so I should have staid till morning had not the sleepy porter come yawning in to tell me it was twelve o'clock, and then often I have gone home, cold, benumbed and damp, my clothes steaming up as I dried them." [12]

Such details about copying lead to larger conclusions about life and creativity in a museum culture, for in the museum the reverence for art quickly turns into a kind of irreverence that allows the museum crowd to imitate and copy at will. Although one may assume that the museum functions as the preserve of the unique work of art, it is more accurately the despoiler of originality and the arena of duplication. Surprisingly, Walter Benjamin's essay "The Work of Art in the Age of Mechanical Reproduction" never directly discusses the museum's complicity in the "far-reaching liquidation" of the "contemporary mass movement." When Benjamin claims, however, that "by making many productions it [the technique of reproduction] substitutes a plurality of copies for a unique existence," he could be describing the museum, where the aura of art withers and authenticity is exchanged for reproducibility. [13] The transition from aristocrat's cabinet to people's museum parallels what Benjamin calls the exchange of art's "cult value" for its "exhibition value." The aristocrat needs to ensure the exclusivity of his work of art and thus shuns the common gaze; the museum, in contrast, invites all inside its doors, encouraging students to copy the masters, to turn those copies into prints, and to turn those prints into mass merchandise. To know, for example, that many of Keats's visions of classical beauty were modeled after Tassie gems (inexpensive plaster reproductions of ancient coins and medals) is to understand how sublimity can be linked to reproducibility. Keats's rarefied vision becomes reified.

Keats's two museum poems, "On Seeing the Elgin Marbles" (1817) and "To B. R. Haydon" (1817), cannot be adequately understood under the rubric of escapist Hellenism alone. The titles themselves are undeniably topical. Here Keats refers to the discoverer and propagandist, respectively, of the most-prized purloined antiquities of the nineteenth century. Lord Elgin's activities are the age's most vivid example of the politics and economics of art. In 1799 Thomas Bruce, the seventh earl of Elgin, was appointed British ambassador to the Ottoman government. Elgin quickly realized that his political post afforded an opportunity for antiquarian activities, particularly in Turk-occupied Greece. Although he claimed that he intended only to make drawings and copies of the sculptures, his dismay at the crumbling condition of the Parthenon and his disgust for the barbarism of the Turks compelled him to rescue the stones. When he had finished, Elgin had taken fifty slabs, two half slabs of frieze, and fifteen metopes.[14] By 1815 twenty-two ships had removed to the British Museum what is today almost half the surviving sculpture of the Parthenon.

Elgin's sale of the marbles to the British government was delayed six years; his initial demand for £64,440 and a peerage was rejected. He considered opening a private museum and charging for the exhibit; he also supposedly received offers for the marbles from other countries. All the while Elgin attempted to fuel publicity for his marbles. Only later did financial difficulties force him on 7 June 1816 to accept the British government's offer of £35,000. Elgin was able to stipulate that all future earls of Elgin be named to the British Museum's board and that the collection always remain intact and be known as the Elgin Marbles. Haydon's prophecy was realized: "You have immortalized yourself my Lord by bringing [the marbles]."[15] But criticism of Elgin was equally potent. Byron found ample opportunities to make Elgin the object of his satire:

> Let ABERDEEN and ELGIN still pursue
> The shade of fame through regions of Virtu;
> Waste useless thousands on their Phidean freaks,
> Misshapen monuments and maimed antiques;
> And make their grand saloons a general mart
> For all the mutilated blocks of art.

Byron's disapprobation of Elgin and his crowds peaks in "The Curse of Minerva":

> Be all the bruisers cull'd from all St. Giles'
> That art and nature may compare their styles;
> While brawny brutes in stupid wonder stare,
> And marvel at his lordship's "stone shop" there.
> Round the throng'd gate shall sauntering coxcombs creep,
> To lounge and lucubrate, to prate and peep.[16]

Aware of both Haydon's enthusiasm and Byron's vitriol, Keats articulated his own, very different response to the Elgin Marbles when Haydon accompanied him to the gallery in March 1817. Although Keats does not share Byron's political and moral outrage, his sonnets do articulate ambivalence, darkening once again the glow of Haydon's encomium. In "On Seeing the Elgin Marbles" Keats finds in the Hellenic form no still, beautiful otherworld but rather a reminder to the gazer that he dwells in the world—"mortality / Weighs heavily on me." Each marble "tells me I must die," Keats writes. Likened to a "sick Eagle," Keats cannot enjoy even the momentary transport of stanza 7 in "Ode to a Nightingale." Because the marbles represent in equal measure atemporal grandeur and time-wasted ruins, the heart experiences "an undescribable feud" and "most dizzy pain." The marbles are signs simultaneously of an empire's greatness and of its demise, its "sun" and its "shadow." Keats's sonnet reminds us that, although the museum is in part the preserver of past cultures, it is equally, even more potently, the ossuary that houses the dead. In this respect, "On Seeing the Elgin Marbles" resembles Shelley's "Ozymandias"; both poems envision the ruin only to shift the focus from the pure aesthetic of the *non finito* to questions of origin, culture, and appropriation. But Keats's choice of setting—the modern-day museum instead of the sands of the native desert—intensifies the sense of cultural death. In Keats's hands we see how the romantic fragment poem can evolve into the Victorian museum poem. Keats's lines capture the meditative moment in the museum, the pondering—as Haydon calls it—"on the change of empires." [17] For Keats the Hellenic ideal is not restorative but problematic.

The Hellenic is further compromised in "To B. R. Haydon." It is tempting to interpret Keats's opening apology, "Haydon! forgive me that I cannot speak / Definitively on these mighty things," as acknowledgment of his ambivalence. But Keats's objective in this sonnet is to compromise—nay, obliterate—the Hellenic by thoroughly contextualizing it within British culture and by praising one specific man's culture. The poem draws the reader's attention away from the marbles, leading him or her to gaze on the rightful owner of the statues—"that all those numbers should be thine." As a historical painter and ardent propagandist for public art, Haydon emerges the clear victor of Keats's sonnet. Keats pays tribute to the nationalist of the art world, to the man who once claimed, "My life has been connected with my glorious Country's Art." For Haydon, Elgin's acquisition marked a triumph for British taste: "I have lived to see [the marbles] purchased by an English Parliament, and contributed by my efforts towards influencing their purchase! I have lived to see the nobility and the people of my own country, crowd to look at . . . the graces of the Elgin Marbles . . . and I shall yet live to see the triumph of English art, and the fame and glory of English artists!" [18] Keats apparently agreed. The problematic Hellenism of the first sonnet gives way to the patriotism of the second. Keats's timid confession of poetic inadequacy in the sonnet's octave yields to the bold apotheosis of Haydon in the sestet. The two rhetorical questions of line 10—"Whose else? In this who touch thy vesture's hem?"—defiantly claim Haydon's hegemony. By the sonnet's end Haydon is enthroned in a reign of judgment, worshiped for his taste. The paradox of the collectible is apparent: Haydon's worshiping makes him worshiped; the collection pays obeisance to the collector. And Keats, first unsettled by his experience in the museum, ends the champion of the museum—in a sonnet that bristles with confidence on its surface yet seems to strain with deeper uncertainty.

Almost a hundred years later, Thomas Hardy turned to the Elgin Marbles in his poem "In the British Museum" (1912). An interrogator (most likely, the poet in the museum) opens the poem, inquiring of a museum visitor what he sees in "that time-touched stone" before him. In his search for meaning, the interrogator refers to the museum's informants, presumably its guards and guides:

> *It is only the base of a pillar,* they'll *tell you,*
> *That came to us*
> *From a far old hill men used to name*
> *Areopagus. (emphasis mine)*

But the poet returns to the hermeneutical moment directly before him, to the gazer who can impose his own meaning because the stone is blank, because "nothing is there." Although the gazer admits his ignorance, "I know no art," he presents his Christianized interpretation—"But I am thinking that stone has echoed / The voice of Paul." The gazer has chosen to see these marbles, despite their alterity so evident in Hardy's next Elgin poem, as the monument to Paul's address to the Athenians. Like other poems focused on the museum, this lyric depicts the crowd and its homespun interpretations, suggesting that for every museum piece there are two acts of appropriation: the originary, or archaeological, and the

ongoing, or interpretative. Hardy's poem reconstructs the moment of
art's reception before the museum's mass culture. For this man is merely
"a labouring man, and know[s] but little, / Or nothing at all." Nevertheless, he judges.

Hardy's treatment of this museum visitor remains gentle, however;
he is not attacked like Byron's bruisers from Saint Giles. Hardy's very
different motive for this poem lies buried in the twice-repeated, resonant
verb "echoed." The laboring man describes how Paul's words were intimate with the stone, how they "pattered," a verb that conveys the double
imprint of linguistic flow and physical impression. (The first line's "time-
touched stone" confirms this.) Having heard, having been touched, the
palimpsestic stone stands before the museum crowd as an emblem of late-
Victorian, modern Gothic existence. This vision of life—one that informs Hardy's oeuvre—depicts Victorian culture as at times enchanted,
at times haunted by lost empires.[19] An epigonic writer in an epigonic
epoch, Hardy feels the magnitude and the burden of history. In another
museum poem, "In a Museum," Hardy imagines the delights of being
thus haunted. This lyric (a revision of romantic bird poems) fantasizes
about reanimating a museum's fossilized prehistoric bird so that it might
join the "contralto voice" the poet heard just the other night. To hear
this "full-fugued song" is to imagine the "universe unending."

But reanimation can bring with it a curse. "Christmas in the Elgin
Room" (1905), Hardy's last poem to be published in his lifetime, returns
to the Elgin Marbles. Here Hardy reanimates the marbles, allowing the
ghosts of the museum to speak for themselves. By listening to the marbles
at the moment of their acquisition (hence the subtitle, "British Museum:
Early Last Century"), Hardy heightens the burden (both of pathos and
of guilt) at the heart of the museum enterprise. The poem opens in confusion; the pilfered gods cannot properly understand the signals of their
new culture. The celebratory ringing of Christmas bells, which for
Christian British culture signals "a day of cheer / And source of grace,"
becomes a dissonant clanging for the statues, "All loth to heed / What
the bells sang that night which shook them to the core." Hardy makes
his readers feel the dread, the conflict, the loss that fill this elegant gallery.
In the museum two cultures, as represented by their gods, the Christian
Christ and "Zeus' high breed," clash. And Hardy reminds us that the
Elgin acquisition is the second Christian triumph over classical Greece:

> *We are those whom Christmas overthrew*
> *Some centuries after Pheidias knew*
> *How to shape us.*

This poem is powerfully debunking: it exposes the day dearest to sentimental Victorian Britain, the day of supposed Christian goodwill, as a day of ill will—"Before this Christ was known, and we had men's good will"; and it depicts the edifying museum as a prison—an "exile," "this hall that blears us captives with its blight," "this gaunt room / Which sunlight shuns, and sweet Aurore but enters cold." Like other museum poems, "Christmas in the Elgin Room" functions as a critique of culture, condemning British artistic imperialism: "O it is sad now we are sold—/ We gods! for Borean people's gold."

Concerned with the exchange of gods for gold, "Christmas in the Elgin Room" is a meditation on fortune, in two senses of the word: fate or situation and (financial) success. The museum is the place where fortunes are made or broken. When Robert Browning turns to the art world in his painter monologues, he, too, studies fortune. Andrea del Sarto hears the jingle of the great monarch's gold chain in his ear, and Fra Lippo Lippi finds his meat and drink at Cosimo de' Medici's table. Himself an artist of uncertain fortune, Browning seems to commiserate with Pictor Ignotus's agony. Equally drawn to and repelled by the marketplace, Pictor Ignotus cannot determine his fortune. At first he idealizes the public life, "Of going—I, in each new picture,—forth":

> *Oh, thus to live, I and my picture, linked*
> *With love about, and praise, till life should end,*
> *   And then not go to heaven, but linger here,*
> *Here on my earth, earth's every man my friend.*

Reality, however, disrupts his fantasy:

> *These buy and sell our pictures, take and give,*
> *Count them for garniture and household-stuff,*
> *   And where they live needs must our pictures live*
> *And see their faces, listen to their prate,*
> *   Partakers of their daily pettiness,*
> *Discussed of,—"This I love, or this I hate,*
> *   This likes me more, and this affects me less!"*[20]

Browning immerses his painter figures, even Pictor Ignotus, who finally retreats, in the marketplace's worldly activities of buying and selling, taking and giving, audience approval and rejection. Art for Browning is a social production involving the interchange of producers, products, and consumers. A critic's comment made in reference to "Fra Lippo Lippi" pertains to Browning's general treatment of the visual arts: "But this account of activity and change exceeds the bounds of pictorialism and deconstructs its essential characteristics of static and superficial verisimilitude. This is now narrative." [21] Browning narrates artistry as activity and change, as it is affected by history and society. His characteristic preoccupation with the clutter of existence is telling: he appears as interested in the artifact as in the artist who made it. Thus his figures often interact with objects; the artistic generations confront one another through that which is transmissible, the work of art itself. Del Sarto, for example, wrestles with the spirit of Raphael as it is embodied in the copy Giorgio Vasari sent him of the Urbinate's work. Psychological and moral blueprints for the dramatic monologue, however, encourage readers to focus on selfhood at the expense of history and context. This hermeneutics based on a cult of personality has privileged the painter poems at the expense of a related genus of poem Browning composed, the painting or art-object poem. Here Browning most intensely explores the ramifications of art as commodity. To compose poems about the art object itself is his clearest acknowledgment of the marketplace.

"A Likeness" (1864) is such a poem. The poem alludes to the museum, yet it also portrays the life Victorian museum culture fostered beyond its walls: the bourgeois collector's life in the Victorian house-museum he constructs. [22] The triviality of this poem is deliberate. Browning intends to show art thrust amid the clutter of mundane existence. He demystifies the art world and portrays the incredible tedium to which art is exposed. The poem consists of three vignettes, each depicting a different owner and his or her attitudes toward the art object. As the poem opens, the portrait hangs in the dining room of a bourgeois couple, who treat it as "garniture and household-stuff." The wife dismisses it as a "daub John bought at a sale." The scene depends on caricature: the disengaged, ailing husband with corns; the wife suspicious of her husband and jealous of the portrait; and the dull-witted cousin with the half-interested interrogation. The scene closes on the portrait overseeing the prosaic activities of chitchat and the clinking and stirring of tea things.

Next the portrait becomes the property of a bachelor no less stereotypical in his youthful preciosity. For him the portrait holds an unprivileged place among the "other spoils / Of youth." Using a favorite stylistic device, Browning lists the miscellany of bachelorhood (so that form mirrors matter):

> *masks, gloves, and foils,*
> *And pipe-sticks, rose, cherry-tree, jasmine,*
> *And the long whip, the tandem-lasher,*
> *And the cast from a fist . . .*
> *And the cards . . .*
> *And a satin shoe . . .*
> *And the chamois-horns . . .*
> *And prints . . .*
> *And the little edition of Rabelais.*[23]

Again, the vignette ends with small talk. Just as the wife sees in the portrait what she wants to, the bachelor's friend imagines it to be Jane Lamb, his dancing partner one evening in Vichy.

The poem's final section transports the likeness to the home of a leisured yet salaried gentleman. Details reveal the society he keeps:

> *When somebody tries my claret,*
> *We turn round chairs to the fire,*
> *Chirp over days in a garret,*
> *Chuckle o'er the increase of salary,*
> *Taste the good fruits of our leisure,*
> *Talk about pencil and lyre,*
> *And the National Portrait Gallery.*[24]

The art collector and his friends are connoisseurs who relish poetry, music, and the museum—particularly that most refined of museums, a portrait gallery. The first-person voice of the final section emphasizes the role of proprietor who stores the "Fifty in one portfolio." And the beginning clauses of each stanza highlight the ethos of proprietorship: "All that *I own*," "*I keep* my prints," and "Then *I exhibit* my treasure" (emphasis mine). The verbs mark the inevitable progression from consumerism to collection to the museum. Art rests in polite company, in the company of men who attend the National Portrait Gallery, who are connoisseurs left at the poem's end bartering for artistic goods. In light of this poem, a remark by Dwight Culler seems misdirected: "Browning has no use for the connoisseur, whether of women or of pictures, but only for the creative artist, who can sometimes, in rare and unforeseen conditions, experience the revelation of beauty for one tremendous moment."[25] "A Likeness" depicts not "rare and unforeseen conditions," "one tremendous moment," or that "creative artist"; rather, it charts the random transmission of an art object through different kinds of societies and its unremarkable reception by different kinds of audiences. In one way, the intrigue of "A Likeness" lies in the old question, "if the mute object could talk, what tales would it tell?" But the pathos of the poem derives from how silent the likeness is, how it becomes everything and anything its owners desire, how its owners speak for it.

Rossetti's poem "The Burden of Nineveh" (1870) also captures the moment of an artifact's transmission, an artifact as monumental as Browning's likeness is small. This poem relies on an important nineteenth-century British discovery overshadowed perhaps only by the Elgin Marbles. Between 1845 and 1851 Sir Austen Henry Layard excavated the ruins of Nineveh as part of a more extensive nineteenth-century exploration, fueled by the allure of the East, of Egypt and Sinai. When Layard began his search, England possessed only a small collection in the British Museum. "A case scarcely three feet square inclosed all that remained . . . [of] Nineveh . . . [and] Babylon." Layard's ambition was thus firm: "I determined . . . to accept the charge of superintending the excavations, to make every exertion, and to economize as far as it was my power—that the nation might possess as extensive and complete a collection of Assyrian antiquities as . . . it was possible to collect."[26] In 1849 George Putnam published Layard's two-volume account *Nineveh and Its Remains,* which highlights the winged bull as his greatest acquisition and which immediately became a best-seller. Rossetti must have been familiar with Layard's popular tale, for, in a stanza that was edited from the final version of "The Burden of Nineveh," he describes the maids "just fresh from 'Layard's Nineveh.'" And the details of stanza 12 rise "fresh" from Layard's account:

> *The consecrated metals found,*
> *And ivory tablets, underground,*

Winged teraphim and creatures crown'd.
When air and daylight filled the mound,
    Fell into dust immediately.

The opening stanza of "The Burden of Nineveh" captures the moment when the poet and the artifact are positioned at the threshold of the museum. As the swinging door thrusts the poet out, the museum's portal prepares to receive the bull:

And as I made the swing-door spin
And issued, they were hoisting in
A winged beast from Nineveh.

The liminal status of creator and creation alike vivifies the act of committing and transmitting art. Rossetti's tenuous position registers his ambivalence toward the institution of the museum, an ambivalence he was able to articulate only through numerous revisions of the poem. The 1856 version of the opening stanza reads:

I have no taste for polyglot:
At the Museum 'twas my lot,
Just once, to jot and blot and rot
In Babel for I know not what.
    I went at two, I left at three.[27]

The earlier mindless, mechanical activities of jotting, blotting, and rotting (and their absurd internal rhyme) become the delicate lingering of the 1870 version. And by 1870 the jocose perception of the museum as a house of polyglot or a Tower of Babel has disappeared. Moreover, "the Museum" becomes "our Museum," the possessive indicating perhaps Rossetti's admission of his own involvement in the museum world. As Rossetti's seriousness about the museum intensifies, it becomes a place of "prizes."

Many critics wish to find in Rossetti and the Pre-Raphaelites a legacy of romanticism. Oswald Doughty's infamous labeling of Rossetti as a Victorian romantic persists among some readers. However, the opening tableau of "The Burden of Nineveh" envisions a Victorian rather than a Romantic artist, paralleling what Carl Woodring sees as the century's movement away from nature toward art and culture.[28] The museum thus replaces the mountains as the site of a poet's reverie, however uneasy that reverie has become. As a Victorian artist, Rossetti finds his place in the museum, and his personal investment in this place is apparent in a stanza that was later excised:

> *Here, while the Antique-students lunch,*
> *Shall Art be slang'd o'er cheese and hunch,*
> *Whether the great R. A.'s a bunch*
> *Of gods or dogs, and whether Punch*
> *Is right about the P. R. B.*[29]

When museums open and the demographics of the art world change, art is exposed to public scrutiny. Rossetti finds his own enterprise, as with all art, the concern of a new class of museum goers and museum students. He acknowledges that art now leads not to the alienation but to the education of the people. Thus he watches with interest the "school-foundations in the act / Of holiday, three files compact." The transmission of the winged bull becomes an emblem for the reception of Rossetti's own art.

When "they" (who, we assume, are the museum bureaucrats) of the first stanza complete the moving of the beast, Rossetti proceeds to describe its new "unblest abode," the gallery's interior:

> *Now, thou poor god, within this hall*
> *Where the blank windows blind the wall*
> *From pedestal to pedestal,*
> *The kind of light shall on thee fall*
> *Which London takes the day to be.*[30]

The interior of the museum ensures a certain epistemology, its spatialization a certain conceptualization. A paradox thus emerges: although the museum owes its prominence in part to the burgeoning nineteenth-century interest in historiography, its effect on exhibits can be homogenizing. The encyclopedic, totalizing enterprise of the museum can obscure historical difference.[31] Thus Rossetti's British Museum houses all the gods together:

> *did any god*
> *Before whose feet men knelt unshod*
> *Deem that in this unblest abode* (86–90)
> *Another scarce more unknown god*
> *Should house with him, from Nineveh?*

Rossetti's opening meditations on past and present, Assyrian and British, stop; by the poem's end distinctions between Nineveh and London are blurred, and the winged beast is now the god of London. The dim light, the blank window, the blind wall, the eternal recurrence implied in the phrase "From pedestal to pedestal," the schoolchildren learning the bull as a fact—all suggest the cold, undifferentiating, and undiscriminating gaze in the museum. The privileging of the exhibition value, Benjamin tells us, strips the totem of its useful and independent existence; what matters is its "being on view."

Stanza 11 highlights these issues while raising startling new concerns:

> *Why, of those mummies in the room*
> *Above, there might indeed have come*
> *One out of Egypt to thy home,*
> *An alien. Nay, but were not some*
>   *Of these thine own "antiquity"?*
> *And now,—they and their gods and thou*
> *All relics here together,—now*
> *Whose profit? whether bull or cow,*
> *Isis or Ibis, who or how,*
>   *Whether of Thebes or Nineveh?*

(101–10)

Ideally founded on order and hierarchy, the museum levels the room above and the room below—"All relics here together."[32] The thrice-repeated "and" of line 106 and the closing string of urgent questions mimic the museum's heaping effect. But in the stanza's most curious lines Rossetti claims that Nineveh had museums of her own—"but were not some / Of these thine own 'antiquity'?" In the 1856 version Rossetti called the Egyptian mummy of line 104 a "pilgrim" rather than an "alien." This alteration indicates his increasingly more accurate understanding of the irreverent and hostile undertaking of museum acquisition.

Thus emerge the poem's central revelations: with empire comes art; without imperialism there would be no museums; without death there is no life, or, in more politically specific terms, without the fall of one empire there cannot be the rise of another.[33] It is, therefore, the charming alienage of the "brown maidens" and the "purple mouths" that captures the British gaze. It is the "dead Greece" and the "very corpse of

Nineveh" or the "dead disbowelled mystery" that entertain British "living eyes." The poem's second and third lines ("the prize / Dead Greece vouchsafes to living eyes") points to the crux of life's dependence on death. Does the British archaeologist bring Nineveh back to life or destroy it? As Rossetti's twelfth stanza confirms and British discovery narratives often unwittingly attest, discovery necessitates destruction. Nineveh's fragility ensures Britain's triumph. Or, as the following lines more accurately indicate, Nineveh's queenly reign—

> *Delicate harlot! On thy throne*
> *Thou with a world beneath thee prone*
> *In state for ages sat'st alone*

—makes it an eventual "kingly conquest." Thus the lesson learned in the museum is the "zealous tract: 'Rome,—Babylon and Nineveh'" that charts the rise, conquest, and fall of great empires. And such will be London's demise. Rossetti uses the site of the museum for his "condition of England" poem, for his critique of British culture. The culture that builds museums will someday be the charnel relics of another culture:

> *For as that Bull-god once did stand*
> *And watched the burial-clouds of sand . . .*
> *So may he stand again; till now,*
> *In ships of unknown sail and prow,*   (171–72,
> *Some tribe of the Australian plough*   176–80)
> *Bear him afar,—a relic now*
>   *Of London, not of Nineveh.*

This burden of Nineveh suggests how these nineteenth-century poems about museums are burdened in another sense: by history and belatedness, preoccupied with audience and the problematics of power and authorization. Such preoccupations reveal the modernity of these poems, for it is modern artists who call museums their inevitable home. As James Heffernan argues in *Museum of Words: The Poetics of Ekphrasis from Homer to Ashbery,* "Twentieth-century ekphrasis springs from the museum, the shrine where all poets worship in a secular age." Most famously, of course, there are Auden's "Musée des Beaux Arts" and Yeats's several visits to municipal galleries. But there is also the discomfort John Ashbery confesses to in "Self-Portrait in a Convex Mirror":

I think it is trying to say it is today
And we must get out of it even as the public
Is pushing through the museum now so as to
Be out by closing time. You can't live there.

And William Empson's "Homage to the British Museum" is a hardly worshipful, ironic treatment of the "Supreme God in the ethnological section" to whom, he writes, "Let us offer our pinch of dust." [34] Here the religion of the museum turns out to be a shady, shabby affair centered on a straw god; and the congregation vacillates between smugness and confusion, overwhelmed by the surfeit of the museum visit.

Having once jealously guarded the golden apple with the Hesperides—"watch the treasure / Of the wisdom of the West . . . / Hoarded wisdom brings delight"—Tennyson much later in his life composed his imperial odes for the queen. "Ode for the Opening of the International Exhibition" (1862) and "Ode on the Opening of the Colonial and Indian Exhibition" (1886) mark the laureate's promised return to the palace of art with others—in effect, the official sequel to the brash production of Tennyson's earlier days. [35] Gone is the solitary lingering in the palace; indeed, the palace has changed back into the palace of and for the age, the Crystal Palace, which Tennyson praises as the prototype for the International Exhibition: "a feast / Of wonder, out of West and East." Gone, too, is the tension of conflicting impulses that bristled with the soul's guilt as Tennyson now speaks without oppositionalism—"with one voice"—proclaiming, "Let us dream our dream to-day" in celebration of a museum culture where "Britons [must] hold your own!" As these imperial odes suggest, the museum was, paradoxically, the realization of both nineteenth-century British national democratization and British international hegemony. This double complicity made the museum the site of critiques of culture in verse. The museum politicized art in unprecedented measure, and poetry of the age captured this transmogrification. As the popularizer of art, the museum was a new and necessary, if sometimes hostile, arena for the nineteenth-century artist. Poems about museums permitted the poet an oblique way of addressing his increasingly intrusive public. Moreover, they allowed the poet to weigh the other burdens of history and tradition. In capturing the negotiations between their creators and the museum culture they half critique, half embrace, nineteenth-century museum poems record the widening demographics of the art world and offer a political and cultural poetics that reflects the phenomenon of art gone public. As Browning wrote about the art of abandoned churches and its exposure to the gallery, "The works on the wall must take their chance." [36]

VI

An Empire's Great Expectations: Museums in Imperialist Boy Fiction

My plan was made with a view to strike the Nile at its head, and then to sail down that river to Egypt. . . . I had in my mind . . . collecting the fauna of those regions, to complete and fully develop a museum in my father's house, a nucleus of which I had already formed from the rich menagerie of India, the Himalaya Mountains, and Tibet. . . . There are now but a few animals to be found . . . [that] have not fallen victims to my gun. Of this the paternal wall is an existing testimony . . . every year I marched across the Himalayas, and penetrated into some unknown portions of Tibet, shooting, collecting, and mapping.

—John Speke, *What Led to the Discovery of the Source of the Nile*

INDIANA JONES AND THE LAST CRUSADE (1989), the final episode in the Indiana Jones adventure series, begins with a flashback, which Steven Spielberg uses to convey to the movie audience the making of the hero-man, Indiana Jones. From this retrospective we learn small but pertinent details: the origin of Indiana's signature fedora, the source of his skill with a whip, the genesis of his aversion to snakes. More importantly, however, this flashback reveals the originary moral moment that fuels Indiana's repertoire of adventures. While on a wilderness exploration trip with his scout troop, young Indiana discovers looters at work in a cave excavating buried treasure. When the thieves uncover the priceless cross of Coronado, their greedy jubilation sparks the hero's indignation. "That cross is an important artifact! It belongs in a museum!" he cries and, snatching the cross from the thieves' hands, runs from the scene. Later, with the thieves in hot pursuit, the young Indiana urgently repeats, "This should be in a museum!" It is thus that Indiana embarks on his first adventure and, most significantly, discovers in himself a powerful drive to collect and preserve art for the public good. This curatorial imperative comes to define the adult Indiana Jones and shape the course of his life. Indeed, it becomes his motto, as distinctive as his dusty fedora. For, as the movie turns to events in the life of Indiana the man, we find the protagonist in the midst of a nearly identical crisis (the cross having fallen again into the wrong hands) and witness him trying once again to reclaim it. We hear the by-now-familiar cry—"That belongs in a museum!" This time, however, Indiana's cry is answered: the vignette closes with his entrusting the cross of Coronado to a museum official, who assures him that it will make a fine addition to the Spanish Collection.

As a champion of the museum, Indiana is a protector of the cultural good, the inspired rescuer of such icons as the ark of the covenant and the Holy Grail. Pitted time and again against the sinister alterity of assorted Nazi and Eastern foes, Indiana never fails to ensure the continuity of Western civilization. Headquartered in his academic office, a virtual warehouse of cultural relics, Indiana plays out his role as keeper of the archive and guardian of important origins and heritage. His archaeological adventures are the means of achieving cultural stability; crisis erupts only as the way to recoup the status quo. Such heroics embody what Robin Wood in *Hollywood from Vietnam to Reagan* calls the political conservatism of the Indiana Jones series, which never tries to revise or debunk but rather recovers. It is not surprising, then, that the young Indiana, appearing in his scout uniform as the cultural novitiate, grows up to be Indiana the archaeologist and cultural hero. Indiana offers a potent blend of the maverick tamed by the faithful civil servant, for, unlike Clark Kent and Superman, who schismatically represent the prosaic and the heroic, the academic Indiana and the traveling Indiana unite in the solitary, romantic figure of the archaeologist. As the collector of art, Indiana Jones can do all—decipher, ruminate, travel, and withstand natural disaster. And he embarks on endless, fantastic adventures—all because he possesses a keen sense that certain things belong in museums.

Such whimsical musings on a celluloid hero might be pardoned for the culturally charged issues they invoke; for, as Jack Zipes has persuasively argued, fantasy is a sociopolitical text. In short, the success of the

Indiana Jones series reminds us of our inheritance: the museum is one of the greatest legacies bequeathed us by the Victorians. The young Indiana takes us back to the twilight of the century that gave birth to the civic museum. An obvious alliance between Victorian museum founding and empire building underlies such institutions as the South Kensington, which housed both British textiles and colonial Indian artifacts. As "a source of empire," that which "differentiates 'us' from 'them,'" the South Kensington variously showcased colonized otherness and home supremacy, thereby erecting the hierarchy of colony and metropole essential to imperialism.[1] Likewise, representations of museums helped generate and circulate what historians have called the growing popular imperialism of the century; these images promoted the fantasy that collecting brought the world home and thus domesticated all the world into home. In short, the elements of Spielberg's adventure fantasy—empire, boyhood and adult-male heroics, collecting, collectors, and collections—suggest a question worth examining: what is the function of the museum in Spielberg's source material, the numerous Victorian children's tales, more specifically boys' tales, focused on collecting and exhibiting? As an enterprise or institution within the adventure tale, the museum gives a political gloss to what Bruno Bettelheim has identified as the three questions central to both fairy tales and a child's development—"What is the world really like? How am I to live my life in it? How can I truly be myself?"[2] The represented museum teaches a young and un(in)formed audience about heritage, about what it is (for the purposes of this study) to be English, thereby transforming children into citizens and boys into men who will honor the narrative of nationalism.

The ties between children's literature and the museum are due in part to the centrality of museums in the lives of nineteenth-century children. Many etchings of nineteenth-century museum scenes portray an art-loving crowd diverse not only in gender and class but also in age. Whether with parents or with school classes, children stand prepared to be educated by the museum's holdings: "Exhibitions, galleries, and museums, are part and parcel of popular education in the young and the adult: they stimulate that principle of inquisitiveness natural to man, and with the right sort of food: they instil knowledge, drop by drop, through the eye into the mind, and create a healthy appetite, growing with what it feeds on: they make the libraries of those who have no money to expend on books, and are the travels of those that have no time to bestow on travel: they are schools in which the best and only true politeness may be taught."[3] While the grand, civic museums fulfilled Victoria and Albert's plans for mass education, the museum enterprise was also brought into the home in order to instruct and entertain children further. Conveying to its young audience that the world was to be contained, collected, assembled in one place for observation and possession, a wide range of museal activities was available. For example, panoramas for the home were a popular item for sale at print shops. The *Illustrated London News* often boasted foldout panoramas, in particular a twenty-two-foot miniature of the Great Exhibition. *The Ascent of Mont Blanc,* a popular diorama at the Egyptian Hall in 1852, could be purchased in miniature for the home. And children played collecting games like the Panorama of Europe: A New Game and a Day at the Zoo, where the objective was to paste bars over exotic animals.[4] Most commonly, children were encouraged to form aquariums, specimen collections, and dollhouses. One domestic taste manual spoke directly to children: "Every house ought to possess a 'Museum,' even if it is only one shelf in a small cupboard, here, carefully dated and named, should be placed the pretty shells you gather on the seashore, the old fossils you find in the rocks, the skeleton leaves you pick up from under the hedges, the strange orchids you find on the downs. Learn what you can about each object before you put it in the museum, and docket it not only with its name, but also with the name of the place in which you found it, and the date."[5] Such diverse manifestations of museum culture invited children to collect, organize, and display—for pleasure and for gain.[6]

But adventure literature was the most obvious avenue by which the museum came home to children. The real-life prototypes for Indiana Jones—such men as Giovanni Belzoni, Austen Henry Layard, Richard Burton, Captain Marryat, and John Speke—were heroes in three respects. First, they explored. Second, as scouts for the museum enterprise, they explored in order to collect, whether, like Belzoni, for a public institution, the British Museum, or, like Speke and Marryat, for the personal ambition of erecting private collections. Third, their travels and collections often ended in narration.[7] For example, after his 1819 exploration of Egypt, Belzoni published his account in 1821 and was further mythified when in 1843 Sara Atkins published the fictionalized *Fruits of*

Enterprize Exhibited in the Adventures of Belzoni in Egypt and Nubia—
which went through nine editions between 1821 and 1841. Layard's narrative was a best-seller in railway bookshops, and Marryat became known
as the "seafaring Dickens," publishing a collection of children's tales and
a Juvenile Library and profiting £20,000 from his most popular book
alone.[8] Such men were both the heroes and the manufacturers of imperialist boy fiction, narrating and fictionalizing the museum enterprise
while ordaining innumerable Victorian boys into a community of collectors. Their narratives were usually formulaic, replete with the indomitable hero (often clever with disguises), the indolent natives, and the
saboteurs and double agents sent by the competing governments. Securing the artifacts for the home museum was the undisputed concord fiction, and brash cadence and bold rhetoric were indispensable. The heroic
collectors were characteristically both male and masculine, unburdened
by female presence except for the occasional native woman or "chocolate
nymph."[9] Akin to the Victorian tradition of imperialist boy literature
like *Boys of the Empire* and *The Boy's Own Paper,* these narratives of identity construction turn boys into men who fulfill conventional prescriptions for masculine virtue (action, aggression, patriotism).[10] Central to
such initiation, the represented museum usually plays a conservative part,
upholding traditional gender roles, "acquisitive aggression in men and
dutiful nurturing of this aggression by women."[11] Samuel Smiles's ethos
of self-help, a distinctively Victorian "muscular morality," often fuels the
museum enterprise within the tale, which in turn promotes a breed of
heroic masculinity considered by many Victorians both the normative
and the ideal extension of the separate spheres, the kind of maleness that
well serves an empire's recruits.[12]

In order to investigate the museum's role in fashioning the imperial
male, I will focus on two late-Victorian fictions, Rudyard Kipling's *Kim*
(1901) and Edith Nesbit's *The Story of the Amulet* (1906). Such museum
tales illuminate an often overlooked corner in children's literature studies,
for, although scholars have long discussed the centrality of the fantastic
voyage to children's tales, they have given far less attention to the significance of acquisition on these journeys. Yet with its distinctive spatiality,
its capacity to hold the world in a capsule or under one roof, the museum
perfectly embodies what Angus Wilson has identified as the two principal
ways in which a child imagines the world. It showcases both a "world

contracted" and a "world traversed": "The first is that transformation of a small space into a whole world which comes from the intense absorption of a child. The second is the map-making of hazards and delights which converts a child's smallest journey into a wondrous exploration." [13] (The urtexts for much nineteenth-century voyage literature, *Gulliver's Travels* and *Robinson Crusoe,* show that, in the end, journeys lead to exhibition—whether it be of a great goatskin cap, an umbrella, a parrot, or a Brobdingnagian insect stinger.) By heralding the museum as civilization's triumph over the native, such fiction appears to address the age's deep anxiety that anarchy would supplant culture. It enlists young readers in the project of *Kulturwerk,* immersing them in what Norbert Elias has identified as the civilizing process—a process that makes readers more confident of their domain, more self-assured of their status as heirs. As Philip Fisher has argued, in the museum "we will find, between our ancestors and our descendants, our 'place.'" [14] While Nesbit articulates a possible socialist and feminist counterresponse to imperialist boy fiction, her tale ends up equally committed to what Zipes in *Fairy Tales and the Art of Subversion* has called "normative expectations" and "dominant cultural patterns." For both Kipling and Nesbit the museum instructs its readers on the necessity of making the world one's own and making it powerful as well as exciting; it links inextricably the processes of self-realization and world building. For both authors the central political lessons of the museum prevail: how to fashion a world and how to make that world imperial and/or utopic.

Kipling's *Kim* presents the making of a boy into a man—a white man, a good man, to echo Father Victor. During the course of the novel Kim's identity changes, and so does India's; at the center of such reconfigurations stands the Lahore Museum, or Wonder House, as the natives call it. The novel opens on the Lahore's threshold and on the "open-mouthed wonder" of the lama who has traveled far to behold the Wonder House's displays. The spectacle the museum visitor provides and the specular feast he enjoys signal the cataclysmic change that has altered colonized India. The museum enterprise has transformed the very dimensions of life itself; India has become a world contracted: "There were hundreds of pieces, friezes of figures in relief, fragments of statues and slabs crowded with figures that had encrusted the brick walls of the Buddhist *stupas* and *viharas* of the North Country and now, dug up and

labelled, made the pride of the Museum."[15] Chapter 2 continues to focus
on the lama's confusion, a virtual vertigo brought on by both the museum and the other quintessential colonizing structure, the railroad, as
they transform India's landscape into manageable space. A counterforce
to the provincialism characteristic of India, the museum has pieced together the country's entire story, including details concerning the lama's
way of life, for it is the arcane that piques a collector's curiosity. When
the curator admits his familiarity with the lama's home, four months'
march away, the incredulous lama must ask, "And thou—the English
know of these things?" (7). No corner, no region, is left unexplored in a
world turned increasingly cosmopolitan by the museum's presence. As
representative of the metropole Britain far away, the museum also enforces India's position as colony. In the Wonder House the lama falls to
his knees at the feet of the curator, as do the peasants, "hurrying up to
the Wonder House to view the things that men made in their own province and elsewhere" (4). Through an uncanny transformation India has
accepted its status as an object of study and surveillance, acknowledging the authority of the museum to place India on view: "The Museum
was given up to Indian arts and manufactures, and anybody who sought
wisdom could ask the curator to explain" (4). In the Lahore Museum we
witness the transmission of objects, which leads to the transference of
information and thus power. The lama and the curator play their respec-
tive roles in their own exchange of gifts, with the curator offering recording devices—eyeglasses, pencil, and notebook—and the lama bestowing
what he calls, in so many words, a piece of himself, an ancient, curiously
wrought pen case far removed from its use value but quite valuable as an
artifact. In the Wonder House wise man meets wise man; lama confronts
curator, and the lama must concede to the wiser man.

Kim cultivates his own wisdom at the museum's doors. It is not
surprising that the "Little Friend of all the World" is good friends with
the museum's staff. As the receptacle for all the world, the museum is
appropriate ground for Kim's training in espionage. Well suited to India's
new order, the cosmopolite Kim is a speaker of many languages, an aggregate of numerous appearances and identities. His blend of East and
West is appropriately figured in the tale's opening image: Kim boldly
straddles the Zam-Zammah, the great gun on display before the museum. Yet his sitting astride the cannon is an even more powerful emblem

for his dominance. As we learn, the Zam-Zammah is "always first of the conqueror's loot" (1). And Kim has earned this position of power by winning the king-of-the-castle game against his friends Chota Lal and Abdullah. Singing his song, "All Mussalmans fell off Zam-Zammah long ago. . . . The Hindus fell off Zam-Zammah too" (4), Kim learns at an early age to "hold the Punjab" (1). Before the museum he enacts his destiny as a white colonizer by playing a boyhood game that mimics the Great Game of adults. Kim, in fact, is not a blend of East and West but rather white—"a poor white of the very poorest" (1). His amulet will uphold the grand narrative of social mobility that is already confirmed by his familiarity with the museum sahibs. His cultural inevitability is revealed at the museum's doors: he will emerge as the remarkable boy with vision, the prophet of battle, the boy whose star means war.

Kim's association with the Lahore Museum has taught him the power of watching and of collecting information. For example, the novelty of the lama, and his desire to possess it, initially prompts Kim to go with the priest: "This man was entirely new to all his experience, and he meant to investigate further: precisely as he would have investigated a new building or a strange festival in Lahore city. The lama was his trove, and he purposed to take possession" (12). Even when Kim leaves the training ground of the museum behind, his new schools do not undo the central lesson of the museum. Saint Xavier's, Lurgan's shop—the Lahore's double, with its "ghost-daggers and prayer-wheels from Tibet; turquoise and raw amber necklaces; green jade bangles, curiously packed incense-sticks in jars"— and even his discipleship under the lama sharpen Kim's collecting skills (152). At the end of his training in mensuration, after Lurgan's jewel game and his cultural grand tour with the lama, Kim emerges the avatar of imperialism. At Saint Xavier's he has worked toward the day "one will command natives" (125). He has excelled at mapmaking, the skill that enables one to carry away a picture of any country. And he has successfully played the highest stakes in Lurgan's memory game, moving from "veritable stones" to "piles of swords and daggers" to "photographs of natives" (158). Kim's heroism recalls the connections Benedict Anderson has drawn among the power institutions of the census, map, and museum—those systems of surveillance that, as they count, map out, and organize the colonized, are instrumental to the colonialist.

As a collector, Kim finds himself in the company of many: the Lahore curator, Mahbub, Creighton, Lurgan, and even Hurree Babu. The
novel penetrates "straight to an ethnologist's heart" and watches as the
Great Game, as the competition for the "wonderful account," unfolds.
The Lahore Museum turns out to be a front for the British Secret Service, a "government's house" for spies posing as ethnologists. The British
use the museum to watch the people they govern and to gather information on the alien culture. As the Lahore curator weightily acknowledges, "I am here . . . to gather knowledge" (7). And Kipling attributes
Hurree's ethnographic knowledge to his governmental position: "His
store of local legends—he had been a trusted agent of the State for fifteen
years, remember—was inexhaustible" (239). Indeed, as John McClure
has claimed, "*Kim* is Kipling's richest dream"; however, Kipling's dream
here is not one of idealistic tolerance, as McClure goes on to argue.[16]
Rather, Kipling's museum emerges a utopia based on surveillance, a Ben-
thamite panopticon; it is the tale's central setting, indefatigably watchful
even in its seeming absence from the rest of the tale.[17] Under the museum's grand conception, under the rubric that can make sense of it all,
the teeming Grand Trunk Road, the mazy bazaars, the "happy Asiatic
disorder" can fall into line and into labels, classes, and categories (64). In
this political system that upholds the truism knowledge is power, "there
is no sin so great as ignorance," to quote the Great Game's leader, Col-
onel Creighton (119). Kim's affiliation with the ethnological surveys will
make him the ideal ruler—one who does not rule from ignorance, one
who knows "by the look of the large wide world unfolding itself before
him . . . that the more a man knew the better for him" (163). The novel's
later contrast between the northern invaders and Kim confirms his superiority: their crude understanding of native custom deposes them from
the Great Game while Kim has been able to make India his home.

A utopia of comprehensive knowledge, Kipling's museum is utopic
in another, related way. In its roles as cultural provider and preserver of
local traditions, the museum allows the cloak of beneficence to fall over
the maneuverings of political power. Orientalist in conception, Kipling's
museum–cum–government-front makes possible a kind of rule more effective because more ingenious than rule based on force. The museum
helps India to believe in the necessity of British governance and in its
own dependency. The lama's fable of a shackled elephant's reliance on a

calf relates, with some pathos, India's acceptance of its own colonization. So too does the lama, who initially feels betrayed by the revelation that Kim is white, come to accept his dependence on a sahib. As his journey to the River of the Arrow draws to a close, he increasingly relies on Kim, who accepts the often conflicting responsibilities of a white man's burden: "Kim's shoulders bore all the weight of it—the burden of an old man, the burden of the heavy food-bag with the locked books, the load of the writings on his heart" (270). Like the curator whose gift of glasses compels the lama to see with sahib eyes, the museum in its business of history and tradition making offers its vision to all. Ever watchful in its monitoring yet benevolent in its guardianship, the museum emerges the tale's deepest imperialist fantasy.[18]

Although the museum's ties to political strategy in *Kim* seem indisputable, some readers have argued that *Kim* is an anti-imperialist text, distinctive in its inclusivity or what they variously call its "generous magnanimity," its "ecumenical understanding," its "warm affection." McClure writes, "In his stories, written in the 1880s and '90s, Kipling uses many of these same crude dichotomies [white and black, civilized and savage] to defend imperialism, but in *Kim* (1901) he breaks with convention, offering instead a powerful criticism of racist modes of representation."[19] Yet from the central schism between Kim's star of war and the lama's star of peace to the incontrovertible split between collector and collectible, without which the ethnological survey could not proceed, *Kim* is a tale rife with dichotomies. For example, when Hurree, the collectible—"hopelessly trying to be like 'us'"—attempts to become the collector, we laugh.[20] Even the infinitely rounder character of the lama is kept in his place by the comedy of his perpetual stupefaction and subsequent dependence on Kim. Directly before the lama liberates his soul in the novel's closing pages—before, in short, he threatens to "get out of [the collector's] hand"—Kipling resituates him within the Lahore collections, identifying him with "the stone Bodhisat . . . who looks down upon the patent self-registering turnstiles of the Lahore Museum" (287). *Kim*'s inclusivity might be, rather, the thoroughness of a museum's job well done, its warm affection, a museum's censuslike appetite for detail. Inspired by his father's South Kensington satellite museum, the model for the Lahore, Kipling may have produced *Kim* as his museum piece. It is not surprising that museal metaphors often appear in discussions of this novel—from J. H. Millar's 1901 review, where he calls it a "portrait-gallery" and a "panorama," to McClure's praise of its "vivid catalogues" and "catalogues of wonders."[21]

Although the novel's central relationship between chela and priest *is* one of warm affection and while, like most imperialist boy stories, *Kim* celebrates the delights of fraternity, loneliness plagues Kim (Mahbub asks, "And who are thy people, Friend of all the World?" [136]). From Kim's nickname to Hurree's Dickensian discussion of mutual friends, the novel repeatedly draws us to the theme of friendship in order to highlight it as absent, complicated, or compromised. *Kim* is ultimately a strange and strained love story about an uncertain kind of love. This otherwise confident adventure story repeatedly turns to tentative discussions of love, as characters seek the foundations for friendship in a world in which so many relationships are based on the utility of information exchange. Witness the following conversation between Mahbub and Kim:

> *"What are a few rupees"*—the Pathan threw out his open hand care-*lessly*—*"to the Colonel Sahib? He spends them for a purpose, not in any way for love of thee."*
>
> *"That," said Kim slowly, "I knew a very long time ago." (132)*

In short, the final effect of the museum in *Kim* is to fashion a protagonist who is a highly successful public man but an ambiguous private friend. Operating through its mix of familiarity and distance, the doubly utopic museum has fashioned a cynic's hero. Kipling proposes two images of Kim in the epigraphs to chapters 14 and 8: the man who can hear his "own unanswered agonies" in his "brother's voice" and the two-sided man, "with two separate sides to [his] head." While the museum has formed an identity for the hero-man, it is a hard one to fathom, a challenging one to know and love. Aloof and slippery, well versed in the arts of detection and disguise, Kim is equally the disciple of the "tortuous and indirect" Creighton, a "man after his own heart" who remains one of the most intensely enigmatic characters in literature. While Kim's two mentors, the spiritual lama and the secular Mahbub, compete over the boy's sleeping body in the novel's final pages, we wonder who will gain mastery over him. As a tale about genuine power and private ambiguities, Kipling's *Kim* has found the persistent question "Who is Kim—Kim—Kim?" difficult to answer.

Nesbit's *The Story of the Amulet* trades in one protagonist for four and opens in London instead of far-flung India; however, the museum again makes its appearance early and emerges central to the characters' growth. The tale opens with four children, Cyril, Robert, Anthea, and Jane, who must spend their summer vacation apart from their parents. Resigned to the tedium of days passed under a nurse's supervision, the children soon realize that their London address on Fitzroy Street is near the British Museum. Like Kim on the Zam-Zammah, these children sense in the museum's proximity new possibilities that initially promise pure playfulness, though they prefigure a more serious game: "You can, for instance, visit the Tower of London, the Houses of Parliament, the National Gallery, the Zoological Gardens, the various Parks, the Museums at South Kensington, Madame Tussaud's Exhibition of Wax-works, or the Botanical Gardens at Kew." [22] Even rainy days are enlivened with museum games at home, with "reproducing the attitudes of statues seen either in the British Museum, or in Father's big photograph book" (175). Nesbit's tale functions most simply as a child's introduction to the museum, sparking a young audience's interest in and familiarity with museums. Nesbit literally invites her readers, "You know what a mummy-case is like, of course? If you don't you had better go to the British Museum at once and find out" (42). To help readers visualize an ancient form that appears before the children, Nesbit recommends, "You can see it in our own British Museum at this day" (140). Repeatedly, she draws on the riches of the museum to construct her fantasy, as do the children. [23] When Anthea is puzzled about the pharaoh's house in Egypt, she wonders if "it's like the Egyptian Court in the Crystal Palace" (225). And, as the children's travels unfold, others confuse the magic for the museum. For example, Nurse thinks the children are going to a Royal Academy exhibition when Anthea announces they are off to see old relics. And the learned gentleman believes that Anthea has seen ancient beads in the British Museum—in a place she simply pretends is Babylon.

In this magical museum culture of turn-of-the-century London, the children visit a curiosity shop, where they discover a broken amulet that sends them on many fantastic journeys. As a museum artifact, the amulet is a synecdoche for the museum itself. First, as the central detail in Nesbit's Egyptology, this antiquity reminds us of the exotic nature of museums. Moreover, as the archway for the children's time travel, this curiosity emphasizes the inclusiveness of museums. The amulet becomes the vehicle for the story's playfulness, and the museum, by extension, becomes the juncture of all times and places. The British Museum sends the children into the past, to Egypt 6000 B.C., Babylon, Atlantis, England 55 B.C., and Tyre. It brings the past to the present: when the Psammead grants the Babylonian queen her desire to travel to present-day London, she spends an afternoon in the British Museum, "at home" surrounded by the Babylonian exhibits. The museum can even transport the children into the future, where they will conclude their quest by gaining wisdom both small and great, for the amulet not only marks the threshold of the children's adventures but also holds the solution to their problem. If they can restore the amulet to its missing half, their parents and youngest sister will be restored to them. Like Kim, Nesbit's children use the museum to secure their home.

The queen's visit and the children's journey into the future, however, suggest Nesbit's ambivalence toward the museum. In the British Museum the queen feels simultaneously too much at home and too estranged. First she shatters the display glass in order to repossess what she considers her rightful property, then she requests that the museum relinquish her possessions. What follows is a fantastic image of the British Museum surrendering its collectibles; "an enormous stone bull . . . great slabs of carved stone, bricks, helmets, tools, weapons, fetters, wine-jars, bowls, bottles, bases, jugs," and more float out into the courtyard (161). The collection seems to come to life once again when the children go to enjoy the exhibits at Saint George's Hall in Langham Place and reencounter their nemesis, Rekh-mara, the Egyptian priest whom they know from their travels. In these scenes the museum declares its volatile status as the site where cultures mix, where the past haunts the present, and where the familiar and the strange coexist. The menace behind the fantasy, evident in *Kim* only by a counterreading of the Lahore's young chief ethnologist and spy, rises more swiftly to the surface here, out of the interstices of possession, dispossession, and repossession, and the museum emerges a contested site while the issue of cultural property grows increasingly vexed. For these brief episodes Nesbit envisions what might be called an antimuseum, a collection divested and dispersed—a collection in which the collectible, momentarily, fights back.

When the children enter futuristic London through the British

Museum, Nesbit holds the museum enterprise up to closer scrutiny. Her construction of London as a Fabian utopia makes overt the latent critique of culture that runs through the tale. Although the British Museum still exists, it has become, again, something of an antimuseum—less urban, guarded, and institutionalized and increasingly pastoralized. The museum walls and courtyard quickly give way to a city cleaner and brighter (where even the pigeons gleam like "new silver") and, more importantly, to a family unit now intact. Here we finally meet a contented child, Wells, named "after the great reformer." The exception to the tale, Wells reminds us that many neglected children have haunted Nesbit's story. Abandonment, in fact, has been the very impetus for the narrative. And the central figure of the story, the fragmented amulet, is itself abandoned in modern London, a deracinated object searching for its counterpart. The happy Wells thus becomes the key to Nesbit's most subversive political agenda—a gendered critique of the "muscular morality" and unchecked cosmopolitanism that inform imperialist boy fiction and the museum enterprise within it. Like many artifacts transmitted to a culture because of war, the broken amulet is in modern-day London because of Napoleon's expeditions. Moreover, the business of empire has taken the children's father away to Manchuria and at the same time "invalidated" their mother with the care of an invalid child far from home in Madeira. Teasing out the darker implications of cosmopolitanism, Nesbit's tale warns how the pursuit of culture can fracture lives, for the cosmopolite's desideratum—to be citizen of the world—is also to be nowhere at home, that is, rootless. This tension between the longing for home and the menace of homelessness divests the museum of instrumentalized fantasy and offers instead what Zipes calls an authentically liberating—because radical—vision.

But such radical visions are eclipsed. What becomes increasingly evident is how resonant and complexly invested an image the museum is for Nesbit. At times the battleground marked with the scars of history and politics, her museum ultimately stands restored, of both its collections and its deepest significance. Only in the museum of the future can the children finish their quest, for here the amulet appears to them whole, on display in its final resting place under glass. Subsequently, the museum allows the children to go home; in fact, it has taught them that there is no place like home and that home comes in both personal and national dimensions. Travel through the amulet has fostered in the children a citizen's concern and duty as well as a cultural pride. Every journey has been a cultural lesson—about other cultures but more profoundly about their own. The exotic has served ultimately to confirm the familiar. When introducing himself and his siblings to strangers in new lands, Cyril recites, "We come from the world where the sun never sets. . . . We are the great Anglo-Saxon or conquering race" (70). Pledging his allegiance, he claims that they are children of the sun, blessed with famous men—"Alfred the Great, Shakespeare, Nelson, Gordon, Lord Beaconsfield, Mr. Rudyard Kipling, and Mr. Sherlock Holmes" (127)—and fine things, such as "St. Paul's, and the Tower of London, and Madame Tussaud's Exhibition" (211). With each trip Cyril's nationalism grows stronger (until he cries "Union Jack, Printing Press, Gunpowder, Rule Britannia"), and the imperialist boy within him flourishes. One culminating episode, a magic-lantern exhibition at Camden Town, depicts a teacher's sermon steeped in the predictable Smilesian rhetoric packaged for boys: "And I hope every boy in this room has in his heart the seeds of courage and heroism and self-sacrifice, and I wish that every one of you may grow up to be noble and brave and unselfish, worthy citizens of this great Empire" (284).

The children end their adventures safe in their home, happy in their home culture, and a bit wiser. But Nesbit's story weaves an important subtext, for the amulet's magic charms not only the children but also Jimmy, the impoverished, hardworking archaeologist who lives above them. At first Jimmy's function seems to confirm the story's main message. As a jaded adult who nevertheless has a penchant for antiquities, Jimmy is willing to be transformed by the amulet and by the museum enterprise it embodies, a powerful testimony to the transfiguring power of imagination. Moreover, he represents what scholars of children's literature identify as the child-adult, an acceptable and identifiable figure for a young audience because of his regressive nature. For example, on a trip to Atlantis, he explains to the children: "When I was your age I was called Jimmy. . . . Would you mind? I should feel more at home in a dream like this if I—Anything that made me seem more like one of you" (181). Yet Jimmy remains stubbornly different, vestigially adult, and the home the tale finds for him is equally distinct. When the children travel to futuristic London, they encounter this "learned gentleman," now happy and famous in a prosperous home filled with "many more books than the Fitzroy Street room, and far more curious and wonderful Assyrian and Egyptian objects" (257). For Jimmy happiness and home have meant a fairy-tale career, and the museum-case label promises him immortality as a museum donor. Reauthorizing him, even renewing him, the museum, with the travels and visions it has offered, has granted him fame: "And they can't upset my theories . . . they can't, though they've tried. Theories they call them, but they're more like—I don't know—more like memories. I *know* I'm right about the secret rites of the Temple of Amen" (259). Finally the champion of antiquarians, a bookish sort of Indiana Jones, Jimmy establishes an imperium of professional success guaranteed by his magical wedding with the soul of Rekh-mara. This marriage of collector and object, and Jimmy's renovation thereby, is Nesbit's most marvelous, most fitting representation for the thrill of possession.

The museum aided in Victorian Britain's empire building by popularizing imperialism, capitalizing on the burgeoning image culture of the nineteenth century. As an image in children's fiction, the museum helped to mold boys into an empire's heroes: what certain dreams are made of. Jimmy's presence in Nesbit's novel, however, suggests the museum's greater readership and its broadest appeal. The museum in fantasy, the fantasy of the museum, serves to recapture for the adult that moment when one first makes all the world the self, when one forces all objects to respond to the self in that more generalizable form of empire making called self-fashioning. Jimmy permits us a parting glance into the psychology of collecting, into the psychological motivations that invest the museum in the first place with such powerful political instrumentality. In her *Companion to the Most Celebrated Private Galleries of Art in London* (1844) Mrs. Anna Jameson identifies four types of art collectors: "those who collect [pictures] for instruction," "those who collect pictures around them as a king assembles his court—as significant of state," "those who collect pictures as a man speculates in the funds," and "those who collect pictures for love, for companionship, for communion." Jean Baudrillard is more to the point: "It [the collection] means every bit as much as our dreams." Undeniably the museum's greatest lure is its promise of order and control: in museums we satisfy our "insistent search for an ordered world." Yet we collect in order to exhibit for many other reasons: to internalize (to make a book "my own book"), to retrieve (a souvenir "promises" that an event, a place, an experience can come again), to recollect (to indulge nostalgia), to belong (collectibles are tokens of membership), to legitimate (collecting entails weaving narratives of meaning), to enhance (displayed exotica offer respite from the mundane), and to idealize (holding the world in a capsule, a shelf, a cabinet). Walter Benjamin's *märchenhaft* "Unpacking My Library" best describes the passion of possession: "The most profound enchantment for the collector is the locking of individual items within a magic circle in which they are fixed as the final thrill, the thrill of acquisition, passes over them. . . . One has only to watch a collector handle the objects in his glass case. . . . To renew the old world—that is the collector's deepest desire." As Baudrillard succinctly puts it, "It is all my own, the object of my possession."[24]

In their broadest applicability, then, museum tales for children form a master pattern, arising out of the intersection of museum and fantasy, that characterizes an age's desires. This pattern helps make sense of so curious a text as Moncure Conway's *Travels in South Kensington* (1882), an adult's guide to the museum cloaked in the guise of a fantastic voyage. Like *Kim* and *The Story of the Amulet,* Conway's book presents a sage figure, Professor Omnium, who invites the protagonist into the museum. This realm, a place both contracted and traversed, defies the limits of time and space, securing all the world for the protagonist on his visit. The delight rests in the professor's paradox: "Come, go round the world with me here in London! I do not propose to leave London. We can never go round the world, except in a small limited way, if we leave London."[25] Conway's textual hybrid tells a tale told time and again when we survey either the museum in fantasy fiction or the fantasy fiction central to many nineteenth-century museums. One need only look at the pediment of the British Museum or the original facade of the South Kensington to witness the progressivist plot the museum endorses both outside and inside its walls: while *The March of Civilization* unfolds above the doors of the British Museum, Britannia rules the center of the globe, and the Crystal Palace stands forever over the portal of the South Kensington. The Natural History Museum's west and east wings, ornamented with friezes of live and extinct species, meet in the center, at a statue of Adam—all in tribute to the glory of man (plans for a statue of Eve were canceled). Richard Owen's vision of Britain as "the nation that gathers together thousands of corals, shells, insects, fishes, birds, and beasts" re-vises the concept of Christian congregation into a nationalist commu-nity of collectors: the writing on the (museum's) wall proclaims that the nation that gathers together grows strong together.[26] Contemporary re-views frequently declared that with the museum—with the collective act of home improvement that collection represented—epic grandeur had returned to modern life: Owen was a new Aeneas, and the Natural His-tory Museum a new Troy. For many Victorians the South Kensington Museum was a magical kingdom or, as they called it, an Albertopolis. On seeing the Crystal Palace in 1851, Thomas Macaulay exclaimed in a letter, "I made my way into the building; a most gorgeous sight . . . beyond the dreams of the Arabian romances. I cannot think that the Caesars ever exhibited a more splendid spectacle." *Punch* fantasized about placing all of London under glass in order to make the Crystal Palace—renamed the Crystal Way—a permanent and all-inclusive feature of London life: "London might be a garden in a state of perpetual bloom—an illimitable Eden under a glass shade!" Dickens, too, was confident that the Great Exhibition embodied the "progress of Humanity, step by step." And in 1887 the Reverend J. G. Wood could dream of a utopian museum that transformed "the despised Tom, Dick, and Harry" into the "Thomas H. Huxleys, Richard Owens, and Henry Gosses of the next generation."[27] The museum entrepreneur William Bullock could aspire to move to America and build a utopia in Cincinnati called Hygeia.

In his poem about childhood and museums, "The Pitt Rivers Mu-seum, Oxford" (1984), James Fenton calls the museum "the kingdom of your promises / To yourself." Given this promise of self-promise or po-tential, it becomes less curious that Kipling's and Nesbit's stories revolve around the image of an amulet. These charms suggest that the museum is not only the archive, not only Indiana Jones's temple of origins; it is also the site of the telos, for the museum packages the past for the present in order to ensure a certain kind of future: "[Collection], for all its love of the past, gathers futures."[28] The museum tales I have examined are charmed tales of an individual's entitlement and an empire's destiny. Edward Said's investigations into the inextricability of culture and em-pire lead one to argue that the museum, as one of the greatest houses of culture, cannot be divorced from the self-definition of a nation. Along similar lines, James Clifford has maintained that collecting is a distinctly

Western fantasy, what he calls "the restless desire and power of the modern West to collect the world."[29] As he points out, not all cultures collect in order to exhibit—certainly not the Igbo, not Native Americans. "Culture-collecting" based on a salvage paradigm, Clifford argues, facilitates the processes of "Western identity formation."[30] And so, in the childhood of the British empire, in the childhood of its fledgling citizens, stories of collecting were indispensable. Adventure tales "were, collectively, the story England told itself as it went to sleep at night; and, in the form of its dreams, they charged England's will with the energy to go out into the world and explore, conquer, and rule."[31] Today, the reverberation of Indiana Jones's cry in our movie theaters and homes reminds us that we crave the same stories, that we dream the same dreams, even though we are told we live in a postcolonial, postmodern world built on the museum's ruins.[32] As blockbusters at the Metropolitan Museum of Art grow to be even bigger business, as the commodity museum of Chicago's Nike Town extends its presence to new cities, as the museal work of Walt Disney takes modern shape in the utopian community of Mike Eisner's Celebration, we realize that the "collective architecture of the nineteenth century [still] provides housing for the dreaming collective" and that the fantasy of the museum is still with us, even as it grants us deeper cultural insight into an empire on which the sun has now set.[33] Certainly this is appropriate, for behind our museums rests another motivation: to memorialize or, as Benjamin says, "to renew the old world." Modeling children into citizens, turning boys into men, and recalling adults to their earliest fantasies by offering the utopia of a world thoroughly coded as known and ordered, these tales of the museum are tales of a culture's great expectations realized.

VII

A Gallery of Readings: The Museum in Decline

What can you challenge in a Temple?

—Rem
Koolhaas

IN WILLIAM MORRIS'S socialist-utopian romance *News from Nowhere* (1891), William Guest travels into the future in order to tour a twenty-second-century London whose main districts are still familiar to nineteenth-century readers: Hammersmith, the gardens of Kensington, the shops of Piccadilly, Trafalgar Square. Before Guest travels by boat up the Thames, however, his itinerary includes a final stop in Bloomsbury, where he rests so that the tale's matter of substance—Hammond's recounting of the social unrest that led to the uprising that then provided the blueprint for utopia   can unfold. In short, within the pastoralized space of Morris's ideal future world, in order to learn about his society's present state and future condition, Guest must move inside the British Museum. The museum is little changed (even the pigeons still roost there), and Guest can immediately recognize it as "an old friend"; however, he observes that trees now flank the courtyard and the railings are gone. Nor is there any need for crowd control, for only one citizen of Nowhere, Old Hammond, pays heed to the museum's collections. No longer a guarded national treasury, the museum plays back the history of its own institutional inception and reverts into a home, the suitable dwelling place for an aging antiquarian.

This shabby British Museum is the stark centerpiece of Morris's ghostly post-Victorian London. In the refashioned cityscape that greets him, Guest notes certain buildings now defunct, London's "dead follies," and others transformed: from the houses of Parliament to Westminster

Abbey, the booming metropolis of London has become a landscape of markets and fields. Guest's many discussions corroborate what he sees: from the prison to the school, Victorian institutions have vanished. And the museum is part of this institutional overhaul. Although Hammond's great-grandson Dick mentions that his society preserves some tokens from the past, he characteristically shows little understanding of or interest in the enterprise of museums. Rather, Dick values the "great clearance" of Westminster Abbey, the destruction of "the beastly monuments to fools and knaves, which once blocked it up."[1] He has little tolerance for the act of or the necessity for commemoration. At Trafalgar Square, Dick remains unenlightened about the National Gallery's purpose, failing to understand either the concept of national or gallery. He confesses, "I have sometimes puzzled as to what the name means: anyhow, nowadays wherever there is a place where pictures are kept as curiosities permanently it is called a National Gallery" (80).

This deliquescence of both the museum's imposing facade and its monumental function—Dick admits that these "silly old buildings serve as a kind of foil to the beautiful ones which we build now"—suggests its obsolescence in the land of Nowhere (69). This museum in ruin serves to open this chapter, which continues the work of chapter 4 in presenting a gallery of readings that feature meetings in fictionalized museums—yet with two important differences. First, the focus here is on neither bildungsroman nor marriage fiction. Instead, the novels examined below expand on the discussion Forster's *Maurice* could only evoke in its conclusion as it began to explore the political dimensions of private, erotic life. Fully developed political novels, these tales are what might be called diagnostic narratives, social criticism targeted at the future of a society committed to imperialism and industrialism. Second, within these narratives the museum is exposed to the harsher treatment that both irony and dystopia generate; not resisted, revised, embraced, or rejected, the museum lies, in effect, in ruin. The authors discussed in this chapter take up Rem Koolhaas's provocative question.[2] Challenging the museum's monumentality and trespassing on the sacred space of the museum as temple, they provide the counternote to the utopic rhetoric with which this book began as well as complicate the museal romance described in the preceding chapter.

Repeated encounters in museums articulate John Galsworthy's full-blown critique in *The Man of Property* (1906) of a man and a society too acquisitive for their own and others' good. In this first volume of Galsworthy's examination of the institution called the Forsytes, late-Victorian museum culture stands as a testimonial to Soames's degraded love for Irene, who falls victim to the ferociously possessive clan of the Forsytes. As characters meet time and again in the museumlike spaces of late-Victorian zoos, clubs, and botanical gardens, the tribe's enervated humanity grows more appalling. The derelict museums of this aging society give way to an analysis of representations of museums in ruins in H. G. Wells's *The Time Machine* (1895) and Morris's *News from Nowhere*—tales of time travel that find in the museum, itself a time machine, a resonant site. Given the function of these two futuristic narratives as recessionals, as invocations to reflect on and recollect one's present construed as one's past, the moribund museum becomes a cenotaph, a memorial that invites the reader to ponder the imbalance of cultural gain and loss that the museum signals. Despite their divergent modes of social realism, science fiction, and utopian romance, all three tales depict "selves in a 'post-cultural' crisis" and take up "the possibility of dramatizing the failures of a whole social order." They share as their focus what Lionel Trilling called the defining Edwardian question: "Who shall inherit England?"[3]

Composed near or after the end of Victoria's reign, these three narratives are what Stephen Arata identifies as "fictions of loss" that use the represented site of the museum to explore the decadence of a society grown shabby, a society that has lived too long and too well. Accordingly, the subject matter of Galsworthy's "story of dissolution" is, in his own words, the "spiritual limitation" of the upper class; similarly, and again to use the author's own phrasing, *The Time Machine* portrays "degeneration following security."[4] As Arata argues, particularly for the fin-de-siècle imagination, signs of abundance readily turned into markers of excess. Such slippage or ambiguity informs the following description of museum-rich West End London from *Tono-Bungay:* "All these museums and libraries that are dotted over London between Piccadilly and West Kensington, and indeed the museum and library movement throughout the world, sprang from the elegant leisure of the gentlemen of taste. Theirs were the first libraries, the first houses of culture; by my rat-like raids into the Bladesover saloon, I became, as it were, the last dwindled representative of such a man of letters as Swift. But now these things have escaped out of the Great House altogether, and taken on a strange independent life of their own." Whether the city's collections are for Wells a sign of cultural health or decline remains unclear, yet what remains among the remains, Wells's "last dwindled representative," recalls that other lone survivor from nineteenth-century fiction, Mary Shelley's last man, Verney. In the closing chapters of *The Last Man* (1826), which would prove prophetic of the century's final anxieties, Shelley imagines the end of the world to be a museum, what Verney calls a "desolate world" where the wealth of "the earth's million cities" is "stored up for my accommodation." Left to wander the "storied streets" and the "hallowed ruins" of Rome, Verney must endure an exhausting and inexhaustible tour of a world museumified.[5] Whether the vision be, as it is here, the museum as end or whether it be the ends of museums or museums left standing, or crumbling, in the end, the readings below demonstrate the compatibility of the museum's representational use with the "eschatological impulse" of the century's turn.[6] Imagining the museum's end serves as a means to envision the end of all things. If, as I have argued throughout this book, a museum's greatest triumph is to shore fragments against a culture's ruin, then one of the gravest images imaginable is of the museum itself in ruin.

Gallery A: A Museum Elegy

The Forsytes collect. Their great pursuit is property, their great ambition to conquer London and make it their own. As the titular man of property, Soames Forsyte leads his clan of collectors in its acquisitions. The perfect Forsyte, he collects all fine things, including his wife, for whom he is building a house in which to contain her. Throughout the course of the novel Soames repeatedly retreats to his private home gallery to muse over his collected paintings, to gain a private pleasure and fulfill a personal need to assert his will to control. Possession is his glory. The family dinner in chapter 2 of part 2 is, accordingly, magnificent in its international abundance: the Forsytes have conquered the world, making it submit to their appetites for sugar, French olives (Soames is disappointed that they are not Spanish), Russian caviar, German plums, Egyptian cigars, and Turkish coffee. Thus unfolds *The Man of Property,* the first tale in the long saga to chronicle the rise of the Forsyte clan (spanning from 1821 to 1926) as a product of the industrial revolution—"the upwardly mobile, acquisitive, new rich of peasant stock who made their money in the economic growth of London and England."[7]

Proliferating everywhere to be seen by everybody, the Forsytes function in the novel as representatives of their culture. As young Jolyon says, "A Forsyte is not an uncommon animal. There are hundreds among the members of this Club. Hundreds out there in the streets; you meet them wherever you go."[8] Galsworthy's analysis of this great family serves as a meditation on late-Victorian society, for Forsytes "are never seen . . . without habitats. . . . Without a habitat a Forsyte is inconceivable" (84). Galsworthy figures that habitat as a museum culture, replete with all its various sites of collection: men's clubs, opera houses, boardrooms, dioramas, parks, zoos, and botanical gardens. The narrative moves from one institution to the next, stressing the institutionality of existence at the turn of the century. And the Forsytes themselves are the novel's greatest institution, powerful in their organization. Whether it be Swithin's engagement dinner for June, the dance at Roger's, or the death of Aunt Ann, the ritual of family celebration turns the Forsytes into a museum of sorts; family becomes a series of collected moments, a spectacle the reader observes. One critic thus argues, "the tribal ceremony represents a moment of passage, a record of an achievement or a loss, a moment of being that stands still, that expands in space and time as if developing strength and meaning."[9] Initially the novel explores the reasons for such institutionality by juxtaposing rich descriptions of club-room interiors and a nihilistic vision of the city. London pulses with atomistic fitfulness: "The stillness, enclosed in the far, inexorable roar of the town, was alive with the myriad passions, hopes, and loves of multitudes of struggling human atoms" (241). The surrealism of London does not elude Galsworthy: "The fog was worse than ever at Sloane Square station. Through the still, thick blur, men groped in and out; women, very few, grasped their reticules; . . . cabs loomed dim-shaped ever and again, and discharged citizens bolting like rabbits to their burrows. And these shadowy figures, wrapped each in his own little shroud of fog, took no notice of each other" (260–61). "In the great warren, each rabbit for himself . . . driven underground," one can understand how collecting becomes the desperate solution to aggregate existence, the final response to—and of—the crowd (261).

The modernity of Galsworthy's urban vision, his sense of the horror of underground life, prompts him to investigate collecting as a necessary defensive gesture. Yet, in this "ironic saga, without heroes or epic battles," Galsworthy also reveals acquisitiveness to be, if not the tragedy, then certainly the pathos of the Forsyte family. It is their folly twice over, for the Forsytes are both a dying and a dangerous clan. In this "finest written portrait of the passing from power of England's upper middle class, people who make money and property the measure of all things," the Forsytes—representing tribalism at its most enduring and insidious—are the key institution, among others, that the novel depicts in order to expose their obsolescence.[10] They, like the novel's numerous men's clubs, underscore both the generational gap between old Jolyon and young Jolyon and the age itself as one of departure from the old school. As the organic metaphor of the novel's opening paragraph suggests, the Forsyte family tree will parallel "the rise and fall of nations," "flourishing with bland, full foliage, in an almost repugnant prosperity, at the summit of its efflorescence" (3). In capturing the life of a family at its zenith, Galsworthy explores the dangers inherent in organizing life and treating existence as an organization. Such a world, Galsworthy reveals, thwarts the possibility of human happiness and love. When Soames spies on his wife and her lover, Bosinney, in the park at night, he witnesses passion's desperate attempt to escape what Galsworthy calls its "remorseless enemy, the 'sense of property'" (242). Soames's calculated determination to possess Irene kills both the love available to him in marriage and Irene's love for Bosinney. He is left a degraded man.

In two key scenes Galsworthy uses the backdrop of institutions that are sites of collection, the zoo and the botanical garden. Appropriately, young Jolyon is present in both scenes, serving as a new, corrective presence in an old and timeworn spot. And we watch through his eyes. The afternoon in the zoo verges on burlesque as the distinction between animal and human dissolves. Galsworthy clearly hopes to ironize the distinctive charm of the bourgeois elite. Like the zoo animals, the crowd stands collected in its captivation: "In front of the long line of cages they were collected in rows" (155). A "well-fed man," "the fat man," sneers at the tigers for their hunger, and his pinched wife "in a Paris-model frock and gold nose-nippers" reproves him (156). Later that day Rachel Forsyte and her sister Winifred pose "like two of the birds they had been seeing at the Zoo" (158). Although Galsworthy deflates human pretension here by a standard ploy of fabliau comedy, he is also offering a new political consciousness, espoused by young Jolyon: "In [old Jolyon's] eyes . . . the pleasure of seeing these beautiful creatures in a state of captivity far outweighed the inconvenience of imprisonment to beasts. . . . It was for the animals' good. . . . Indeed, it was doubtful what wild animals were made for but to be shut up in cages!" (156).

Later in the novel young Jolyon watches a more urgent meeting at the botanical garden between Bosinney and Irene. Young Jolyon visits the gardens to copy nature for his paintings, paintings that he hopes will succeed in the marketplace. In his first description of the gardens Galsworthy stresses the artifice of the place. Marked by the man-made ponds and the gardeners' constant sweeping of the leaves, it is a spot of collection and organization. To the gardeners' "tidy souls," Galsworthy writes, the "gravel paths must lie unstained, ordered, methodical, without knowledge of the realities of life" (245). In such a spot young Jolyon discovers Irene waiting for Bosinney. As voyeur, Jolyon gazes on her beauty, assessing its attributes and determining the ways in which she resembles none of the conventional forms of female beauty: witch, domestic doll, angel, or victim. Jolyon grows irritated at having to share his vision with other men who pass by, issuing "furtive stares," wanting "an excuse for peeping," and "scrutiniz[ing]" with "a queer expression about [the] lips" (246). The strong language of these phrases captures the men's desire to objectify Irene. Such a scene is foreboding because it suggests that her status as a collectible is inevitable and that the spot chosen as the lovers' retreat is the very pride of the culture that will ultimately thwart their love. In short, they have nowhere to go. The collision of gender, sexuality, class, and culture in *The Man of Property* spells Bosinney's demise; more broadly, it reveals a society nostalgic, elegiac for the old order, desirous of the wrong things, hopelessly and dangerously fossilized, museumified.

The main event of the plot of *The Man of Property* is the building of Robin Hill, a house that is for Soames "a kind of storage place for Irene along with his landscapes and other art objects, a house of protection for a fading relationship that he proposes to capture and contain."[11] Yet it is both richly ironic and just that this construction project results in the deconstruction of Soames's Forsytian ethos and the destruction of his brand of happiness. Nowhere more clearly do we see museum culture in decline than in watching the representative man of property at home. With ownership his greatest fantasy, Soames is compulsive, even furtive about his picture buying (note the effect of the phrase "after dark" and the plural "hours" below): "He had stopped to look in at a picture shop, for Soames was an 'amateur' of pictures, and had a little room in No. 62 Montpellier Square, full of canvases, stacked against the wall, which he had no room to hang. He brought them home with him on his way back from the City, generally after dark, and would enter this room on Sunday afternoons, to spend hours turning the pictures to the light, examining the marks on their backs, and occasionally making notes" (51). In the saga's later volume *In Chancery* (1920) Soames's fantasy only deepens as he cherishes undiminished hopes for a collector's destiny: "He would retire, live privately, go on buying pictures, make a great name as a collector" (600). He even dreams that Robin Hill will "become one of the 'homes of England'" (402). Soames longs to bequeath his property to his son and his son's son: "And the aesthetic spirit, moving hand in hand with his Forsyte sense of possessive continuity, dwelt with pride and pleasure on his ownership thereof" (402). Still later, in *To Let (1921)*, Soames dreams on. In a dilatory two-page effusion of catalogic prose, Soames cannot resist imagining Timothy Forsyte's house turned into a house-museum: "Would it not be almost a duty to preserve this house . . . and put up a tablet, and show it? 'Specimen of mid-Victorian abode—entrance, one shilling, with catalogue'" (700). The plan to build and to hold, however, proves elusive for Soames; his bricks-and-mortar project slips away—first because the architect he hires becomes Irene's lover, then because his progeny, by a second wife, turns out to be not a son but a daughter, who is rejected by Irene and young Jolyon's son and ejected from residence at Robin Hill because of Soames's most scarring act of property, the rape of Irene. In the end, Irene returns to live at Robin Hill with her new lover, young Jolyon, beyond the reach of Soames's collector's grasp. Soames's fate is to endure the irony that his most desperate act of possession leaves him dispossessed; in this allegory of possession he is destined to represent a culture in decline, what Galsworthy calls an "imperialism" that characterizes "the 'possessive' instinct of the nation on the move" (*In Chancery*, 363).

Gallery B: The Order of Things in 802,701

In H. G. Wells's scientific romance the time traveler journeys into a future garden world studded with the colossal ruins characteristic of Eloi architecture. Here, in the year 802,701, he is drawn to enter the Palace of Green Porcelain, which he deduces immediately to be a museum. From this point the reader's sense of foreboding intensifies as Wells's false utopia turns dystopic. "Here," writes Bernard Bergonzi, "the Arcadian spell is finally cast off." [12] Although early versions of the core narrative of *The Time Machine* reveal the changes Wells made to the characters, the scenario of a museum visit remained one of his earliest and most constant conceptions. A friend of Wells's describes the original account: "The Chronic Argonauts stir up these weary idlers, and even make it fashionable to read books. The priests take their visitors to see a vast museum, but themselves grow bored and leave the pair to explore alone, warning them against the passages which lead 'down.'" [13] Some questions arise: Why was Wells, even in early versions of this fantasy, certain of the suitability of the museum scene? Why is it important that the time traveler journey into the future only to find the past as imaged in the museum? Why does the palace lurk on the narrative's periphery in the two chapters preceding the time traveler's actual visit, tantalizing both the narrator and the reader with invitations to step inside its doors? In the plot the museum functions as an aid to the time traveler's survival. Just as Robinson Crusoe ransacks the shipwreck for supplies, the time traveler pilfers the museum. Like Defoe's ship, Wells's museum brings a necessary bit of the traveler's world into the new world, and here, in this warehouse of usable goods, the time traveler discovers his weapons against the Morlocks: matches, camphor, and a mace. The museum shows the hero to be both adventurous and resourceful.

Yet the description of this "latter-day South Kensington," especially in contrast to Wells's typically sketchlike prose, is highly detailed, suggesting more intricate motives for the museum scene. As the reader accompanies the time traveler and Weena on their tour of the palace, the

pace of the narrative slows: we begin in the gallery of paleontology, journey through the mineralogy and natural history sections, the library,
the collection of machines, then move through various halls devoted to
chemistry, arms, and ethnology. It seems important to Wells's purpose
that the time traveler date the building. Although small parts of the building, such as the inscription over the facade, are incomprehensible to the
time traveler, it is nevertheless revealed to be a familiar place. The time
traveler easily deduces that this museum is "latter-day," a strange vestige
of something familiar, something Victorian, and the museum's configurations reveal the collections to be Victorian in kind. The foci of the
collections testify to the concerns of nineteenth-century science and
industrialism, right down to "the old familiar glass cases of our own
time." [14] And the facade of the palace, with its exotic, lustrous pale-green
tint, recalls the design tendencies of Victorian orientalism. This bit of
Wellsian architecture begins to uncover the museum's more complex
function as an emblem for the cultural values Wells attacks, for, as John
Reed has noted, "Wells's architectural vision was closely bound up with
his social and moral views." [15]

Masquerading in the narrative as the past, the museum facilitates
Wells's critique of the present, which faces a future of diminishing possibilities. Like the White Sphinx, like all the dilapidated colossi of the
Eloi world, the palace, with its indecipherable inscription, becomes part
of the illegible monumental architecture of the future, thereby fulfilling
the aim of science fiction, which Darko Suvin has defined as the "literature of cognitive estrangement." [16] This inscrutable text only adds to the
time traveler's heuristic confusion; unable to read both the proverbial
and the symbolic writing on the wall, the time traveler struggles to de-
code the unclear destiny of civic culture. Yet this very inscrutability is
Wells's message, articulate of an antimonumentality that marks a culture
under the siege of entropy. As it "contains the reliques of high technological civilization," the derelict museum signals the death of techno-
culture, undercutting Victorian culture's investment in industrialism and
scientism. [17] A showcase of devolution, signifying an area of "human
activity . . . diminished by the decline into the future," Wells's palace
challenges the Darwinian model on which most Victorian museums organized their exhibits. [18] As we have seen, the flowering of museum culture in the nineteenth century was inseparable from the technological

advances realized in nineteenth-century industry and science. The South Kensington was committed to displaying industrial arts, and the many Victorian exhibitions, particularly the Crystal Palace, were devoted to exhibiting mechanical wonders. Museums, moreover, were founded on the positivistic faith that the objectivity of science could map out the secrets of the world. It is telling, then, that the time traveler longs most to linger in the gallery of machines, a popular feature of many Victorian exhibitions. Here he feels most at home.

The Palace of Green Porcelain, in effect, exists as everything a museum should not be. Wells's museum is an image not of reconstitution but of degeneration; its fate proves to be a reversion to the green world, a fate that exposes the time traveler, once the undisputed insider to the intimate club-land world of the novella's opening chapter, to be an alien transplant to the inhospitable outdoor world of the Eloi. If museums aspire to construct wholes from available fragments, the museum of *The Time Machine* is, in contrast, full of nothing but fragments. Wells repeatedly uses the motif of fracture, detailing the smashed windows and cases, the broken skeletons, the tattered books. The triumph of the museum enterprise, as we have seen, is rescuing humankind from the ravages of time and historicity. In Wells's futuristic museum, however, time has triumphed: "Though the inevitable process of decay . . . had been staved off for a time . . . with extreme sureness if with extreme slowness [it was] at work again upon all its treasures." The museum thus becomes an image of "universal decay," offering up the "spectacle of old-time geology in decay" and the inversion of "the conquest of animated nature" (61). The eerie sense of diminution—"that was all!"—on the site of original abundance unsettles the time traveler and his audience. The time traveler's vision of the museum's tattered books, so decomposed he fails at first to recognize them, speaks of the vanity of human wishes: "Had I been a literary man I might, perhaps, have moralized upon the futility of all ambition. But as it was, the thing that struck me with keenest force was the enormous waste of labour to which this sombre wilderness of rotting paper testified" (63). As the ultimate rendering of the void, the anti-museum is Wells's most aggressive check on Victorian progressivism. Although any decrepit civic building could have suited Wells's purpose, a museum in ruins most dramatically bears witness to the dead culture.[19]

Originally the champion of sweetness and light, Wells's museum becomes the inferno of the preying, subterranean Morlocks. In the gallery of machines the time traveler senses the presence of the Morlocks; at the end of the hall lies one of the many subterranean passages leading down into their factory world. The museum, and particularly the machine gallery, is the appropriate setting for Morlock activity: here they dismantle the exhibitions in order to execute their own creations below. Wells's analysis of the hyperindustrial world of 802,701 leads to a critique of mass museum culture, the final manifestation of which leaves the proletariat in command. The museum is both the habitat where the Morlocks flourish and the medium they must decimate in the frenzy of production that fuels an advance that more closely resembles a decline. Again in ironic inversion, the place of enlightenment transforms into the place of darkness, and, as John Huntington has observed, both spatially and symbolically "it blurs the line between up and down." [20] It also blurs the line between protagonist and antagonist, for here the time traveler reveals his most Morlockian side as he assembles his weapons to become a worthy opponent, as he reenacts the Promethean feat of stealing fire, and as he longs to murder the Morlocks. Such aggression and appetency infect all of the characters in the novella. Not only the Morlocks dismantle the collections; the Eloi do, too, for the time traveler finds "traces of the little people in the shape of rare fossils broken to pieces or threaded in strings upon reeds" (61). Even Weena rolls a sea urchin down a case. And the time traveler takes whatever he wants, smashing the cases that hold his objects of desire. In a particularly irreverent moment he performs a comic dance on the museum floor—part cancan, step dance, and skirt dance. Yet his most fascinating gesture comes as an "irresistible impulse": "I wrote my name upon the nose of a steatite monster from South America that particularly took my fancy" (64). These acts of vandalism bespeak a thug mentality that informs all the pillaging of this scavenger society. Each has in some way taken a hand to the museum, participating in its delegitimation. By definition and function a "monument of an intellectual age" and an expression of cultural optimism and strength, the "latter-day South Kensington" is now a "derelict museum," an antimuseum that proves to be the very inversion of its own ideals.

Although the time traveler and Weena first enter the Palace of Green Porcelain "seeking a refuge there from her Fear," the secrets housed in the palace accelerate the time traveler's horrific awakening to the dreary future of humankind (56). This horror at the heart of the museum takes clearer and more sinister shape in a later tale by Wells, *The Croquet Player* (1936). In this frame narrative the narrator, an "effeminate" and "tame" croquet player who sports a "cherubic face" and an "ineffective will" and who is exceptional only in his "exceptionally uneventful life," listens to the tales of Dr. Finchatton, who is haunted by his experiences in Cainsmarsh. An archaeological-dig site, Cainsmarsh is infected by a miasma that prompts the inhabitants to commit brutish acts of violence and fills the doctor with an indescribable unease and sense of guilt. According to Finchatton, in our archaeological transgressions, in the digging up of old bones, we are as brutal as Cain. In the climax of the tale, a chapter called "The Skull in the Museum," Finchatton visits a museum in Eastfolk, where he witnesses the "thick louring beetle-browed skull" of his human ancestor and cries out to the little curator, "That in our blood!"[21] For Finchatton the "threat of that primordial Adamite" is twofold: first, our ancestor proves our connection to the brute ("the animal rages again," cries Finchatton); second, he symbolizes the burden heaped on us by recorded history, a legacy that breaks, Finchatton repeats, "the Frame of our Present." Explaining his cryptic phrase, the doctor continues, "We have poked into the past, unearthing age after age, and we peer more and more forward into the future. And that's what's the matter with us" (63). Finchatton's tale shatters the once circumscribed world of the narrator, "enclosed in the same pleasant round of harmless and fruitless activities," exposing it forever after to the recurrent nightmare of the skull once again come alive (12).

In this tale that recounts "not an ordinary ghost story" and that might most aptly be called the museal gothic, we discover we are haunted in particular ways (10). With a present that proves to be our distant past, we emerge the modern brute. Moreover, our present is burdened by all that it has inherited. Whether it be our savage roots or the forbidden knowledge of our panicked accumulation, our inheritance turns out to be a baneful legacy. Both curses inform Finchatton's dream in which the skull, grown colossal, is surrounded by its descendants, sufficiently gruesome in their antlike frenzy but more disturbing in their sheer number. The return of this "ancestral brute" to our contemporary lives, and to the post–World War I fiction of Wells, reconnects us to its fictional ancestors, the Morlocks, who also horrify us as our future hideously transformed into a regressive primitive. As John Huntington argues, the palace houses "the paradox of a progress that is a regression."²² Although in many respects the anti–Darwinian inversion of a museum's ideals, the Palace of Green Porcelain, read in this different light, reveals both the menace inherent to museums and the dark lesson of Darwinism that fuels the museal gothic of Wells's recurring vision: atavism. As Finchatton's psychotherapist explains, "But we men, we have been probing and piercing into the past and future. We have been multiplying memories, histories, traditions; we have filled ourselves with forebodings and plannings and apprehensions. And so our worlds have become overwhelmingly vast for us, terrific, appalling" (88). Like *The Croquet Player,* which portrays the "sunset of civilization" (98), *The Time Machine* tells a sobering tale of an aging universe, what Bergonzi has labeled an "ironic myth," that forecasts the end of that religion called Victorianism, whose shrine was the museum. Yet *The Time Machine* is also a clarifying or corrective tale, "any archaeologist will tell you as much": "There has been no real change, no real escape. Civilization, progress, all that, we are discovering, was a delusion" (*Croquet Player,* 89). The Palace of Green Porcelain is like the "evil old skull," "an explanation that was itself an enigma" (81). Yet, when decoded, the palace's crumbling architecture unearths our connection to the lower animals and is the ruin that marks what Wells called "the Age of Frustration." It also compels us to face the central question of Wells's fiction: "How shall Man live through his own coming of age?"²³ How shall we endure our end?

Gallery C: A Thing of the Past

By calling his character Old Hammond an antiquarian rather than a curator, Morris has the deprofessionalization of his post parallel the obliteration of the museum's institutional cachet in Nowhere. In its mission to decontextualize art, the museum participates in what Morris saw as the fatal transmogrification at the heart of Victorian society: the cleavage of art from daily life. Patrick Brantlinger has described the world of Nowhere in language suitable to detailing the museum's demise: "What is missing is 'great art' along traditional lines, the work of individual geniuses. In place of the high, rare achievement of the 'humanistic tradition,' Morris offers collective freedom to create and to enjoy." The museum's canon-making abilities depend on a dangerous elitism at odds with the ethos of Nowhere, an elitism equally at odds with Morris's passionate sense that "the great scandal at the heart of capitalist triumph [was] the systematic occlusion of the worker from the archaeological and historical record of modern times."[24] To set this record straight, Morris invents an imagined world where art is indistinct from functionality; ornament enhances everyday creations, and the artisan has replaced the artist. Thus outmoded, the museum is also unnecessary in Nowhere because utopia has abolished all notions of empire. Old Hammond claims, "We have long ago dropped the pretension to be the market of the world" (101). Later he devalues nationalism as "foolish and envious prejudices" (117). The factionalism indispensable to imperialism gives way to global harmony based on variety. Hammond explains that people no longer wish to rob one another; they would rather be "serviceable and pleasant to each other" (117). He condemns the "transparent pretext[s]" of Victorian imperialism, the rationalizations for "some bold, unprincipled, ignorant adventurer" to loot alien societies and divest them of their native culture in order to westernize them. He is most horrified by the tale of "the time when Africa was infested by a man named Stanley" (125–26).

Morris's use of the verb "infested" leaves little doubt as to his views of, as Hammond ironically phrases it, civilization's dealings with "noncivilization." Accordingly, in his judgment of Victorian imperialist appropriation, Hammond points to the museum: "In there" he has "read books and papers . . . telling strange stories" (126). Throughout the rest of the Bloomsbury discussion the museum retreats, functioning as a largely unrealized backdrop for dialogue. Yet at this moment the museum comes into sharp focus in order to be implicated in the transgressions of Victorian political ambitions. For Morris the museum has served two gods, modern capitalism and the imperialism that feeds its global expansion, and it is these two shibboleths that become his targets for attack. As E. P. Thompson has passionately examined in his political biography of Morris, imperialism for Morris "was the inevitable and most vicious outcome of the 'Century of Commerce.'"[25] In his rethinking of cultural values, Morris exposes civilization to be "organized misery," reliant on cant, vice, and hypocrisy. And the museum, the assumed agent of enlightenment, becomes a propaganda machine and, even more mendaciously, the facilitator of political wrongdoings.

Despite Morris's attempt to imagine a world free of museums and thereby liberated from the clutter of Victorian materialism and commercialism, the British Museum ultimately resists easy cancellation from *News from Nowhere.* What is for many readers a flaw in the tale (what E. P. Thompson laments as "the lack of eager intellectual life"; what Northrop Frye decries when he writes, the utopians "have, quite simply, no time to think"), what is for even more readers a weakness in utopian literature in general, gives way to the tale's greatest richness, housed as it were within the museum.[26] Indeed, as we saw at the outset of this chapter, Dick, the dutiful citizen of Nowhere, admits that he is puzzled about the purpose of a National Gallery. Yet Morris also gives us Dick's wife, Clara, who is known in the text primarily for her desire. The glimpsed narrative of her extramarital yearning suggests her greater infidelity to the prescriptions of utopia. In similar fashion, Ellen's grandfather, the Old Grumbler, admits that the "books of the past days" are "much more alive than those which are written now" (174). In their nascent, nagging dissatisfaction with this "epoch of rest," these two figures point the way to the tale's most important character cluster: Ellen, Henry Morsom, and Old Hammond. All three are immersed in what might be called museal projects. In her cross-examinations of Guest, Ellen is committed to the archival work of digging into the past; she is, as many readers have noted, the muse of history within the tale. Morsom, "a country edition" of old Hammond, is a curator of "a biggish hall which contained a large collection of articles of manufacture and art from the last days of the machine period to that day" (199). And Hammond proves to be Guest's second, and superior, guide because he can articulate a Tiresian wisdom founded on his knowledge of both the past and the present, gathered not only by virtue of his advanced age but also from his work in the museum.

In many ways a voice critical of the past, Hammond also treasures the museum for all it represents: art, narrative, history. He confesses, "Yes, I am much tied to the past," and Dick claims about his great-grandfather, "He looks upon himself as a part of the books, or the books a part of him, I don't know which" (89, 86). By contrast, the citizens of Nowhere are "not great readers," and history is no longer part of their education, if one can call their commitment to intuitive intelligence such (166). Members of the utopian generation have little use for the house of history that the museum is because they feel no trace of yearning or nostalgia for any time or place. Unresponsive to tales and to history, these dwellers of Nowhere strike the text's encoded reader, a reader of historical tales, as narratively uninteresting. Hammond, too, grows impatient with the happy naïfs of Nowhere: "Though it is pleasant enough to see these youngsters moving about and playing together so seriously . . . yet I don't think my tales of the past interest them much. The last harvest, the last baby, the last knot of carving . . . is history enough for them" (88–89). Guest seems grateful for Hammond's ambivalent response to Nowhere: "I rather felt as if the old man, with his knowledge of past times, and even a kind of inverted sympathy for them caused by his active hatred of them, was as it were a blanket for me against the cold of this very new world" (133). The frigid perfection of Nowhere creates pangs even in the hearts of its dwellers. Clara laments that their world is not interesting enough to be represented in painting or books, and she admits that Hammond "makes us feel as if we were longing for something that we cannot have" (162). The troubled utopia uncovered in these counter-textual moments of longing and absence points to the tension that most readers sense in reading this tale: Nowhere depicts the end of history, but it also represents the obliteration of historical awareness. As Frye explains, "this society of young people who have torn themselves loose from the fetters of history have still to face the question of historical continuity."[27]

This pending death of historical consciousness galvanizes Ellen, Morsom, and Old Hammond into a restless commitment to their museal projects: to remember and recollect. Yet it troubles most deeply the text's central character, William Guest, who worries that the fate of the nineteenth century will prove to be erasure from the record. In what James Buzard describes as the tale's ethnographic interruptions, Guest alludes to himself as the outsider in Nowhere; these breaks in the narrative, according to Buzard, assure the reader that Guest the ethnographer, and by extension Morris, despite his immersion in an alien culture, is still one of us.[28] Yet to be one of us is to face the specter of aphasia, and the breaks, far from reassuring, threaten to fracture into the void of amnesia. Too often for comfort, Guest is deemed the nobody in Nowhere, the vanishing or invisible man who proceeds under "the cap of darkness"—a fate that is realized as he watches the denizens of the future, even Ellen in the end, forget him (179). In constructing a world without museums, then, *News from Nowhere* becomes a different kind of fiction of loss that imagines a world without history and memory. Yet the tension that initially arises in the tale when Guest must rely on two guides, due to Dick's limited understanding, ultimately soothes by redirecting the narrative interest away from the pastoral spirit and toward the revolutionary leanings of Hammond. These leanings, in turn, take us back to the museum's roots in insurrection, permitting the museum itself to capture ultimately the energy of the narrative and the spirit of Morris himself. Only on the museum's foundations can the true labor of historical continuity commence.

The three narratives discussed in this chapter share certain key affinities. All three attack the nineteenth century for its hubris: its scientism, commercialism, industrialism, materialism, imperialism, capitalism. While the precise focus or terms of the attack vary among the tales, all three authors use the novel as a form of social criticism—what Wells called "the criticism of laws and institutions"—and are eager to experiment with the novel's form as well as its aim.[29] Moreover, the goal of each narrative is to move beyond Victorian culture, to conceive of community beyond the problematics of possession. In this respect, these tales from authors on the cusp ultimately reject, rather than answer, Trilling's question, "Who shall inherit England?" Instead, with fin-de-siècle exhaustion and Edwardian belatedness, they emerge tales of disinheritance. Not surprisingly, then, these three authors boast a heightened awareness of the passage of time, most piquant in the hypernumeracy of Wells's chosen year, 802,701, but apparent also in references to hours, dates, years, and linear accounts of process riddling all three tales. Invariably, these narratives turn to the museum as the site that best commingles past with present. But the most important kinship among the tales is their shared narrative voice, which has been variously described as that of the detached observer, the scientist, the psychoanalyst, the ethnographer but which might also be aptly identified as that of the curator. Despite their differences, *The Man of Property, The Time Machine,* and *News from Nowhere* are what Buzard calls "ethnographies of ourselves," attempts to preserve a cultural memory by permitting the outsider (or, in these fictions, the insider posed as the outsider) to assume a privileged position within, to become, that is, the insider.[30] All three texts ultimately reveal an odd relation to the very site they challenge. The museal project inspires what one critic calls the "fin-de-siècle zoo" of late-Victorian gentlemen that opens *The Time Machine* and what a contemporary reviewer deemed Wells's "diorama of prophetic visions of the dying earth."[31] It informs Galsworthy's taxonomy of a species, a fact he makes explicit in his preface to the saga when he positions himself retrospectively, "looking back on the Victorian era," "we shall not look upon its like again," and a fact he makes forcefully in ending with the following trope: "If the upper-middle class, with other classes, is destined to 'move on' into amorphism, here, pickled in these pages, it lies under glass for strollers in the wide and ill-arranged museum of Letters. Here it rests, preserved in its own juice: The Sense of Property."[32]

Yet it is Morris's utopian romance that best demonstrates the outsider's metamorphosis into the insider, so evident in the curatorial spirit that flames Guest's delight: "I fairly felt as if I were alive in the fourteenth century" (61). So too, after Hammond and Guest query whether they are strangers or familiars, Guest decides to imagine himself as "a being from another planet," an agreed-upon ruse that informs their dialogue (89). Morris's ambivalence about the museum as a thing of the past turns a tale of rest into a counternarrative of restlessness. It reminds us that Morris was primarily a reteller of old tales, a poet whose proclivity fell toward collections of works. It reminds us of his love for the artifact, of his founding in 1877 of the Society for the Protection of Ancient Buildings when he feared that his own society would silence the tales that monumental architecture can tell. Morris's "archaeological socialism" reminds us that the museum is the house of both history and memory.[33] As Old Hammond says about futuristic London's effaced East End, "but some memory of it abides with us, and I am glad of it" (99). Such a confession echoes the close of *The Time Machine,* where the time traveler's audience admits that the blank and black future is "lit at a few casual places by the memory of his story" (83). Tragic though his situation seems, Guest must be glad that he is not simply stranger or familiar but "strangely familiar" and can envision Trafalgar Square with two sets of eyes, equipped with the double vision of "this fair abode of gardens" and "a phantasmagoria of another day" (77). Ultimately, Morris has moved us toward what might be called a new museology and thus forward to this book's conclusion with the century's greatest scholar of memory, Sigmund Freud.

Coda: In Freud's Study

I sat upon the shore
Fishing, with the arid plain behind me
Shall I at least set my lands in order? . . .
These fragments I have shored against my ruins.

—T. S.
Eliot, *The*
Waste Land

BY WAY OF CONCLUSION I want to turn briefly to the still image of
Sigmund Freud's collection-filled study in London, a public museum
since 1986. Today, when one enters 20 Maresfield Gardens, the more
than two thousand pieces of ancient art that crowd Freud's study and
adjoining consulting room arrest one's gaze (figs. 11 and 12). The physical density effected by the room's numerous, multilayered collectibles
seems to correspond to the multilayered psyche of Freud himself. Here
Freud committed every available space to the display of his collection:
cabinets, shelves, tables, mantelpiece, pedestals, desk—all exhibit meticulously arranged antiquities. This overdetermined space of collection
testifying to Freud's passion to acquire is an emblem that serves to re-
capitulate my central arguments about museum culture, for in his voca-
tion and avocation Freud was devoted to reconstituting fragments into
wholes and to peering inside selves and lost cultures. Moreover (and the
visitor's immediate sense of the study as a sanctuary confirms this), Freud
sought to find through his collecting the "new home" of a respectable
profession and a reconstructed lineage safeguarded from Nazi appropriation.[1] Freud's study—one final Victorian house-museum—thus embodies the connections I have attempted to establish among museum
building, utopia, and rootedness or home-liness. Born in 1856, Freud
grew up in an age dazzled with the new science of archaeology and the
fresh possibilities of an open art market. But as a transitional figure,

Fig. 11. Sigmund Freud's desk. (Courtesy of the Freud Museum, London)

Freud—and our continued museumification of him—suggests, too, that the will to erect museums persists in the twentieth century.

Until the 1986 opening of the Freud Museum and the 1989 traveling exhibition *The Sigmund Freud Antiquities: Fragments from a Buried Past* in America, Freud's penchant for collecting was a lesser-known fact of his biography. It is perhaps professional justice that curators were responsible for exposing him as a curator in his own right. But the larger commitment to preserving the life of Freud had long been a goal for many. When Freud died in 1939, Anna Freud kept her father's study and collections intact. Her will later requested that her father's house be turned into a museum upon her death. Initially, Freud's study had been transplanted to London because family and friends hoped to save him and his reputation from Nazi appropriation and Freud would not calmly repatriate without his collections, his personal and self-constructed fatherland. Even before escape to London seemed a viable option, a family friend enlisted Edmund Engleman to photograph Freud's study in fear that the Nazis would

Fig. 12. Sigmund Freud's study. (Courtesy of the Freud Museum, London)

dismantle his collections; this archive of images later formed the foundation for Vienna's Freud Museum. Perhaps people wanted to collect the
collector not only because of his celebrity but also because Freud had so
effectively taught the importance of remembering and retrieval.

Although the 1989 traveling exhibition held as its obvious premise
that Freud was a collector, it did not, ironically, convey the complexity
of collecting as an activity.[2] The exhibition showcased only sixty-seven
select items from Freud's display cases, isolating each piece in a vitrine.
Treating the collectibles as decontextualized, aestheticized masterpieces,
the exhibition could not reproduce the importance that accumulation
and arrangement held for Freud. Yet Freud had claimed that the aesthetic
value of his acquisitions did not greatly interest him. Some scholars have
tried to identify what Freud valued by establishing a one-to-one correspondence between individual pieces in the collection and Freud's various theories—for example, between his sphinx statue and his Oedipus-
complex theory or his baboon of Thoth and his interest in primitivism.[3]

But the larger questions remain: What does Freud's personal collection in total signify? How can one explain his all-consuming anxiety over the plight of his collections when, in the face of the *Anschluss* of Austria, he fled to London in 1938? To his sister-in-law Minna Bernays, Freud expressed his concern at the time: "In the fateful first days of next week, the commission on which the fate of the collection depends is supposed to come here. The shipper is lurking in the background."[4] Friends and family, particularly Freud's son Ernst and Freud's maid, worked hard to realize Freud's greatest wish: to reconstruct his study from Berggasse 19, Vienna in his new homeland. They transported furniture, two thousand volumes from the library, and the cherished collection. Indeed, after his arrival in London, Freud announced jubilantly, "All the Egyptians, Chinese and Greeks have arrived, have stood up to the journey with very little damage, and look more impressive here than in Berggasse."[5]

It was in Berggasse in the 1890s that Freud had begun to collect antiquities, focusing predominantly on Egyptian art but also acquiring Greek, Roman, Near Eastern, and Asian artifacts. Freud preferred statuary and insisted on originals but settled at times for well-known reproductions. Although he often carefully rearranged his collections, he always kept the faces of his many statues turned inward, to face him and his analysand. Even the select figurines that line Freud's desk in serried files, and particularly the privileged Pallas Athena, were turned as though to observe him at his writings. It is these many faces that continue to command such an intense presence of their own and to acknowledge the now absent collector who once stood surrounded by them. Their collective gaze unblinkingly recalls Freud's dominant impulses toward order and interiority. Here Freud peered into the minds of Viennese women; here he conducted self-analysis the same year he began collecting artifacts. Only within the shrine of his profession, within his half-private, half-public study, did Freud find suitable space for the display of his treasures.[6] And this complex space—the space of a respectable professionalism and an intense interiority—suggests the complex ways in which collection functions as not only the house of the ego but also the haven of the id. It is the space of the master, of mastery and self-mastery. Here, by means of select retrieval, Freud reconstructed his identity; here he sought to discover a new lineage and a new, legitimate science.

Scholars make much of the fact that Freud began his collecting only a few months after his father's death in 1896. In collecting, Freud seemed to find an anodyne for his grief, calling his first acquisitions a "source of exceptional renewal and comfort."[7] He could discover a new father, who, unlike Jacob Freud, would stand as an authentic patriarch of culture. Moreover, Freud could repress his Jewishness by finding new forefathers, who in turn could fashion an alternative, "legitimate" lineage for their new son. Freud confessed that his collection brought him "strange secret yearnings . . . perhaps from my ancestral heritage—for the East and the Mediterranean and for a life of quite another kind: wishes from late childhood never to be fulfilled and not adapted to reality."[8] Such late-childhood wishes were, if not fulfilled, then certainly fueled by a long-standing romance Freud held for museums. Courtship letters between Freud and Martha Bernays show him to be enchanted by the fantasy worlds of museum collections. He calls the Louvre "a world as in a dream."[9] On visiting the study of his mentor, Jean-Martin Charcot— one of his surrogate fathers—Freud describes its "wealth" to Martha, concluding that it was, "in short, a museum."[10] Here one can locate the inspiration for Freud's conception for his own study, what Virginia Woolf later called "something of a museum, 'for there were all round him a number of Egyptian antiquities he had collected.'"[11] In *Gone Primitive* Marianna Torgovnick argues that Freud's construction of a new lineage was politically motivated. Collecting enabled him to garner a bourgeois respectability and cultivation that distanced him from the Nazi conception of Jews as a vulgar, primitive race. As a European intellectual, as a spiritual citizen of antiquity, Freud hoped to escape fatal ethnic stereotyping and become the embodiment of the culture he analyzed. Originally the threatening, disordering other in the eyes of the Nazis, he refashioned himself into an advocate of the Apollonian.

Collecting promised Freud not only civic but also professional respectability. Hoping to publicize and popularize psychoanalysis, he allied himself and his new science to the established and exciting discipline of archaeology. Freud presented himself as an excavator and collector of the buried life, reconstructing selves instead of cities. His great admiration for Heinrich Schliemann encouraged him to continue the analogy, hoping to appropriate some of the excitement Schliemann's heroic discoveries generated.[12] Freud found Schliemann's excavation of "Priam's treasure" utter bliss: "There is happiness only as fulfillment of a child's wish."[13] A self-proclaimed Schliemann of the mind, Freud felt ennobled by the comparison: "It is as if Schliemann had again dug up Troy, which had hitherto been deemed a fable."[14] He often turned to archaeological metaphors in his writings to explain the workings of psychoanalysis. In *Dora,* for example, he likens himself to "a conscientious archaeologist." And in *Civilization and Its Discontents* he draws a lengthy "analogy from another field." "We will choose," he begins, "as an example the history of the Eternal City," and then goes on to explore the similarities and dissimilarities between excavated Rome and the human mind.[15]

Freud's analogy is persuasive: Both the archaeologist and the psychoanalyst explore the depths below the surface; both insist that the present is founded on the many layers of past existence. Both collectors retrieve lost fragments that can then be reconstituted into newly presented wholes—into reassembled cities and comprehensive diagnoses. The solace, the triumph in fact, of both disciplines is that very little is ever lost, for much can be recovered by transforming the diachronic into the synchronic. But the limitless gaze of the probing scientist-collector, Freud argues, ensures the more certain triumph of psychoanalysis, for walls can be torn down and eternally lost, but personality can always be collected by being recollected. Freud envisions his professional task to be a digging down deep through the sedimentary levels of consciousness. From the mental rubbish he uncovers, the psychoanalyst then constructs an ordered prognosis—ultimately assembled as collected thoughts in his writings. As Peter Gay maintains, "Freud's point in compiling his catalogue was to reduce a bewildering array of erotic pleasures to order."[16]

The prevalence of order was a utopic fantasy for Freud. In the essay "Thoughts for the Times on War and Death" (1915) he articulates his anxiety over the world war in light of its disordering power, its whimsical remapping of Europe—or what he calls "the future that is being shaped."[17] For contrast, Freud offers a vision of prewar Europe as a museum. With prose grown dilatory, he formulates a museum idyll:

> *This new fatherland was a museum for [the citizen of the world], too, filled with all the treasures which the artists of civilized humanity had in the successive centuries created and left behind. As he wandered from one gallery to another in this museum, he could recognize with impartial appreciation what varied types of perfection a mixture of blood, the course of history, and the special quality of their mother-earth had produced among his compatriots in this wider sense. Here he would find*

cool, inflexible energy developed to the highest point; there, the graceful
art of beautifying existence; elsewhere, the feeling for orderliness and
law, or others among the qualities which have made mankind the lords
of the earth.[18]

With the cool passion and lyricism of an Apollonian, Freud privileges a utopic pan-Europe because it resembles a museum founded on objectivity, order, and law. In effect, he weeps for the loss of structure, the structure that he appears to salvage through his own collection. His treasury would promote the analysand's mental peace but also testify to the doctor's prowess, assuring patients that Freud the psychoanalyst could competently retrieve and assemble. Indeed, the Wolf Man found that in Freud's study "there was always a feeling of sacred peace and quiet."[19] In her *Tribute to Freud* H. D. also records the calm and order of his study. Using the collection as an objective correlative for the doctor's method, she writes: "There were others present and the conversation was carried on in an ordered, conventional manner. Like the Gods or the Goods, we were seated in a pleasant circle; a conventionally correct yet superficially sustained ordered hospitality prevailed. There was a sense of outer security."[20]

But, as her description implies, H. D.'s peace seems far more tenuous than the Wolf Man's. Her sense of outer security suggests her inner tribulation, her frustration with the correct but superficial order that prevails in her doctor's study. The entire tribute is similarly volatile, at times imploding with H. D.'s trepidation and exploding with Freud's rage. ("I did not know what enraged him suddenly.") First publishing the book under the title "Writing on the Wall" in 1945 in order to record her sessions with Freud in Vienna and London, H. D. intended it to be a tribute, dedicated to "Sigmund Freud the blameless physician"; however, already in the assignation of blamelessness—a curious, double-edged hedge—her ambivalence is clear. As her discomfort around Freud mixes with reverence for him, H. D.'s prose grows more overtly incriminating in the passage below, where she finds in Freud's Greek glass cabinet an apt emblem for the analyst's method:

Thoughts were things, to be collected, collated, analyzed, shelved, or
resolved. Fragmentary ideas, apparently unrelated, were often found to
be part of a special layer or stratum of thought and memory, therefore
to belong together; these were sometimes skillfully pieced together like

the exquisite Greek tear-jars and iridescent glass bowls and vases that
gleamed in the dusk from the shelves of the cabinet that faced me where
I stretched, propped up on the couch in the room in Berggasse 19,
Wien IX. The dead were living in so far as they lived in memory or
were recalled in dream. (14)

While this passage identifies Freud's skill at recuperating the lost and the fractured, the discursive excess of past participles in the first sentence— "collected," "collated," "analyzed," "shelved," "resolved"—functions like a linguistic shudder. Moreover, the concatenation of infinitive verb forms more urgently signals H. D.'s unease in uncovering a professional omnipotence that shakes her calm. Here H. D. appears to ask, can one person have such agency over thoughts as to turn them into things?

Throughout her tribute H. D. returns incessantly to Freud's collections, which serve sometimes as the rich background, sometimes as the foreground against which the power relations between doctor and patient are played out. Freud the collector is a powerful figure that H. D. both idealizes and finds menacing. She calls him "the Old Man of the Sea" and his collections "the treasures he had salvaged from the sea-depth" (97). Later she likens him to "a curator in a museum, surrounded by his priceless collection of Greek, Egyptian, and Chinese treasures; he is 'Lazarus stand forth'" (116). Referring to the collection again, "the Professor knew . . . that . . . he himself was included in the number of those Gods [that he] himself already counted as immortal," H. D. concludes that collecting has made Freud sage, indeed divine (63). Even when he commands her to interact with chosen collectibles, testing her on their significance, her judgment of them, her assessment of their symbolic weight, the collectibles remain to H. D. proof of her vulnerability and evidence of Freud's power, for Freud knows too well her passion: "He knew that I loved Greece. He knew that I loved Hellas" (69). It is by means of his collection, in short, that Freud the aging doctor is able to probe the passion of the young female with the "delicate" voice. It is by this means that Freud goads H. D. into admitting her transference, confessing her love for her analyst. Among the doctor's collections, in essence, H. D. erects the same kind of relationship she has had with the men of culture who haunt her tribute—Havelock Ellis, D. H. Lawrence, and Ezra Pound. In the space of collection, the space of mastery and the master, H. D. experiences an eroticism that is highly painful.

H. D. repeatedly perceives herself to be a fluidity, "my imagination wandered at will," that Freud then harnesses and hardens into diagnosis. In a lengthy analogy she envisions herself "drifting," part of the immense, unknown forces of the oceanic current or the primeval forest. Her depleted initiative permits her only to see the "old Hermit who lived on the edge" and have him "talk to me, to tell me, if he would, how best to steer my course" (13). H. D.'s remark about a certain intaglio in Freud's prized collection of rings, "the royal signature, usually only the initials of the sovereign's name," is followed by a more suggestive observation, which she tellingly deflects by putting it in parentheses: "(I have used my initials H. D. consistently as my writing signet . . . though it is only, at this very moment . . . that I realize that my writing signature has anything remotely suggesting sovereignty or the royal manner)" (66). The gendered binaries with which she constructs her tribute—the uncontrolled, oceanic female in the hands of the controlling and sovereign male doctor-collector—seem only fostered by Freud's highly erotic and gendered sense of his work. Indeed, it was these intaglio rings that Freud gave to his closest colleagues to wear—in the spirit of a secret society or men's club that would carry on the duties of psychoanalysis when, Freud claimed, "I am no more." Freud himself wore a ring engraved with the head of Jupiter, leader of the gods. In confessing that "there is a boyish and perhaps romantic element too in this conception," Freud seems to admit that the old alliance of collector and conquistador is very much in place in his study.[21] Certainly, the erotics of Freud's collecting supports Jean Baudrillard's intriguing claim (which owes its insight to Freud's writings) that the collection is much like the seraglio: "There is a strong whiff of the harem about all this, in the sense that the whole charm of the harem lies in its being at once a series bounded by intimacy (with always a privileged final term) and an intimacy bounded by seriality."[22]

As a series of singular objects—intaglios, Roman glass, oil lamps, red-figured vases, black-figured perfume flasks, sphinx amulet, fertility totem, scarab, reliquary, Cyprus bottle, Book of the Dead, Bodhisattva, Pallas Athena, Eros, Artemis, Venus, Shabti figure of Djehutyemheb—Freud's collection-filled study provides the coda for this book on Victorian museum culture; its resonance, in spite of its silence, recapitulates what I consider the key structures of meaning that museums erect. In his emulation of Schliemann, in his desire to be a boyish romantic, Freud takes us back to the issues raised in chapter 6: the fantasy of imperial myth, the utopian impulse to collect, the archive's ability to construct a certain brand of masculine identity. And Freud's struggles to legitimate his discipline compel us to revisit the realm of chapter 5: the marketplace and the burdens of those writers struggling within it. Moreover, Freud's museum idyll of a pan-Europe is another kind of museum poetry, articulate of a would-be insider's longing to belong, lyrical over the dialectics of here and there, miniature and monumental, present and past that—as we have seen throughout this book—inform a museum's work. H. D.'s sessions in a doctor's collection-filled study represent a final rendezvous in the museum, an intense encounter with culture and power, gendered in ways similar to Eliot's and Brontë's museum scenes examined in chapter 4 yet also rich in memory like the museum scenes constructed by Morris, Wells, and Galsworthy examined in chapter 7. In his attempt to build a home, Freud is like Soane is like FitzGerald; and with FitzGerald one comes full circle back to the romance of appropriation. The will to domesticate the exotic reinvokes that other key nineteenth-century scientist, Charles Darwin; and Freud's international celebrity recalls the museum's interlocking sites of city and empire. Freud's love of structure and order also conjures the hard, antiseptic bodies with which this study opened: the Iguanodon, the Whale-bone Lounge, Wyld's great globe, the middle-class museum-going public. As a member of the European intelligentsia, Freud reminds us of the larger intellectual scene against which the nineteenth-century London cityscape and its museums arose; transposed to London, he reminds us of the cultural exchange central to museums, the cosmopolitan world order museums invariably signal. In sum, as a profound investigator into the foundations of culture and selfhood, Freud—and his collection, now a museum within a museum—has permitted me to ask one final time why the Victorians—and, by extension, we—collect in order to exhibit.

But perhaps Freud's collection-filled study most eloquently articulates the museum's double potency as monument and memorial. As I have argued throughout this book, the rise of museums cannot be separated from Victorian England's industrial, commercial, and cultural power. An undisputed symptom of a healthy public sphere, museums—in their construction, popularity, and presence—marked nineteenth-century London's ascent to the stature of a world city. Yet it seems clear, too, that museums are memorial to loss. Articulate of cultural gain as well as decline, architectural expressions of consolidation as well as consolation, "museums express modern ambivalences, even dilemmas."[23] Freud's study reminds us that, despite the diverse acts of accumulation and inventory and the various sites of exhibition this book has examined, the kinship of the collectors within has been their milieu. Christine Boyer eloquently describes the age: "For many who lived in its whirl, the nineteenth century represented a world of ruins and fragments, emptied of meaningful traditions and authentic memories that once connected the present to the past. In such a world, everything seemed to be collectible."[24] Freud's gallery of memory reminds us of the museum's contradicting impulses and effects—that there is desire and despair in making sense of a world, that dispersal is a counterforce to assemblage, and that commemoration slips into mourning. Although both monuments and memorials foster and cultivate our collective memory, the labor of memorials is the more somber work of marking crises in memory, crises that form one of modernity's deepest scars. To be in Freud's study is simultaneously to dwell inside his home and to listen to his laments regarding the terror of homelessness. In this final way Freud's study keeps us from an easy return to where this book began, in the house of Robert Kerr's English gentleman, for the house that was a museum is now the wasteland. With time Kerr's English gentleman has bequeathed his legacy to Eliot's Fisher King, who attempts to shore fragments against his ruin. Kerr's construction is now, at best, an attempt at reconstruction. And thus the monumental has slipped toward the memorial.

Notes

Introduction

1. H. G. Wells, *Tono-Bungay*, 99; *Official Catalogue*, 50.
2. Kerr, *English Gentleman's House*, 356, 357.
3. Doré and Jerrold, *London*, 161. Subsequent citations appear in the text.
4. In "Vicarious Excitements," Pollock argues that Doré and Jerrold's text portrays London as two discrete cities, the London of the East End and the London committed to charity work. While Pollock's reading of the shifting urbanism marks an important and fresh investigation into Doré and Jerrold's project, I would claim that the text's inevitable trajectory is from the East End to the museum, as evident in the final chapter's final words. The notion of London as a museal city also helps explain the text's seemingly schizophrenic attention to both grime and beauty. In effect, the connoisseur's eye can turn anything into the picturesque; and to the visual collector even charity becomes an aestheticized object. Thus Pollock seems to miss the text's final categorical move.
5. *Times,* quoted in Pollock, "Vicarious Excitements," 48.
6. The work of Doré, Jerrold, and Taine allows me to raise a question central to the museum's enterprise, which is fundamentally engaged in the construction of identity. These views from the British eye and the French eye invite us to gaze on a country both as it wishes to know itself and as it appears in the eyes of others. When I later discuss the American Moncure Conway's *Travels in South Kensington*, the key visual as well as political triangulation for the century will stand complete. This historical paradigm holds in miniature within the Great Exhibition itself: Britain's plans for the exhibition were motivated by the desire to surpass the French in mounting exhibitions. Surpass it did; however, the United States—with its youthful vigor and raw strength—emerged during the course of the exhibition the new and unexpected contender.
7. Taine, *Notes on England*, 231–32. Subsequent citations appear in the text.
8. Donato, "Museum's Furnace," 226.
9. Altick, *Shows of London*, 509.
10. Ruskin, *Deucalion*, 84.
11. Ruskin, "Use of Museums," 200. See Casteras, "Germ of a Museum," and Boyer, *City of Collective Memory,* for fuller discussions of Ruskin's museological plans and practice at Saint George's Museum.
12. Hudson, *Museums of Influence*, 10.
13. Henry James, "London," 13.
14. Fisher, *Making and Effacing Art*, 6.
15. Bataille, "Museum," 25.
16. Such confidence is also evident in one of Henry Cole's later projects, *Universal Art*

Inventory (1867), which lists the worldwide locations of the best examples of artistic production in various categories for the purpose of an "International Exchange of Copies of Works of Fine Art." It is equally telling that the British section of the Paris Exhibition of 1867 showcased not only the best of the South Kensington's reproductions but also the institution's reproductive capabilities.

17. Gibbs-Smith, *Great Exhibition of 1851,* 17–20.

18. Because there were no price tags affixed to the objects displayed in the Crystal Palace, some critics have argued that the Great Exhibition had little effect on Victorian commodity culture. However, I am persuaded by arguments made to the contrary in such books as Richards's *Commodity Culture of Victorian England* and Buck-Morss's *Dialectics of Seeing.* To separate the site of production from the site of consumption presents a clear difficulty, as the presence of the seventy-six-page "Official Illustrated Catalogue Advertiser" in the back of the Great Exhibition catalog might suggest. Even without price tags, the Crystal Palace refashioned Britain's identity into what *Punch* called the world's "Crystal Store." As both advertising language and commerce in 1851 indicate, the Great Exhibition improved trade in Britain. Thus the *Times* reported examples "of the extensive sales at present in progress in the Exhibition," like the "splendid collection of tools shown by Whitworth [which] has been bought by the Austrian government" ("Sales in Progress of Exhibits," 4). But the most striking evidence that the British were being educated as consumers is the South Kensington's announcement in its 1857 guidebook that museum labels in its educational collections would include prices.

19. "Open House at Crystal Palace."

20. Taine's description of the British Museum Library resembles a prison tour. The library seems uncannily similar to Jeremy Bentham's panopticon: "The reading-room is vast, circular in form, and covered with a cupola, so that no one is far from the central office. . . . Each seat is isolated; there is nothing in front but the woodwork of the desk, so that no one is annoyed by the presence of his neighbour" (*Notes on England,* 230).

21. See Coombes, *Reinventing Africa,* for an informative discussion of the Victorian museumification of Africa.

22. Cole, *Catalogue of Objects,* 1, 2; Conway, *Travels in South Kensington,* 89; Owen, "On the Extent," 126.

23. The British Museum shop used to sell a T-shirt that perpetuated such nervous joking. On the shirt an average visitor stands scratching his head, puzzling over a signpost that points one way to Egypt, another to Greece, another to Nineveh, and so on. Confused, the visitor can only quip: "And they call this the *British* Museum?"

24. Darwin, *Origin of Species,* 213; Darwin, *Fertilisation of Orchids,* 241; Darwin, *Origin of Species,* 107; Darwin, *Narrative of Surveying Voyages,* 60, 64.

25. Owen, "On the Extent," 2.

26. Perl, "Pieces of the Frame." For one critic's vision of the museum's future, see the last two chapters and afterword of Davis's *Museum Transformed.*

I. The Museum Crowd

1. I am indebted to Desmond, "Central Park's Fragile Dinosaurs," for the facts concerning the Iguanodon.

2. Such a grammar of conquest is under attack at a twentieth-century American insti-

tution, the Museum of Jurassic Technology in Los Angeles—a kind of antimuseum dedicated to exposing the logic of the museum enterprise. One of its most resonant displays is a rather unspectacular and shabby habitat case of a jackal. Although a visitor can hear the howlings of the animal throughout the museum, it is only on direct encounter with the case that one realizes that the animal's howls are human-generated. A hologram flashes an image of an obese man sitting on a chair howling, an image strategically superimposed on the jackal's head, recalling to this visitor's mind the nineteenth-century Iguanodon. These sieges on the interior of the other demonstrate Rugoff's point that museums are acts of "imaginative reconstruction" ("Beyond Belief," 72). For a full-length treatment of Los Angeles's most curious collection and the often inscrutable intentions of its curator, David Wilson, see Weschler, *Mr. Wilson's Cabinet of Wonder.*

3. Bataille, "Museum," 25.

4. An article from the *Times* of 6 October 1863 likens a natural history museum to a panorama that fuses parts into wholes: "A national museum ought . . . to be the means of keeping before men's eyes and thoughts the unity of knowledge and the mutual dependence and connexion of its different parts. . . . In such a museum there will be seen . . . a sequence and an order pervading alike the whole and every part, and logically binding together by a chain of correlation all the subjects on which men's minds are exercised" (Owen, Miscellaneous Manuscripts).

5. Owen, "On the Extent," 69, 67. Owen's passion for the "crystallised body" looks ahead to my discussion of Mr. Venus in chapter 3. Is not the whole museum enterprise taxidermic in impulse and effect? The hard body of the Iguanodon is also interesting in light of spectators' attempts to possess the beast by stealing fragments of it. "Within months, whole rows of teeth had disappeared from the models, leading a contemporary writer to conclude that in their enthusiasm the 'culprits supposed they were carrying away the real teeth of preserved animals'" (Desmond, "Central Park's Fragile Dinosaurs," 67). This desire to take possession of the hard body generates Haraway's concern about the taxidermic practices of natural history museums today: "Taxidermy fulfills the fatal desire to represent, to be whole; it is a politics of reproduction" (*Primate Visions,* 30).

6. Boyer, *City of Collective Memory,* 195; Barthes, quoted in Boesky, "'Outlandish Fruits,'" 310.

7. "Gigantic Whale."

8. Rembrandt Peale arranged a similar diversion in the United States when he held a dinner party (with room for thirteen guests and a piano) inside one of the mammoth skeletons he and his father had exhumed from the Hudson River Valley (Altick, *Shows of London,* 305).

9. Mumford, *City in History,* 561. To read further on how the museum is and is not like the street, see Jukes, *Shout in the Street,* particularly the section "Street as Museum."

10. Foucault, "Of Other Spaces," 25, 27, 26.

11. "Mr. Wyld's Globe."

12. Wyld, *Notes to Accompany Wyld's Model,* 2. Subsequent citations appear in the text.

13. "New Use of Globe."

14. One need only glance at a work such as Lysons's five-volume *Collectanea,* a panoramic view of early-nineteenth-century "Public Exhibitions and Places of Amusement," to see that time and again witnesses borrowed heavily from the grammar of the panorama to describe Wyld's globe. Here follows a typical advertisement for a panorama:

*The PUBLIC are most respectfully informed, that the SUBJECT at
present of PANORAMA,
is a view, at one glance, of the CITIES
OF LONDON AND WESTMINSTER
comprehending
THE THREE BRIDGES
Represented in ONE PAINTING.*

The panorama ensconces viewers in the world it simulates, making them feel "as though they themselves were there"—wherever "there" happens to be. The panorama appears to free viewers from the limitations of time and space. Through optical illusion, it exhibits the whole world in a small room—the vista, on a comparatively miniature canvas. Such a grammar of visuality and spatiality informs the Victorian museum experience as well.

15. "Journey round Globe"; "Mr. Wyld's Model."
16. Wyld's globe seems the low-culture, or mixed-culture, analogue to the Nash project of Regency London. Although John Nash's central aim was to connect the royal palace in the south with a picturesque park and royal pavilion in the north, he also wished to create a main artery linking the city to Sir Robert Smirke's British Museum. The grand city planner Nash clearly understood how a site of exhibition can function as a hub or center around which a city organizes itself. For a detailed description of the Nash project, see Fox, *London—World City.*
17. Sanitizing the image of London for London and the world became the focus of the city's International Health Exhibition of 1884. See Adams, "Healthy Victorian City."
18. Bourdieu and Darbel, *Love of Art,* 112.
19. Elias, *Civilizing Process,* 3, 6; Cole, "Duty of Governments," 6.
20. Cole, "What Is Art Culture?" 6. Complaints from the manufacturers, whose names were exposed on the collection's labels, soon compelled Cole to dismantle the collection and thus conclude his catechism in design taste.
21. *Report from Select Committee,* 2; *Inventory of British Water Colour,* 4; *Report of Proceedings,* 8–9.
22. The social-amelioration defense of museums was a popular impetus for the public library and museum movement in the nineteenth century. In *Museums and Art Galleries* Greenwood defends every town's right to have a museum for reasons such as these: "1.—Because a Museum and a Free Library are as necessary for the mental and moral health of the citizens as good sanitary arrangements, water supply and street lighting are for their physical health and comfort. . . . 7.—Because Museums and Art Galleries not only give widespread pleasure, but are, with Free Libraries, the Universities of the working classes. . . . 9.—Because they are educational institutions for young and old, and education deepens the sense of the duties and privileges of citizenship" (389–90).
23. "Circulation of Objects," 202.
24. "Bethnal Green Museum." Attendance figures suggest the museum's appeal: 1887, 409,929; 1882, 443,692; 1876, 938,794; 1874, 530,676; and 1872, 901,464. Compare with 1990's figure of 236,080 (in-house document, courtesy of the curator).
25. "Editorial," *Modern Society;* "Bethnal Green," 11, 12.
26. *Brief Guide to Various Collections,* 29, 5.

27. "Editorial," *Bazaar, the Exchange, and Mart; Brief Guide to Various Collections,* 36.

28. Laurie, *Suggestions for Establishing Museums,* 15; Adorno, "Valéry Proust Museum," 175; Baudrillard, *Simulations,* 13. Subsequent citations to *Simulations* appear in the text.

29. I thank Michael Levenson for this argument, one not lost on Dickens in "Please to Leave Your Umbrella." Dickens describes a trip to the Hampton Court Palace, beginning with a guard's standard request that the sightseer deposit his umbrella at the door before entering the palace's collections. The author, at first distracted by utopic dreams of eternity spent in this "encompassing universe of beauty and happiness," only later realizes the implications of such a request (423). The umbrella becomes a symbol, a catchall, for an individual's personal property—his "powers of comparison," "individual opinion," "private judgment," "personal experience"—the loss of which marks the price of gentility, in other words, that which institutionalized, collective existence dictates an individual surrender. I thank Karen Chase for alerting me to this article.

30. Donato, "Museum's Furnace," 223.

31. Clifford, "Of Other Peoples," 121.

32. Nietzsche, *On Advantage and Disadvantage of History,* 64. Subsequent citations appear in the text.

33. Valéry, "Problem of Museums," 203. Subsequent citations appear in the text.

34. Valéry, "Fabre Museum," 207. Subsequent citations appear in the text.

35. One might think of Ruskin's recollection: "In that same museum [Crosthwaite], my first collection of minerals—fifty specimens—total price, if I remember rightly, five shillings—was bought for me, by my father. . . . No subsequent possession has had so much influence on my life" (*Deucalion,* 244). Is it not appropriate that the life Ruskin led devoted to vision arose out of this home museum? Consider, too, the interworkings of self and museum in Pater's extremely private museum *The Renaissance* as well as his curatorial return to childhood in "The Child in the House." Given the museum's connections to memorializing and memory, it is tempting to see the Victorian interest in autobiography as in some fundamental way museal and simultaneously to consider the melancholy inherent in the project of reconstructing one's past life, in light of Pater's rumination in "Sir Thomas Browne": "A museum is seldom a cheerful place—oftenest induces the feeling that nothing could ever have been young" (134).

36. Adorno, "Valéry Proust Museum," 175. Subsequent citations appear in the text.

37. Benson and Esher, *Letters of Queen Victoria,* 1:383; *Official Catalogue,* 1; Malraux, *Museum without Walls,* 10.

38. Sherman, *Worthy Monuments,* 238. Linda Nochlin goes so far as to deem the museum schizophrenic: "As the shrine of an elitist education and at the same time a utilitarian instrument for democratic education, the museum may be said to have suffered from schizophrenia from the start. . . . The museum has always occupied an ambiguous position in radical thought and action" (quoted in Davis, *Museum Transformed,* 69).

39. Wallis, *Hans Haacke,* 60; Anderson, *Imagined Communities,* 178; Marx, *Communist Manifesto,* 13, 12–13.

40. Hardy, "Fiddler of Reels," 94.

41. See Weintraub, *Victoria,* and Benson and Esher, *Letters of Queen Victoria.*

42. Strachey, *Queen Victoria,* 240. Subsequent citations appear in the text.

43. Harbison, *Eccentric Spaces,* 150; Boyer, *City of Collective Memory,* 187.
44. Greenblatt, "Resonance and Wonder," 85.

II. *Fugitive Articulation of an All-Obliterated Tongue*

1. Pound, *ABC of Reading,* 66.
2. In his introduction on FitzGerald, Edmund Gosse, writing when the *Rubáiyát* was a "newer" text, makes some curious hedges concerning its overexposure, calling it "this almost too-celebrated pamphlet" and its history "an ancient tale" (Bentham, *Variorum Edition of Writings of FitzGerald,* xviii, xxi).
3. Kermode, *Continuities,* 57; Robert Bernard Martin, *With Friends Possessed,* 221; Schenker, "Fugitive Articulation," 62.
4. Schenker, "Fugitive Articulation," 61.
5. Terhune and Terhune, *Letters of FitzGerald,* 2:514–15. Subsequent citations to this edition of FitzGerald's letters appear in the text.
6. Hayter, *FitzGerald to His Friends,* 154, 41; Benson, *Edward FitzGerald,* 5.
7. We shall soon see, however, how easily compromised FitzGerald's taste for the exotic can be. He confessed his penchant for modernizing: "I advise what I don't practise: for my Salámán just fails in that [it] loses its Oriental Flavor. . . . But I had to choose between being readably English, or unreadably Oriental" (Terhune and Terhune, *Letters of FitzGerald,* 2:164–65).
8. Hayter, *FitzGerald to His Friends,* 143.
9. In light of FitzGerald's claim that he had brought the world home, Edmund Gosse's vision of him as "one who dozed through life among the Northamptonshire turnips" seems misguided. Gosse continues: "His mind seemed to have grown to be like one of those dingles which faintly diversify the country in which he lived, a modest cup of the pasturage, with a definite horizon of hedge-rows quite close around, almost to be touched by an outstretched finger. . . . A life more still, more rurally sequestered, less affected by the world outside, it is impossible to imagine" (Bentham, *Variorum Edition of Writings of FitzGerald,* xi–xii). While Gosse's pastoralized FitzGerald is in keeping with the standard reading of the *Rubáiyát* as a garden poem that bids its readers "Retreat," it presents a half-truth, blinding us to the acquisitive FitzGerald, who had, in Smilesian fashion, helped himself to the world. (Smiles's *Self-Help* appeared the same year as FitzGerald's first *Rubáiyát.*)
10. Benson, *Edward FitzGerald,* 167.
11. John D. Yohannan, quoted in D'Ambrosio, *Eliot Possessed,* 4.
12. Arberry, *Omar Khayyám,* 17; Hayter, *FitzGerald to His Friends,* 129; Said, *Orientalism,* 53, 102.
13. Jewett, *Edward FitzGerald,* 142.
14. In quoting FitzGerald's *Rubáiyát,* I use the text of the fourth edition as it appears in Decker's 1997 critical edition. Citations for ruba'i appear in the text.
15. As we shall see, the most famous image in the poem, the book of verse (and FitzGerald's increasing privileging of it), is an emblem for FitzGerald's westernization of the oral tradition.
16. Parenthetical numerals following quotes from Arberry's translation refer to rubaiyat. Throughout this chapter, I rely on Arberry's much respected translation as the contrasting text to FitzGerald's, and citations appear in the text. Were my aim here to

uncover the true or authentic Khayyám, pitting one translation against another would be heuristically risky and flawed. However, establishing a range of Khayyámic identity and voice and allowing that there are translations more honest than others are necessary steps in examining FitzGerald's ambitions as a translator of Khayyám.

17. In the introduction to his translation of Capellanus's *Art of Courtly Love,* Parry explains that the image of the boy lover is an Arabic convention for the sake of decency: "Among the Arabs public opinion required that if the beloved was a woman she must, 'for decency's sake,' be spoken of as a man and referred to by masculine pronouns, adjectives, and verbs" (10). Such an argument, however, does not invalidate the allure of Eastern boy love for many Western writers who, like FitzGerald, did not realize that this taboo sexuality was a convention.

18. Brower, *On Translation,* 3.

19. See, for example, Lefevere, *Translation/History/Culture;* Venuti, *Rethinking Translation;* Bassnett, *Translation Studies;* and Barnstone, *Poetics of Translation.*

20. Hugo, quoted in Lefevere, *Translation/History/Culture,* 18; Nietzsche, quoted in Schulte and Biguenet, *Theories of Translation,* 14.

21. FitzGerald revised each new edition without referring back to Khayyám's verse, making his work increasingly inauthentic and increasingly his own. In subsequent editions he also deleted references to Khayyám from the poem. With such lines as "But come with old Khayyám," the first edition had reminded readers that someone other than FitzGerald had composed the lines. For a comprehensive look at the changes FitzGerald made among editions, see Wright, *Letters and Literary Remains,* and Decker's critical edition of the *Rubáiyát.*

22. Jewett, *Edward FitzGerald,* 112. See Robert Bernard Martin, *With Friends Possessed,* for an informative discussion of FitzGerald's translations of Calderón. In his preface to *Six Dramas of Calderón, Freely Translated by Edward FitzGerald* (1853), FitzGerald admitted that because he took such liberties in translating he confined himself to Calderón's lesser-known plays

23. Jewett, *Edward FitzGerald,* 150.

24. Bentham, *Variorum Edition of Writings of FitzGerald,* xxx.

25. FitzGerald discussed with delight his capable renovations of an Opie girl he later regretted purchasing. But his greatest desire lay in duping another buyer into purchasing her: "Yesterday I was busily employed in painting over my Opie, which has suffered by heat, or something of that kind. I borrowed Laurence's palette and brushes and lay upon the floor two hours patching over and renovating. The picture is really greatly improved, and I am more reconciled to it. It has now to be varnished: and then I hope some fool will be surprised into giving £4 for it, as I did. I have selected an advantageous position for it in a dealer's shop, just under a rich window that excludes the light" (Terhune and Terhune, *Letters of FitzGerald,* 1 : 309).

26. However much FitzGerald's discovery of Khayyám is a story of artistic appreciation, aggression appears to play a key role in the birth of this translation. Although most critics sidestep the issue of FitzGerald's possible homosexuality, the triangle of Fitz-Gerald, Cowell, and Khayyám presents a homoerotic configuration in which the ambition of both orientalists to resurrect the beloved object intensifies and complicates their own relationship. Correspondence reveals their competition to master the meaning of the Persian verses; FitzGerald would always believe that he had triumphed over Cowell, claiming that he understood Khayyám more deeply than Cowell did

and that Khayyám belonged to him ("he and I are more akin, are we not? You see all his Beauty, but you don't feel *with* him in some respects as I do" [Bentham, *Variorum Edition of Writings of FitzGerald*, xxx]). Also, the publication of M. Nicolas's French translation of Khayyám, which implicitly attacked the authority of FitzGerald's, prompted a reluctant FitzGerald to issue his second edition, which appeared with a counterresponse to Nicolas's claim that Khayyám was a Sufi poet.

27. Although here and throughout the chapter I argue largely through analogy—for example that the translation and consumption of a text mirror building and defending empire—there is evidence to suggest the worth of arguing causality, too. Witness such a comment as the following made by the journalist Moncure Conway on having read FitzGerald's *Rubáiyát:* "Here we are in large-hearted England that takes us all in, whether from America, from Persia, or India . . . that large-heartedness which is now, I believe, the great and living breath of the world" (quoted in Wrentmore, *Letters from FitzGerald to Quaritch,* 124).

28. Said, *Culture and Imperialism,* 14.

29. It seems fitting that in 1856, three years before the publication of the *Rubáiyát,* Fitz-Gerald was reading with intense interest Burton's *Personal Narrative of a Pilgrimage to El-Medinah and Meccah.* And, in the wake of the *Rubáiyát's* popularity, Burton's hopes for the success of his own Persianesque poem, *The Kasidah,* seemed well founded, although they were quickly disappointed. The Burton-FitzGerald connection took yet another form when FitzGerald, on one of his many mental travels, imagined himself Burton's boon companion: "I am travelling (by Book) yet further North . . . to Iceland, with Captain Burton. When he speaks of passing the Orkneys and Shetlands, I felt a thrill of *The Pirate*" (Terhune and Terhune, *Letters of FitzGerald,* 3 : 694).

30. *Rubáiyát* (1910), 14; D'Ambrosio, *Eliot Possessed,* 60.

31. Arberry, *Omar Khayyám,* 7; D'Ambrosio, *Eliot Possessed,* 60.

32. One such commemorative verse, by Graham R. Tomson, appears in the 1898 edition, which includes three such poems:

> *Sayer of sooth, and searcher of dim skies!*
> *Lover of Song, and Sun, and Summertide,*
> *For whom so many roses bloomed and died;*
> *Tender Interpreter, most sadly wise,*
> *Of earth's dumb, inarticulate cries!*
> *Time's self cannot estrange us, nor divide;*
> *Thy hand still beckons from the garden-side,*
> *Through green vine-garlands, when the Winter dies.*

33. One of the most vitriolic attacks on FitzGerald's translation came from Graves, who, collaborating with the Sufi poet and classical Persian scholar Omar Ali-Shah, offered a corrective translation in 1968 called *The Original Rubáiyát of Omar Khayyám.* Graves claimed that "FitzGerald's additions to the Khayyám corpus seem falser than any," calling FitzGerald "a literary dilettante" and his verse at places "clumsy to the point of unintelligibility" (22, 14, 17). Although Graves pondered the biting rhetorical question "And how could a man like FitzGerald who was incapable . . . of writing first-class original work, recreate that of so extraordinary a predecessor?" his own authority was later challenged (11). See Bowen, *Translation or Travesty?,* in which Graves is accused of participating in a "literary hoax as large as McPherson's Ossian" (5). While Burgess grants Graves's translation a measure of accuracy in *Urgent Copy,*

he concludes that the translation—in contrast to FitzGerald's—is "very pedestrian" with "a regrettable lack of . . . magic" (206).

34. Thomas Carlyle called "the Book itself a kind of jewel" (quoted in Robert Bernard Martin, *With Friends Possessed,* 220). In his 1878 review in the *Atlantic Monthly,* Aldrich praised "the compact, flexible stanza in which Mr. FitzGerald has reset the Persian's jewels" ("Persian Poet," 426). Clarence Darrow titled his 1899 review "A Persian Pearl," and Arberry called the adaptation "a veritable jewel of the poetic art" (*Omar Khayyám,* 21). A recent study of FitzGerald ends with the following analogy: "Like the ancient Persian ornaments of gold and gems, which were made small and precious so that their nomadic owners could carry their treasure wherever they went, FitzGerald's *Rubáiyát* will easily accompany man as he travels through the centuries" (Jewett, *Edward FitzGerald,* 159). In her commemorative verse that adorned a 1932 edition, Blind capitalized on the trope—"I read the Persian Poet's rhyme of old, / Each thought a ruby in a ring of gold" ("On Reading *Rubáiyát,*" 175). The list of examples goes on.

35. My turn here to discourse owes much to Stewart's study of the relationship between objects and narrative in *On Longing.* Moreover, the transformative powers of the miniature, the collection, and the souvenir Stewart uncovers seem to match those of FitzGerald's *Rubáiyát:* making the external world interior, making it "mine" (the possessor's), collapsing the large and unknown into the held or possessed, making time space (retrieving the past for the present). Stewart's treatment of the miniature book is perhaps most relevant to my argument; she sees in the miniature's showcasing of mechanical ingenuity an emblem of the possessor's control over the content within the book's tiny covers. It should not surprise us when she identifies the smallest printed book in the world as an edition of *The Rose Garden of Omar Khayyám.*

36. Familiarity becomes the shibboleth marking the talismanic quality of the *Rubáiyát.* The legends of the *Rubáiyát*'s power to bring people together as a family, a club, a union of converts abound. Below is one such story in which Moncure Conway, writing for the *Nation,* describes how the poem could bond strangers in eternal friendship. This narrated moment rivals the "Klopstock!" scene in *Die Leiden des Jungen Werthers* for Sturm und Drang: Thomas Hinchliff, the first British reviewer of the *Rubáiyát,* "was once at sea near Panama, in a formidable storm, when some on board were expressing doubts whether they could weather it. Hinchliff said: 'He knows about it all—He knows—He knows!' Instantly his hand was seized by an American, named Clarke, who cried, 'You have been reading Omar Khayyám.' The two men fairly embraced, on account of the ancient Persian, and remained friends through life" ("Omar Khayyám Cult," 305).

37. Norton quoted in Schenker, "Fugitive Articulation," 52; Walker quoted in Cadbury, "FitzGerald's *Rubáiyát,*" 547.

38. John Hay continues in the same speech: "There is not a hill-post in India, nor a village in England, where there is not a familiar friend and a bond of union. . . . I heard [the quatrains] quoted once in one of the most lonely and desolate spots of the high Rockies. We had been camping on the Great Divide, our 'roof of the world,' when in the space of a few feet you may see two springs, one sending its waters to the Polar solitudes, the other to the eternal Carib summer. One morning at sunrise, as we were breaking camp, I was startled to hear one of our party, a frontiersman born, intoning these words of sombre majesty." He goes on to quote ruba'i 45 ("Address," 10–12).

39. In his monumental *After Babel* George Steiner movingly describes this naturalization

of text: "The foreign text is felt to be not so much an import from abroad . . . as it is an element out of one's native past. It has been there 'all along' awaiting reprise. . . . Archaism internalizes. It creates an illusion of remembrance, which helps to embody the foreign work into the national repertoire" (365). Thus, FitzGerald's turn to Bernard Quaritch, an antiquarian bookseller, when the *Rubáiyát* was rejected by *Fraser's Magazine* seems fitting. To Quaritch, FitzGerald indicated who had prevailed in this battle between the ancients and the moderns: "You and I might both be laughed at for treating my Omar as if it were some precious fragment of Antiquity" (Wrentmore, *Letters from FitzGerald to Quaritch,* 19).

40. Although the obvious relevant text here is "The Task of the Translator," Benjamin's collector, far more than his translator, serves as the genius of this study. Benjamin's cabalistic sense of the hidden affinities among languages and his belief in the need for reverence and in the translator's ability to bring to life his text are antithetical to the workings of self and other, home and colony that inform both FitzGerald's motives for translating and his uses for his translation—a translation that is, as we have seen, exhausted rejuvenating the translator and his culture.

41. Benjamin, "Unpacking My Library," 59, 64.

42. Borges, "Enigma of Edward Fitzgerald," 77.

43. Schenker, "Fugitive Articulation," 53; Norton, quoted in Schenker, "Fugitive Articulation," 52; Kermode, *Continuities,* 61; George Steiner, *After Babel,* 333.

44. Kerney, "Biographical Preface," 16; Simpson, "Omar Khayyám's Grave," 30.

45. Grant Allen, quoted in Conway, "Omar Khayyám Cult," 305.

46. Edmund Gosse, "The Rose from Omar's Grave," in FitzGerald, *Rubáiyát* (1910), 15.

47. Clifford, "Of Other Peoples," 129.

48. Houghton and Stange, *Victorian Poetry and Poetics,* 341.

49. Bhabha, *Location of Culture,* 10.

50. Wrentmore, *Letters from FitzGerald to Quaritch,* 32.

III. Acquired Taste

1. On the thirty-four models of antique buildings, see Elsner, "Collector's Model of Desire," which contains a fascinating discussion of Soane's Model Room. Elsner's treatment of this house of models as a model house is relevant to my later claim that Sir John Soane was an exemplary Victorian collector. This complete list may be found in Millenson, *Sir John Soane's Museum,* 77–78.

2. It is difficult for scholars to know precisely the date when Soane embraced the idea of a public museum; however, in line with the argument I am positing here, many scholars mark 1823—the year Soane's elder son, John, died—as the date Soane's plans took shape.

3. "House and Museum," 464; Soane, *Description of House and Museum* (1830), 56. Among the many domestic collections of Victorian culture, the homes of Sir Frederick Leighton and William Bullock best demonstrate not only the wide socio-economic range of the house-museum vogue but also its two sources, empire and industrialism. Leighton's trips to the East as well as his imperial connections to friends like Sir Richard Burton and Sir C. Purdon Clarke aided in appropriating exotic cultural artifacts and building materials for the featured room of his house, the Arab Hall.

Home to Leighton's prized collection of Damascus porcelain tiles, the Arab Hall is a stunning example of Victorian domesticated exotic and thus was and is considered the showpiece of his house. By contrast, Bullock's humble beginnings were in Liverpool, where he was a silversmith. In 1805 he launched a new career as a museum entrepreneur by opening the Liverpool Museum in five specially designed rooms in his home. Here, in more than four thousand exhibits, visitors could witness a range of curiosities from "a shoe of Count Borulaski, the Polish dwarf," to feather cloaks from the South Seas; many articles were purchased from the Leverian Museum, donated by the Linnean Society, or—best yet—once "the property of the celebrated Captain Cook" (*Companion to Mr. Bullock's Museum*). In 1812 Bullock moved his collection to London and opened the Egyptian Hall on Piccadilly Street. In 1821 the Egyptian Hall showcased the spoils from Giovanni Belzoni's excavations in Egypt. In 1823 an exhibit based on his own travels called *Ancient and Modern Mexico* made Bullock wealthy. His practice of habitat arrangements eventually served as model for the Natural History Museum in London.

4. Owen, Miscellaneous Manuscripts, 117; Greenwood, *Museums and Art Galleries*, 388.

5. Conway, *Travels in South Kensington*, 85; *Guides to South Kensington Museum* (1879, 1882, 1885).

6. Cole, "Reasons for Converting," 253. In *Selling Culture* Silverman identifies the Reagan era in America as marking a new alliance among government, museums, and department stores (as evident in the Reagan, Vreeland, and Bloomingdale coterie). Her argument is fascinating and influential to my study, yet her conclusions, I would argue, are historically inaccurate. In short, Silverman bases her argument on a highbrow conception of the museum and thus sees the Reagan years as its degradation; however, the museum has always been a politicized and commercialized institution.

7. Haweis, quoted in Rubinstein, *Victorian Homes*, 77; Eastlake, *Hints on Household Taste*, 135, 136; Clarence Cook, *House Beautiful*, 101.

8. Loftie, preface to *Plea for Art*. Subsequent citations appear in the text.

9. The maxim of Matthew 6:19—"Do not lay up for yourselves treasures on earth, where moth and rust consume and where thieves break in and steal, but lay up for yourselves treasures in heaven"—appears to counsel against domestic collecting yet in the logic of Loftie's argument advocates it. Loftie writes, "And if we look on the home here as the prototype of the home hereafter, we may see reasons for making it as a sacred thing, beautiful and pleasant" (*Plea for Art*, 89).

10. Greenwood argues for collecting on the basis of its positive effects on children: "The study of a single branch of natural science . . . may be made the means of cultivating habits of neatness, order, and skill," which will prepare children for what Greenwood calls, with the age's characteristic severity, the "struggle of existence" (*Museums and Art Galleries*, 30). And *Herdman's Miscellany,* one of the many collector magazines that proliferated in the last two decades of the century, offered a front-page feature article, "A Plea for Collecting," focused on the child: "You are aiding him in an amusement that occupies his spare time, keeps him at home, and stimulates a thirst for knowledge on his part that may do him an infinite amount of good."

11. Greenwood makes explicit the hope that many Victorians secretly cherished for the museum. As the palace of art supplants the gin palace, Greenwood maintains that a different sort of craving will replace "another and lower craving which may at one time have held [man] in bondage—that for intoxicants or vicious excitement."

Greenwood goes on to recommend a condition he calls "picture drunkenness or Museum drunkenness" (*Museums and Art Galleries,* 27, 29).

12. Mayhew, *London Labour and London Poor,* 1 : 47; "Bethnal Green Museum," 24 March 1883.

13. In *House and Home in the Victorian City* Daunton argues that the nineteenth century witnessed a "realignment in the use of space," both private and public (14–15), and that "public space lost its ambiguous, semi-private character. At the same time, each house was turned in upon itself as its own private world" (12). Daunton rightly ties this respatialization to the strengthening of the nuclear family unit. Yet we must also see the Victorian period, in all its bureaucratic and reforming zeal, as the epoch of regulated private life in which the public realm of museums, zoos, parks, and gardens informed the private space of the home. For details on the shifting alignment of space within the Victorian middle-class home, see Davidoff and Hall, *Family Fortunes,* where the authors argue that "middle-class housing had to provide more than just a haven for family withdrawal, for the home was also a stage for social ritual and out-ward manifestation of status in the community" (362).

14. In his phenomenological study *Poetics of Space* Bachelard describes the kind of interior space the house-museum encloses: "It is impossible to dream of an old house that is not the refuge of old things—its own—or that has been filled with old things as a result of the simple craze of a collector of knick-knacks" (142). Yet for Bachelard domestic collecting remains a strictly private pleasure. In short, he does not appreci-ate visitors: "To describe [the oneiric house] would be like showing [it] to visitors" (13). His definition of intimate space as that "space that is not open to just anybody" indicates to what extent his love of hiding places and inclusive structures, such as shells and nests, reflects his impulse to exclusivity. Bachelard's primitivist escape into the felicitous space of the hut free of possession, clutter, and crowds is antithetical to the house-museum that subsumes the civic space of the museum within its private walls. Such topoanalysis does not acknowledge the necessary function of the house-museum: exhibiting. Nor does it address the political and cultural agenda raised by the house-museum, which is not always, as this chapter will demonstrate, the felici-tous space that enchants Bachelard.

15. Yonge, *Heartsease,* 26; Yonge, *Daisy Chain,* 153; Dickens, *Little Dorrit,* 161, 163.

16. For more discussion of James's "narratives of possession," refer to See, "James and Art of Possession." Also see Winner, *James and Visual Arts,* for a limited treatment of how the museum permits James to explore "the relation of the self to art, morality, history, and possession" (ix). Tintner's *Museum World of Henry James,* although self-confessedly weak on analysis, presents an excellent catalog of the museum's importance to James and his writing.

17. For this phrase I am indebted to Chase, *Eros and Psyche,* 59.

18. Brontë, *Jane Eyre,* 45. Subsequent citations appear in the text.

19. Much critical attention has been given to these two scenes; scholars have linked Rochester's enactments to such issues as nineteenth-century cross-dressing and Vic-torian theater. I would only add that the institution of the museum also informs the "acquired" abilities Rochester demonstrates in these scenes. In *Madwoman in the Attic* Gilbert and Gubar call Rochester's "puzzling transvestism" "a semi-conscious effort to reduce this sexual advantage his masculinity gives him" (355). Rochester's perfor-mance in drag, however, is not his feminization or diminution but evidence of his

power to charm, to be both man and woman, Western and Eastern—in other words, to possess, magically and otherwise.

20. According to Meyer, "Colonialism and Figurative Strategy," Brontë intended the events of the novel to occur during the 1820s and 1830s, when, "owing to the economic decline of the British sugar colonies in the West Indies, planters imposed increasing hardship on the slaves and increasingly feared their revolt" (166). Seen in this larger context, *Jane Eyre*'s Thornfield Hall may not let the British public forget their own colonial anxieties.

21. Gilbert and Gubar, *Madwoman in the Attic,* 339.

22. Ibid., 347. In *Desire and Domestic Fiction* Armstrong likens Thornfield's third floor to a museum; however, in accordance with Gilbert and Gubar, she calls it "The Woman's Museum," where are stored the remnants of domestic culture, the Victorian novel, and conduct books for women readers. Armstrong then concludes: "It is fair to say that Brontë composes Jane's autobiography out of a series of such rooms" (207). But, as I have argued, this space of the third story, of Thornfield in its entirety, is clearly a space where Jane is not in charge. Indeed, given the logic of the novel's political subtext, Armstrong's phrase is oxymoronic; it is Jane's dispossession that saves her.

23. See Roy, "Unaccommodated Woman," for a discussion of Thornfield within the tradition of country-house literature. As Roy claims, such a famously represented house as Jonson's Penshurst symbolizes order and abundance. By contrast, Thornfield stands largely in disuse and neglect, emblematic of Brontë's critique of the value system traditionally embraced by those to the manor born.

24. Several critics have noted that *Jane Eyre* rectifies female exclusion from the tale of possession to the point of including her in the affairs of colonial acquisition. That Jane comes into her own fortune in the end through her uncle's colonial business has struck many as ironic and/or problematic. Such critics argue that Jane's filthy lucre is evidence of the novel's compromising its own radical political critique. See Roy, "Unaccommodated Woman," and Meyer, "Colonialism and Figurative Strategy."

25. Gosse, *Father and Son,* 8–9. Subsequent citations appear in the text.

26. In her biography of Gosse, Thwaite directs our attention to the *Oxford English Dictionary,* which "gives P. H. Gosse the credit for coining the word 'aquarium'" (*Edmund Gosse,* 27). To Thomas Hardy in 1920 Gosse wrote about his "earliest experiences of Weymouth": "My Father was all this time collecting living specimens for the newly-formed aquariums, and sending them to the Zoo in Regent's Park, and the Crystal Palace and elsewhere" (Charteris, *Life and Letters of Gosse,* 456). Gosse's next sentence speaks to the legacy of his father: "He started, in the Weymouth lodgings, a salt-water tank of his own (Sept. 5, 1853) and this was the first private aquarium ever made. I possessed it, until about 1893, when it fell to pieces" (Ibid., 457). In 1844 P. H. Gosse was sent by the British Museum of Natural History to Jamaica to collect specimens (Thwaite, *Edmund Gosse,* 12).

27. One cannot help but think of a similar meditation on parent-child relations, *Hard Times,* and Dickens's comparison of the Gradgrind home, the "great square" Stone Lodge, with a museum: "The little Gradgrinds had cabinets in various departments of science too. They had a little conchological cabinet, and a little metallurgical cabinet, and a little mineralogical cabinet; and the specimens were all arranged and labelled" (55).

28. Thwaite fails to capture the mood of the autobiography when she describes Gosse's childhood homes: "There is plenty of evidence of pleasure in the early Marychurch years. The house itself became more and more attractive: outside the clematis climbed more luxuriantly up the verandah; the garden and greenhouses and aquaria were full of rich delights. Inside there were brilliant cases of tropical insects and in winter the leaping flames of good fires" (*Edmund Gosse,* 38).

29. Thwaite writes, "Eventually the Sandhurst garden contained no fewer than five hot-houses or conservatories" (*Edmund Gosse,* 45). She also explains how Gosse frequently visited Eliza Brightwen, the wife of his stepmother's brother; her home boasted a museum, menagerie, and aquariums constructed by Gosse's father.

30. This vision of the specter self so haunts Gosse he later refers again to it, to the "one pale-faced child with its cheek pressed to the window!" (78). As critics have pointed out, novelists often use scenes involving reflections in mirrors to capture the deep psychic maneuverings of characters. Yet Gosse's fascination with the reflection in the mirror that is actually the glass case of confinement offers a fresh spin on the convention.

31. A letter sent by Gosse to his father on 3 August 1874 narrates a most successful impersonation: "For never since I was a little boy have I been so ardent a naturalist." Here Gosse tells of his "wild escapade," collecting with a Miss Otte in the pools of Lizard. Has Gosse overperfected the ebullience of this letter? The reader cannot ignore the pathos of the son's attempt to win the father's approval: "How excited I was! . . . The collecting mania has seized us both, I rushed back to the inn, borrowed a hammer and a chisel, begged a picklebottle, and raced back. . . . We were like intoxicated people!" (Charteris, *Life and Letters of Gosse,* 62–63).

32. Gosse's life follows a clear pattern of early immersion in museum culture—at the age of seventeen, in 1867, he began working at the British Museum as a junior assistant, a position he left in 1875 to become a translator—subsequent breaking away to become a poet, and eventual return to the public world of museums. As an older man, Gosse worked on the *Encyclopaedia Britannica,* was a trustee of the National Gallery, and was an active belletrist and committee man. In some sense, Gosse grew up to become his father.

33. Dickens, *Our Mutual Friend,* 63, 191. Subsequent citations appear in the text.

34. A glance at *The Wonderful and Scientific Museum* reveals the relevance not only of its form but also of its subject matter to *Our Mutual Friend* and Dickens's imagination in general. Kirby's love of detail and the organization of the book reflect Dickens's own novelistic art. But more importantly, the six volumes boast an astounding collection of stories relating amazing resuscitations and reanimations. The focus of *The Wonderful and Scientific Museum* is often the body and its perversion or its contents: "Instances of Vegetation in the Human Body," "Extraordinary Instances of Living Animals and Other Substances in the Human Stomach," and "Remarkable Case of a Human Body Found in a Bear Skin" are just a few of Kirby's tales. In light of my larger argument about museum culture's attempt to get inside the body of the other, as well as for its immediate resonance for Mr. Venus the taxidermist and John Harmon's resurrection, Kirby's book is seminal.

35. Some studies take up a straightforward and, I would argue, ultimately reductive interest in the realism of and sources for Mr. Venus. For example, see Cotsell, "Mr. Venus Rises from the Counter." But Shea's "Mr. Venus Observed" is even more

dismissive of Mr. Venus's significance. Shea argues that first the Podsnaps and then the Lammles, either of whom would have made for a deeper social critique than Mr. Venus on the ills of money, were the intended nemesis to Boffin.

36. See "Artistic Reclamation of Waste," where Metz argues that the novel's artist figures, Mr. Venus and Jenny Wren, offer "the only hope of bringing meaning from this common cycle" of denial and hoarding; they prove by example "how chaos may be livable, and in part, and over time, redeemed" (72).

37. In "Dismemberment and Articulation" Hutter identifies Mr. Venus as the namesake of that most famous of parts forced to stand in for the whole, the Venus de Milo. Such an allusion takes us to the world of the museum. Given his primary focus on Mr. Venus the articulator, Hutter tangentially discusses the function of the museum in a society always threatened by, what he calls, "disarticulation." Although this excellent article has influenced my own work on *Our Mutual Friend*, I do not agree with Hutter's final dismissal of the museum: these problems' "importance went far beyond the confines of museums, whether of art or science: this was ultimately a debate about the function of imagination and the nature of historical reconstruction" (151). My premise has been and remains that the museum is the seat of history and epistemology.

38. Paracelsus, *Archidoxes of Magic*, 8. I would like to thank my colleague Kate Greenspan for this intriguing suggestion.

39. Soane, *Description of House and Museum*, 94, 25.

40. Soane ensured his immortality most unusually by planting time capsules in hiding places in his museum and leaving orders that they be opened consecutively in 1866, 1886, and 1896 on the anniversary of his wife's death. The present curator maintains that these capsules, containing nothing more than spectacles, false teeth, and a few letters, were a mere hoax. But what a fascinating hoax! On the very day of death Soane continued to remind people of his presence. Later in the century George Bonomi, curator from 1861 to 1876, secretly stored his own time capsule in one of the museum's cinerary urns. This running joke in the Soane Museum demonstrates the serious desire of the collector to perpetuate his being through time. For the quote, see Britton, "Bull's 'Museum,'" the epigraph to *Union of Architecture*, his tribute to Soane.

41. Soane, *Crude Hints*, 53.

42. Ibid., 59.

IV. A Gallery of Readings: Rendezvous in the Museum

1. *Handbook of 1840*, 6–7.

2. "Soanean Museum," 214.

3. Cole, Miscellanies, 1851–1866, 135. Cole was not alone in his conviction that museums were a right to be enjoyed by all and that society in general would benefit from their presence and influence. In *Nether World* (1889) Gissing offers the following commentary: "Had the British Museum been open to visitors in the hours of the evening, or on Sundays, Bob Hewitt would possibly have been employing his leisure nowadays in more profitable pursuits" (220).

4. Cole, Miscellanies, 1857–1865, 414; Cole, Miscellanies, 1851–1866, 135, 79, 105.

5. Cole, Miscellanies, 1851–1866, 89, 131.

6. These numbers come from interviews conducted by the author with Clive Wainwright, the deputy curator of Furniture and Woodwork Collections at the Victoria and Albert Museum.

7. Cole, Miscellanies, 1851–1866, 105.

8. Conway, *Travels in South Kensington,* 102.

9. Quoted in Altick, *Shows of London,* 419.

10. Levine makes a similar argument in *Highbrow/Lowbrow:* "The primary debate was less over who should enter the precincts of the art museum . . . as over what they should experience once they did enter, what the essential purpose of these temples of culture was in the first place." Later he writes, "the creation of the institutions and criteria of high culture was a primary means of social, intellectual, and aesthetic separation and selection. Here one learned not only how to appreciate art but also how to behave while doing so" (167, 229).

11. Sherman, *Worthy Monuments,* 211. Some critics claim that order is the museum's greatest goal, that museums present first and foremost a series of labels, which are illustrated by displayed objects. Glib but nevertheless interesting, such a claim points to what was perhaps the greatest pride of Victorian curators, their advanced techniques in labeling. Lazarus Fletcher, the keeper of the Minerals Gallery in the Natural History Museum, boasted about his relocation to Kensington: "When the Collection was at Bloomsbury, all the labels were hand-written, and mostly of temporary character; in the course of re-arrangement at South Kensington, printed labels have been designed and furnished for all parts of the collection. . . . There are now nearly 17,000 printed labels exhibited in the Gallery" (quoted in Stearn, *Natural History Museum,* 60).

12. I borrow the phrase "symbolic space of nationalism" from Duncan's lexicon in *Civilizing Rituals.*

13. Richards, *Imperial Archive,* 111.

14. Hobsbawm and Ranger, *Invention of Tradition.*

15. Ruskin, "Picture Galleries," 71, 78, 80, 83.

16. Quoted in Owen, Miscellaneous Manuscripts.

17. Quoted in Altick, *Shows of London,* 222.

18. Mayhew, *1851,* 159; "Pictures for Exhibition of Industry."

19. Alexander, *Museums in Motion,* 215.

20. Newhouse, *Towards a New Museum,* 190, 193.

21. Mainardi, "Postmodern History of Musée d'Orsay," 35–36.

22. Owen, "On the Extent," 22–23; collected by Owen in Miscellaneous Manuscripts.

23. Henry James, *London Life,* 75. Subsequent citations appear in the text.

24. Austen, *Selected Letters,* 109.

25. Boon, "Why Museums Make Me Sad," 255.

26. Bal, "Telling Objects," 103.

27. Brontë, *Villette,* 178. Subsequent citations appear in the text.

28. Newton, *Women, Power, and Subversion,* 94.

29. Gezari, *Brontë and Defensive Conduct,* 4; Boone, *Tradition CounterTradition,* 220.

30. Litvak, "Brontë and the Scene of Instruction," 481; Brownstein, *Becoming a Heroine,* 162.

31. Newton, *Women, Power, and Subversion,* 120.

32. Gezari, *Brontë and Defensive Conduct,* 29.

33. Paxton, "Eliot and the City," 72; Rischin, "Beside the Reclining Statue," 1121. Wiesenfarth calls chapter 19 "the single most allusive chapter of fiction George Eliot ever wrote" ("Greeks, Germans, and Eliot," 93). For detailed "tours" of the Vatican galleries and their significance, see Wiesenfarth, "Greeks, Germans, and Eliot," and McCormack, "Dorothea's Husbands in Vatican Museums."

34. Paxton, "Eliot and the City," 74; Rischin, "Beside the Reclining Statue," 1128.

35. George Eliot, *Middlemarch*, 140. Subsequent citations appear in the text.

36. Paxton, "Eliot and the City," 74.

37. Welsh, *Eliot and Blackmail*, 219.

38. Witemeyer, *Eliot and Visual Arts*, 151–52.

39. Williams, *English Novel*, 84.

40. Beer, *Darwin's Plots*, 154.

41. Andres, "Unhistoric in History," 82, 83; D. A. Miller, *Narrative and Its Discontents*, 130.

42. Forster, *Maurice*, 253. Subsequent citations appear in the text.

43. Strachey, quoted in Holroyd, *Lytton Strachey*, 726; Pritchett, "Upholstered Prison," 450; Summers, *Gay Fictions*, 100.

44. See Hitchcock's movie *Blackmail* for a featured scene in the British Museum.

45. Robert K. Martin, "Carpenter and Double Structure," 39.

46. Forster, "Art for Art's Sake," 90.

47. Forster, "For the Museum's Sake," 290, 293, 297.

48. Robert K. Martin, "Carpenter and Double Structure," 40.

49. Wilde, *Horizons of Assent*, 79.

50. *Report from Select Committee*, 165.

51. Henry James, *American*, 68. Subsequent citations appear in the text.

52. Henry James, "Americans Abroad," 359.

53. Sherman, *Worthy Monuments*, 10.

54. Preziosi, "Collecting/Museums," 281; Bakhtin, *Dialogic Imagination*, 234.

V. *"The Works on the Wall Must Take Their Chance"*

1. Tennyson, "Palace of Art," 289–92.

2. Ibid., 293–96.

3. Hazlitt, *Collected Works*, 6:148. Subsequent citations appear in the text.

4. The multidisciplinary and political nature of cultural studies has helped to reconceive the idyllic thinking about the genial, sisterly relationship between image and text. See, for example, J. Hillis Miller, *Illustration*, and Mirollo, "Sibling Rivalry in the Arts Family." For all the provocative issues they raise concerning the arts, the regime, and the marketplace, however, these interart studies do not acknowledge the important context of the collection.

5. Hagstrum, *Sister Arts*, xxii.

6. Loy Martin's *Browning's Dramatic Monologues* has greatly influenced my interest in the political, cultural, and historical fabric of nineteenth-century poetry. His argument is particularly relevant to my later discussion of "Pictor Ignotus."

7. Lipking, *Ordering of Arts*, 472.

8. Krieger, "Ekphrastic Principle," 127, 125. Also see Krieger's expansion of the essay, *Ekphrasis*.

9. Forman, *Letters of John Keats,* 311.

10. Jack, *Keats and Mirror of Art,* xix.

11. Quoted in ibid., 61–62.

12. Haydon, *Autobiography,* 89.

13. Benjamin, "Work of Art," 221.

14. Hitchens, *Elgin Marbles,* 24.

15. Quoted in Rothenberg, *"Descensus Ad Terram,"* 282–83.

16. Byron, "English Bards and Scotch Reviewers" and "The Curse of Minerva," in *Complete Poetical Works,* 1027–32, 179–84.

17. Haydon, *Autobiography,* 89.

18. Haydon, *Annals of the Fine Arts,* quoted in Jack, *Keats and Mirror of Art,* 23.

19. See Hardy's description of Casterbridge in *The Mayor of Casterbridge,* 76.

20. Browning, "Pictor Ignotus," in *Poems,* 36–39, 50–56.

21. Campbell, "'Painting' in Browning's *Men and Women,*" 16.

22. Browning seems interested in the mentality of the collector in part because, as a poet, he is a collector of sorts. In "One Word More" he refers to his dramatic monologues as a collection:

> Love, you saw me gather men and women,
> Live or dead or fashioned by my fancy,
> Enter each and all, and use their service . . .
> Pray you, look on these my men and women. (*129–31, 140*)

One can conceive of the dramatic monologue as an imperialistic and appropriative genre that collects speakers from all times, all cultures, and all lands. Thus Browning the poet becomes the curator of his own gallery, and his delight is most clearly expressed in his refashioning of the phrase "men and women" into "*my* men and women."

23. Browning, "A Likeness," in *Poems,* 14–24.

24. Ibid., 44–50.

25. Culler, *Victorian Mirror of History,* 202.

26. Layard, *Nineveh and Its Remains,* 17, 267.

27. Boos, *Poetry of Dante G. Rossetti,* 207.

28. Woodring, *Nature into Art.*

29. Boos, *Poetry of Dante G. Rossetti,* 208.

30. Rossetti, "Burden of Nineveh," 71–75. Subsequent citations appear in the text.

31. As Stewart succinctly argues, "The collection replaces history with *classification*" (*On Longing,* 151).

32. I am reminded here of Michel Leiris's shocking comment: "Nothing seems to me so like a whorehouse as a museum" (quoted in Torgoynick, *Gone Primitive,* 75). Rossetti seems equally disturbed by the promiscuity of the British Museum.

33. Rossetti's winged bull is a "wounded artifact" that through its "signs of use" bears witness to "the violence of history" (Greenblatt, "Resonance and Wonder," 81). Again, the artifact speaks a powerful, resonant story.

34. Heffernan, *Museum of Words,* 138; Ashbery, "Self-Portrait in a Convex Mirror," 395–98; Empson, "Homage to British Museum," 1, 15.

35. See also the verse Tennyson wrote to commemorate the laying of the foundation stone of the Imperial Institute (in operation from 1887 to 1893), which Stamp and

Amery have called the "principal architectural expression of the rising tide of late Victorian imperialism" (*Victorian Builders of London*, 168):

> *Raise a stately memorial*
> *Some Imperial Institute*
> *Rich in symbol and ornament*
> *Which may speak to the centuries.*

36. Browning, "Old Pictures in Florence," in *Poems*, 661. Like Keats and Rossetti, Browning spent much time in museums. He first discovered his passion for Italian art in the Dulwich Picture Gallery, a half-hour walk from his boyhood home. As an older man, he was drawn to the museums of Italy, eventually settling in Florence with Elizabeth Barrett. Like Edward FitzGerald, Browning loved to collect. His poem "Old Pictures in Florence" charts an expedition into the "empty cells of the human hive" in search of art deals, capturing the fever of the collector: "I, that have haunted the dim San Spirito / . . . Nay, I shall have it yet!" (241, 244).

VI. An Empire's Great Expectations

1. Said, *Culture and Imperialism*, xiii.
2. Bettelheim, *Uses of Enchantment*, 45.
3. *Blackwood's Magazine*, quoted in Altick, *Shows of London*, 442.
4. Altick, *Shows of London*, 227, 449, 232; Ritvo, *Animal Estate*, 219.
5. C. Montiesor, quoted in Stewart, *On Longing*, 162.
6. The museum's complicity with kitsch demonstrates how widespread, how mass-produced a fantasy the museum was. See Richards, *Commodity Culture of Victorian England*, for a discussion of Sir Henry Morton Stanley kitsch. In the chapter "Selling Darkest Africa" Richards explores how the explorer truly came home—on medallions, matchbook covers, cigarette papers, trays, and pots.
7. See, for example, Belzoni, *Narrative of Recent Discoveries*; Layard, *Nineveh and Its Remains*; Burton, *Personal Narrative of a Pilgrimage*; and Speke, *What Led to the Discovery*.
8. Altick, *Shows of London*, 244; Marryat, *Life and Letters of Captain Marryat*, 2:238.
9. Belzoni, *Narrative of Recent Discoveries*, 335.
10. For a survey of imperialist boy fiction, see Louis James, "Tom Brown's Imperialist Sons." Also consult the chapter "The Boy's World," in Avery, *Nineteenth Century Children*.
11. Zipes, *Fairy Tales and Subversion*, 181. Largely absent from Atkins's text, Mrs. Belzoni emerges courageous only for her patience, as she waits or is left behind. Meanwhile, Atkins's portrait of Belzoni personifies Smiles's self-help by honoring the bourgeois appropriation of Virgil that stands as the motto of Atkins's tale: "Labor Omnia Vincit." Indeed Atkins's frame narrative focuses on a mother's recounting of Belzoni's travels in order to make men of the boys who listen. Inspired, one son vows, "When I am a man, mother, I mean to be a traveller, and to possess as much perseverance as our Belzoni!" Another son, in demonstrating newly discovered diligence, cries, "It was Belzoni who first taught me to exert it!" (*Fruits of Enterprize*, 44, 72).
12. While I realize that gender theory and men's studies have destabilized the notion of masculinity, the construction of masculinities is far from what I have in mind here. Although life in the Victorian age seemed to offer a wide range of options for male

identity, I refer here to the monolithic masculinity Victorian writers usually described as ideal or, to use a vexed word, natural. Such a writer is Ruskin, who in "Of Queens' Gardens" famously describes the separate spheres of women and men, predictably sequestering the woman at home and assigning the man to "rough work in [the] open world" (151).

13. Wilson, *Strange Ride of Kipling,* 1–2.

14. Fisher, *Making and Effacing Art,* 6.

15. Kipling, *Kim,* 6. Subsequent citations appear in the text.

16. McClure, *Kipling and Conrad,* 70.

17. Or, to speak more accurately, "indefatigably watchful *in* and *because of* its seeming absence from the rest of the tale." Foucault's assessment of the panopticon's effectiveness in *Discipline and Punish* is relevant here: "The Panopticon is a machine for dissociating the see/being seen dyad: in the peripheric ring, one is totally seen, without ever seeing; in the central tower, one sees everything without ever being seen" (201–2).

18. As Owens argues more broadly in "Birth and Death of the Viewer," "the protection of culture is an ideological alibi for the project of imperialism—an alibi in which we witness an inversion which, I propose, is the hallmark of protectionist discourse. For it is those who stand to benefit most from the destruction of culture who pose as its protectors" (20).

19. The first two phrases come from Alan Sandison's introduction to Kipling, *Kim,* xiv; the third, from McClure, *Kipling and Conrad,* 70; the full statement, from McClure, "Problematic Presence," 155.

20. Said, *Culture and Imperialism,* 153.

21. Millar, "Review," 270, 271; McClure, *Kipling and Conrad,* 71, 80.

22. Nesbit, *Story of the Amulet,* 198. Subsequent citations appear in the text.

23. Julia Briggs's biography of Nesbit, *Woman of Passion,* relates how important museums—from the British Museum with its mummies to Sydenham's Crystal Palace with its simulated dinosaurs—were to the young Nesbit. Briggs also recounts how Nesbit's conception for *The Story of the Amulet* as well as many further details for the story came from Ernest Wallis Budge, the curator of the British Museum, to whom the book is dedicated.

24. Jameson, *Companion to Private Galleries,* 383; Baudrillard, "System of Collecting," 16; André Favat quoted in Zipes, *Fairy Tales and Subversion,* 178; Benjamin, "Unpacking My Library," 60; Baudrillard, "System of Collecting," 8.

25. Conway, *Travels in South Kensington,* 23.

26. Owen, "On the Extent," 118.

27. Thomas Macaulay, quoted in Asa Briggs, *Victorian Things,* 119; "Immortal Idea"; Dickens, "Great Exhibition," 356; J. G. Wood, "Dulness of Museums," 391.

28. Clifford, "Of Other Peoples," 119.

29. Clifford, *Predicament of Culture,* 196.

30. For a genealogy of collecting in the West, see ibid., 232ff.

31. Martin Green, quoted in Brantlinger, *Rule of Darkness,* 10.

32. This phrase is a barely coded reference to the work of Crimp, whose last twelve years of writings on the museum are brought together in *On the Museum's Ruins.*

33. Walter Benjamin, quoted in Buck-Morss, *Dialectics of Seeing,* 271.

VII. A Gallery of Readings: The Museum in Decline

1. Morris, *News from Nowhere*, 69. Subsequent citations appear in the text.
2. Koolhaas, quoted in Newhouse, *Towards a New Museum*, 149.
3. Bellamy, *Novels of Wells, Bennett, and Galsworthy*, 2; Gill, *Happy Rural Seat*, 99; Trilling, quoted in Gill, *Happy Rural Seat*, 97.
4. Galsworthy, quoted in Gill, *Happy Rural Seat*, 122, 115; Wells, quoted in Arata, *Fictions of Loss*, 26.
5. H. G. Wells, *Tono-Bungay*, 113; Shelley, *Last Man*, 347, 356.
6. I am indebted for this phrase to Arata, *Fictions of Loss*, 1.
7. Sternlicht, *John Galsworthy*, 49.
8. Galsworthy, *Man of Property*, 195. Subsequent citations appear in the text.
9. Hart, "Ritual and Spectacle," 34.
10. Sternlicht, *John Galsworthy*, 49.
11. Hart, "Ritual and Spectacle," 38.
12. Bergonzi, "*Time Machine*," 50.
13. Quoted in ibid., 38.
14. H. G. Wells, *Time Machine*, 60. Subsequent citations appear in the text.
15. Reed, *Natural History of Wells*, 20.
16. Suvin, quoted in Huntington, *Logic of Fantasy*, xi. The sheer shock value of a museum in ruin also facilitates what Huntington believes is the mission of science fiction: to exercise the "reader's imagination by breaking down old assumptions and habits of seeing and by offering new possibilities" (x).
17. Huntington, *Logic of Fantasy*, 72.
18. Ibid., 45.
19. In *Experiment in Autobiography* H. G. Wells describes a boyhood epiphany: "[the earth] already had a past which was rapidly opening out to men's minds in those days. I first became aware of that past in the gardens of the Crystal Palace at Sydenham; it came upon me as a complete surprise, embodied in vast plaster reconstructions of the megatherium and various dinosaurs and a toadlike labyrinthodon" (71). Yet Wells uses this site to more satiric effect in *Kipps* when his lovers rendezvous in the dinosaur's shadow. An 1896 review explained, "The 'stupid little tragedies of these clipped and limited lives' appear symbolised in the Crystal Palace Labyrinthodon beneath whose grotesque figure Kipps and Ann make love. In such a lumpish, clumsy monster Mr. Wells finds gathered up the brooding 'antisoul' of stupidity and fear from the shadow of which Kipps can never escape" (Chalmers Mitchell, quoted in Parrinder, *H. G. Wells*, 125). Wells again challenges the museum's monumentality when, in describing how he wrote the martian attack in *The War of the Worlds*, he targets the district that housed not only the school of his boyhood but London's museums as well: "I completely wreck and sack Woking . . . then proceed . . . to London, which I sack, selecting South Kensington for feats of peculiar atrocity" (quoted in Huntington, *Logic of Fantasy*, 84).
20. Huntington, *Logic of Fantasy*, 46. Huntington points out that this is the one moment in the text where the editor intrudes with a note clarifying the odd spatial configurations of the hall and, by this means, drawing our attention to it all the more. Yet I am not persuaded by Huntington's argument that this moment of slippage or spatial

confusion contains a positive image, a break in "the up-down opposition" and thus "an image of union" (58).

21. H. G. Wells, *Croquet Player,* 58–59. Subsequent citations appear in the text.
22. Huntington, *Logic of Fantasy,* 45.
23. McConnell, *Science Fiction of Wells,* 32, 35.
24. Brantlinger, "'News from Nowhere,'" 43; Skoblow, *Paradise Dislocated,* 14.
25. Thompson, *William Morris,* 260.
26. Ibid., 696; Frye, "Meeting of Past and Future," 313.
27. Frye, "Meeting of Past and Future," 313.
28. Buzard, "Ethnography as Interruption," 460.
29. Wells, quoted in Reed, *Natural History of Wells,* 191.
30. Buzard, "Ethnography as Interruption," 449.
31. Bellamy, *Novels of Wells, Bennett, and Galsworthy,* 56; Mitchell, quoted in Parrinder, *H. G. Wells,* 43.
32. Galsworthy, *Forsyte Saga,* xlii, xlv.
33. I borrow this phrase from Lutchmansingh, "Archaeological Socialism."

Coda

1. Torgovnick identifies Freud's collections as a symptom of his homelessness: "If we enter the place where Freud lived and worked, we can find the idea of homelessness and exile both represented and denied in the very decor" (*Gone Primitive,* 194). The topos of Freud among his collectibles is common. Gay writes, "Here at Maresfield Gardens, enveloped by his reconstituted old environment, Freud lived out the year he still had to live" (*Freud: A Life,* 635). Spitz describes "the maze of Freud's voluminous writings and encircling scholarship" ("Psychoanalysis and Legacies of Antiquity," 54). As this nest imagery suggests, Freud found a haven for himself in his collection.
2. The book that accompanied the exhibition, *Sigmund Freud and Art,* however, is excellent in this respect. The introduction by Gay and Gamwell's essay, "Origins of Freud's Antiquities Collection," have been helpful to me.
3. See, for example, Spitz, "Psychoanalysis and Legacies of Antiquity."
4. Gay, *Freud: A Life,* 15.
5. Richard Wells, preface to *Sigmund Freud and Art,* 12.
6. As Bruno Bettelheim notes, "All these many, many objects were crowded into his treatment room and study; none of them spilled over into the many rooms next door which formed the family living quarters. What more definite statement could Freud have made that his collection was part and parcel of his psychoanalytic interests, and not at all of his life as paterfamilias? It is a contrast that seems to declare: 'Unique though my life as discoverer of the unconscious is, my life with my family is ordinary'" (quoted in Forrester, "Freud and Collecting," 228).
7. Gamwell, "Origins of Freud's Antiquities Collection," 24.
8. Gay, *Freud: A Life,* 172.
9. Ibid., 47.
10. Ernst Freud, *Letters of Sigmund Freud,* 194.
11. Gay, *Freud: A Life,* 640.
12. Gamwell contextualizes Freud within the contemporary archaeological craze: "Hein-

rich Schliemann's first major finds at Troy date to 1873, when Freud was an eighteen-year-old student. The legendary labyrinth of Minos was excavated on the island of Crete in 1900, the year Freud published *The Interpretation of Dreams,* when he was forty-four, and Tutankhamun's tomb was discovered in the Valley of the Kings in 1922, when Freud was sixty-six" ("Origins of Freud's Antiquities Collection," 22).

13. Gay, *Freud: A Life,* 172.
14. Gamwell, "Origins of Freud's Antiquities Collection," 28.
15. Sigmund Freud, *Dora,* 27; Sigmund Freud, *Civilization and Its Discontents,* 16.
16. Gay, *Freud: A Life,* 146.
17. Sigmund Freud, "Thoughts for the Times," 275.
18. Ibid., 277.
19. Gay, *Freud: A Life,* 170.
20. Doolittle, *Tribute to Freud,* 12. Subsequent citations appear in the text.
21. Gamwell and Wells, "Selections from the Collection," 123.
22. Baudrillard, "System of Collecting," 10.
23. Graña, "Private Lives of Public Museums," 98.
24. Boyer, *City of Collective Memory,* 130.

Works Cited

Adams, Annmarie. "The Healthy Victorian City: The Old London Street at the International Health Exhibition." In *Streets*, edited by Zeynep Çelik, Diane Farro, and Richard Ingersoll, 203–12. Berkeley: Univ. of California Press, 1994.

Adorno, Theodor. "Valéry Proust Museum." In *Prisms*. Cambridge, Mass.: MIT Press, 1981.

Aldrich, Thomas Bailey. "A Persian Poet." *Atlantic Monthly* 41 (1878): 421–26.

Alexander, Edward. *Museums in Motion*. Nashville, Tenn.: American Association for State and Local History, 1979.

Altick, Richard. *The Shows of London*. Cambridge, Mass.: Harvard Univ. Press, 1978.

Anderson, Benedict. *Imagined Communities*. 1991. Reprint, New York: Verso, 1994.

Andres, Sophia. "The Unhistoric in History: George Eliot's Challenge to Victorian Historiography." *Clio* 26, no. 1 (1996): 79–95.

Arata, Stephen. *Fictions of Loss in the Victorian Fin de Siècle*. New York: Cambridge Univ. Press, 1996.

Arberry, Arthur. *Omar Khayyám*. London: John Murray, 1952.

Armstrong, Nancy. *Desire and Domestic Fiction*. New York: Oxford Univ. Press, 1987.

Ashbery, John. *Self-Portrait in a Convex Mirror*. New York: Viking Penguin, 1976.

Atkins, Sara. *Fruits of Enterprize Exhibited in the Adventures of Belzoni in Egypt and Nubia*. New York: Charles Francis, 1843.

Austen, Jane. *Selected Letters*. Edited by R. W. Chapman. New York: Oxford Univ. Press, 1985.

Avery, Gillian. *Nineteenth Century Children*. London: Hodder and Stoughton, 1965.

Bachelard, Gaston. *The Poetics of Space*. Translated by Maria Jolas. Boston: Beacon, 1969.

Bakhtin, Mikhail. *The Dialogic Imagination*. Austin: Univ. of Texas Press, 1981.

Bal, Mieke. "Telling Objects: A Narrative Perspective on Collecting." In *The Cultures of Collecting*, edited by John Elsner and Roger Cardinal, 97–115. Cambridge, Mass.: Harvard Univ. Press, 1994.

Barnstone, Willis. *The Poetics of Translation*. New Haven, Conn.: Yale Univ. Press, 1993.

Bassnett, Susan, ed. *Translation Studies*. New York: Routledge, 1980.

Bataille, Georges. "Museum." *October* 36 (spring 1986): 24–25.

Baudrillard, Jean. *Simulations*. New York: Semiotext(e), 1983.

———. "The System of Collecting." In *The Cultures of Collecting*, edited by John Elsner and Roger Cardinal, 7–24. Cambridge, Mass.: Harvard Univ. Press, 1994.

Bazin, Germain. *The Museum Age*. New York: Universal Press, 1967.

Beer, Gillian. *Darwin's Plots: Evolutionary Narrative in Darwin, George Eliot, and Nineteenth-Century Fiction*. Boston: Routledge and Kegan Paul, 1983.

Bellamy, William. *The Novels of Wells, Bennett, and Galsworthy, 1890–1910*. New York: Barnes and Noble, 1971.

Belzoni, Giovanni. *Narrative of the Operations and Recent Discoveries within the Pyramids, Temples, Tombs, and Excavations in Egypt and Nubia*. London: John Murray, 1821.

Benjamin, Walter. "The Task of the Translator." In *Illuminations,* edited by Hannah Arendt, 69–82. New York: Schocken, 1969.

———. "Unpacking My Library." In *Illuminations,* edited by Hannah Arendt, 59–67. New York: Schocken, 1969.

———. "The Work of Art in the Age of Mechanical Reproduction." In *Illuminations,* edited by Hannah Arendt, 217–51. New York: Schocken, 1969.

Bennett, Tony. *The Birth of the Museum: History, Theory, Politics*. New York: Routledge, 1997.

Benson, A. C. *Edward FitzGerald*. London: Macmillan, 1925.

Benson, Arthur, and Viscount Esher, eds. *The Letters of Queen Victoria*. 4 vols. London: John Murray, 1907.

Bentham, George, ed. *The Variorum and Definitive Edition of the Poetical and Prose Writings of Edward FitzGerald*. New York: Phaeton, 1967.

Bergonzi, Bernard. "*The Time Machine:* An Ironic Myth." In *H. G. Wells: A Collection of Critical Essays,* edited by Bernard Bergonzi, 39–55. Englewood Cliffs, N.J.: Prentice-Hall, 1976.

Berman, Marshall. *All That Is Solid Melts into Air*. New York: Penguin, 1988.

"Bethnal Green." *Saturday Review,* 12 April 1882.

"Bethnal Green Museum." *Eastern Argus,* 24 March 1883.

"Bethnal Green Museum." *Hackney and Kingsland Gazette,* 18 April 1883.

Bettelheim, Bruno. *The Uses of Enchantment*. New York: Vintage, 1989.

Bhabha, Homi. *The Location of Culture*. New York: Routledge, 1994.

Blind, Mathilde. "On Reading the *Rubáiyát of Omar Khayyám* in a Kentish Rose Garden." In *The Rubáiyát of Omar Khayyám*. New York: Walter J. Black, 1932.

Boesky, Amy. "'Outlandish Fruits': Commissioning Nature for the Museum of Man." *ELH* 58, no. 2 (1991): 305–30.

Boon, James A. "Why Museums Make Me Sad." In *Exhibiting Cultures,* edited by Ivan Karp and Steven D. Lavine, 255–77. Washington, D.C.: Smithsonian Institution Press, 1991.

Boone, Joseph. *Tradition CounterTradition: Love and the Form of Fiction*. Chicago: Univ. of Chicago Press, 1987.

Boos, Florence. *The Poetry of Dante G. Rossetti*. The Hague: Mouton, 1976.

Borges, Jorge Luis. "The Enigma of Edward FitzGerald." In *Other Inquisitions, 1937–1952*. Austin: Univ. of Texas Press, 1964.

Bourdieu, Pierre, and Alain Darbel. *The Love of Art: European Art Museums and Their Public*. Translated by Caroline Beattie and Nick Merriman. Stanford, Calif.: Stanford Univ. Press, 1990.

Bowen, John Charles Edward. *Translation or Travesty?* Abingdon, Berkshire, U.K.: Abbey Press, 1973.

Boyer, M. Christine. *The City of Collective Memory*. Cambridge, Mass.: MIT Press, 1994.

Brantlinger, Patrick. "'News from Nowhere': Morris's Socialist Anti-Novel." *Victorian Studies* 19, no. 1 (1975): 35–49.

———. *Rule of Darkness: British Literature and Imperialism, 1830–1914*. Ithaca, N.Y.: Cornell Univ. Press, 1988.

Brief Guide to the Various Collections in the Bethnal Green Branch of the South Kensington Museum. London: Eyre and Spottiswoode, 1891.

Briggs, Asa. *Victorian Things*. London: B. T. Batsford, 1988.

Briggs, Julia. *A Woman of Passion*. New York: New Amsterdam Books, 1987.

Britton, John. *The Union of Architecture, Sculpture, and Painting*. London: J. Taylor, 1827.

Brontë, Charlotte. *Jane Eyre*. New York: Penguin, 1966.

———. *Villette*. New York: Dutton, 1957.

Brower, Reuben. *On Translation*. New York: Oxford Univ. Press, 1966.

Browning, Robert. *Robert Browning: The Poems*. Edited by John Pettigrew. New Haven, Conn.: Yale Univ. Press, 1981.

Brownstein, Rachel. *Becoming a Heroine*. New York: Penguin, 1984.

Buck-Morss, Susan. *The Dialectics of Seeing*. Cambridge, Mass.: MIT Press, 1991.

Burgess, Anthony. *Urgent Copy*. London: Jonathan Cape, 1968.

Burton, Richard. *Personal Narrative of a Pilgrimage to El-Medinah and Meccah*. 3 vols. London: Longman, Brown, Green, and Longmans, 1855.

Buzard, James. "Ethnography as Interruption: *News from Nowhere*, Narrative, and the Modern Romance of Authority." *Victorian Studies* 40, no. 3 (1997): 445–74.

Byron, Lord. *Lord Byron: The Complete Poetical Works*. Edited by Jerome McGann. Vols. 1 and 2. New York: Oxford Univ. Press, 1980.

Cadbury, William. "Fitzgerald's *Rubáiyát* as a Poem." *ELH* 34, no. 4 (1967): 541–63.

Campbell, Susie. "'Painting' in Browning's *Men and Women*." *Browning Society Notes* (winter 1984–85): 2–22.

Capellanus, Andreas. *The Art of Courtly Love*. Translated by John Jay Parry. New York: Columbia Univ. Press, 1990.

Casteras, Susan. "The Germ of a Museum, Arranged First for 'Workers in Iron': Ruskin's Museological Theories and the Curating of the Saint George's Museum." In *John Ruskin and the Victorian Eye*, 184–209. New York: Abrams, 1993.

Charteris, Evan Edward. *The Life and Letters of Sir Edmund Gosse*. New York: Harper and Brothers, 1931.

Chase, Karen. *Eros and Psyche*. New York: Methuen, 1984.

"Circulation of Objects to Exhibitions in Aid of Schools of Art for the Purpose of Study." Extract from the Parliamentary Return, 28 April 1870.

Clifford, James. "Of Other Peoples: Beyond the 'Salvage' Paradigm." In *Discussions in Contemporary Culture*, edited by Hal Foster, 121–30. Seattle: Bay Press, 1987.

———. *The Predicament of Culture*. Cambridge, Mass.: Harvard Univ. Press, 1988.

Cole, Henry. *Catalogue of the Objects of Indian Art Exhibited in the South Kensington Museum*. London: Eyre and Spottiswoode, 1874.

———. "The Duty of Governments towards Education, Science, and Art." London, 1875.

———. Miscellanies, 1851–1866. Cole Collection. National Art Library, Victoria and Albert Museum, London.

———. Miscellanies, 1857–1865. Cole Collection. National Art Library, Victoria and Albert Museum, London.

———. "Reasons for Converting the Crystal Palace into a Winter Garden." In Miscellanies, 1835–1852. Cole Collection. National Art Library, Victoria and Albert Museum, London.

———. "What Is Art Culture?" An address delivered to the Manchester School of Art, 21 December 1877. Cole Collection. National Art Library, Victoria and Albert Museum, London.

———, ed. *Universal Art Inventory*. London: Eyre and Spottiswoode, 1867.

A Companion to Mr. Bullock's Museum. London, 1811.

Conway, Moncure. "The Omar Khayyám Cult in England." *Nation* 57 (1893): 304–5.

———. *Travels in South Kensington.* New York: Harper and Brothers, 1882.

Cook, Clarence. *The House Beautiful.* Croton-on-Hudson, N.Y.: North River Press, 1980.

Coombes, Annie. *Reinventing Africa: Museums, Material Culture, and Popular Imagination in Late Victorian and Edwardian England.* New Haven, Conn.: Yale Univ. Press, 1994.

Cotsell, Michael. "Mr. Venus Rises from the Counter: Dickens's Taxidermist and His Contribution to *Our Mutual Friend.*" *Dickensian* 78–80, no. 402, part 2 (1983–84): 105–13.

Crimp, Douglas. *On the Museum's Ruins.* Cambridge, Mass.: MIT Press, 1993.

———. "On the Museum's Ruins." In *The Anti-Aesthetic: Essays on PostModern Culture,* edited by Hal Foster, 43–56. Seattle: Bay Press, 1983.

Culler, A. Dwight. *The Victorian Mirror of History.* New Haven, Conn.: Yale Univ. Press, 1985.

D'Ambrosio, Vinnie-Marie. *Eliot Possessed: T. S. Eliot and FitzGerald's Rubáiyát.* New York: New York Univ. Press, 1989.

Darwin, Charles. *Narrative of the Surveying Voyages of Adventure and Beagle.* In *The Portable Darwin,* edited by Duncan M. Porter and Peter G. Graham, 9–65. New York: Penguin, 1993.

———. *On the Fertilisation of British and Foreign Orchids.* In *The Portable Darwin,* edited by Duncan M. Porter and Peter G. Graham, 224–52. New York: Penguin, 1993.

———. *On the Origin of Species by Means of Natural Selection.* In *The Portable Darwin,* edited by Duncan M. Porter and Peter G. Graham, 105–215. New York: Penguin, 1993.

Daunton, M. J. *House and Home in the Victorian City.* Baltimore, Md.: Edward Arnold, 1983.

Davidoff, Leonore, and Catherine Hall. *Family Fortunes: Men and Women of the English Middle Class, 1780–1850.* Chicago: Univ. of Chicago Press, 1987.

Davis, Douglas. *The Museum Transformed.* New York: Abbeville Press, 1990.

Decker, Christopher, ed. *Rubáiyát of Omar Khayyám: A Critical Edition.* Charlottesville: Univ. Press of Virginia, 1997.

Desmond, Adrian. "Central Park's Fragile Dinosaurs." *Natural History* 83, no. 8 (1974): 64–71.

Dickens, Charles. "The Great Exhibition and the Little One." *Household Words,* 5 July 1851, 356–60.

———. *Hard Times.* New York: Penguin, 1987.

———. *Little Dorrit.* New York: Oxford Univ. Press, 1982.

———. *Our Mutual Friend.* New York: Penguin, 1986.

———. "Owen's Museum." *All the Year Round,* 27 September 1862, 62–67.

———. "Please to Leave Your Umbrella." *Household Words,* 1 May 1858, 423, 458–59.

Donato, Eugenio. "The Museum's Furnace: Notes toward a Contextual Reading of *Bouvard and Pécuchet.*" In *Textual Strategies,* edited by Josué V. Harari, 213–38. Ithaca, N.Y.: Cornell Univ. Press, 1979.

Doolittle, Hilda. *Tribute to Freud.* Manchester, U.K.: Carcanet, 1985.

Doré, Gustave, and Blanchard Jerrold. *London: A Pilgrimage.* New York: Dover, 1970.

Duncan, Carol. *Civilizing Rituals: Inside Public Art Museums.* New York: Routledge, 1995.

Eastlake, Charles. *Hints on Household Taste.* 1868. Reprint, New York: Dover, 1969.

"Editorial." *Bazaar, the Exchange, and Mart,* 15 January 1883.

"Editorial." *Modern Society,* 8 September 1906.

Elias, Norbert. *The Civilizing Process.* New York: Urizen, 1978.

Eliot, George. *Middlemarch.* Boston: Houghton Mifflin, 1956.

Eliot, T. S. *The Complete Poems and Plays, 1909–1950.* New York: Harcourt, Brace and World, 1971.

Elsner, John. "A Collector's Model of Desire: The House and Museum of Sir John Soane." In *The Cultures of Collecting,* edited by John Elsner and Roger Cardinal, 155–76. Cambridge, Mass.: Harvard Univ. Press, 1994.

Empson, William. "Homage to the British Museum." In *Collected Poems of William Empson.* New York: Harcourt, Brace, 1949.

Fenton, James. "The Pitt Rivers Museum, Oxford." In *Children in Exile.* New York: Random House, 1984.

Findlen, Paula. *Possessing Nature: Museums, Collecting, and Scientific Culture in Early Modern Italy.* Berkeley: Univ. of California Press, 1994.

Fisher, Philip. *Making and Effacing Art: Modern American Art in a Culture of Museums.* New York: Oxford Univ. Press, 1991.

FitzGerald, Edward. *Rubáiyát of Omar Khayyám.* New York: Caldwell, 1900.

———. *Rubáiyát of Omar Khayyám.* New York: Dodge, 1910.

———. *Rubáiyát of Omar Khayyám.* Philadelphia: Henry T. Coates, 1898.

———. *Rubáiyát of Omar Khayyám.* 21st and 23d eds. Boston: Houghton, Mifflin, 1893.

Forman, Maurice Buxton, ed. *The Letters of John Keats.* New York: Oxford Univ. Press, 1947.

Forrester, John. "'Mille e tre': Freud and Collecting." In *The Cultures of Collecting,* edited by John Elsner and Roger Cardinal, 224–51. Cambridge, Mass.: Harvard Univ. Press, 1994.

Forster, E. M. "Art for Art's Sake." In *Two Cheers for Democracy,* 88–95. New York: Harcourt, Brace, 1951.

———. "For the Museum's Sake." In *Abinger Harvest,* 290–97. New York: Harcourt Brace Jovanovich, 1964.

———. *Maurice.* New York: Quality Paperback Book Club, 1971.

Foucault, Michel. *Discipline and Punish: The Birth of the Prison.* New York: Vintage, 1979.

———. "Of Other Spaces." *Diacritics* 16 (spring 1986): 22–27.

Fox, Celina, ed. *London—World City, 1800–1840.* New Haven, Conn.: Yale Univ. Press, 1992.

Freud, Ernst. *The Letters of Sigmund Freud.* New York: Basic, 1975.

Freud, Sigmund. *Civilization and Its Discontents.* New York: Norton, 1961.

———. *Dora: An Analysis of a Case of Hysteria.* New York: Collier, 1963.

———. "Thoughts for the Times on War and Death." In *The Standard Edition of the Complete Psychological Works of Sigmund Freud.* Vol. 14. London: Hogarth, 1981.

Frye, Northrop. "The Meeting of Past and Future in William Morris." *Studies in Romanticism* 21, no. 3 (1982): 303–18.

Galsworthy, John. *The Forsyte Saga.* New York: Scribner's, 1934.

———. *The Man of Property.* New York: Scribner's, 1933.

Gamwell, Lynn. "The Origins of Freud's Antiquities Collection." In *Sigmund Freud and Art,* edited by Lynn Gamwell and Richard Wells, 21–32. Binghamton: State Univ. of New York, 1989.

Gamwell, Lynn, and Richard Wells, eds. "Selections from the Collection." In *Sigmund*

Freud and Art, edited by Lynn Gamwell and Richard Wells, 33–132. Binghamton: State Univ. of New York, 1989.

Gay, Peter. *Freud: A Life for Our Time.* New York: Norton, 1988.

———. Introduction to *Sigmund Freud and Art,* edited by Lynn Gamwell and Richard Wells, 15–19. Binghamton: State Univ. of New York, 1989.

Gezari, Janet. *Charlotte Brontë and Defensive Conduct: The Author and the Body at Risk.* Philadelphia: Univ. of Pennsylvania Press, 1992.

Gibbs-Smith, C. H. *The Great Exhibition of 1851.* London: Her Majesty's Stationery Office, 1981.

"Gigantic Whale" (announcement). *Times,* 2 July 1831, 5.

Gilbert, Sandra M., and Susan Gubar. *The Madwoman in the Attic.* New Haven, Conn.: Yale Univ. Press, 1979.

Gill, Richard. *Happy Rural Seat: The English Country House and the Literary Imagination.* New Haven, Conn.: Yale Univ. Press, 1972.

Girouard, Mark. *Alfred Waterhouse and the Natural History Museum.* New Haven, Conn.: Yale Univ. Press, 1981.

———. *Life in the English Country House.* New York: Penguin, 1980.

———. *The Victorian Country House.* New Haven, Conn.: Yale Univ. Press, 1979.

Gissing, George. *The Nether World.* New York: Oxford Univ. Press, 1992.

Gosse, Edmund. "Edward FitzGerald." Reprinted in *The Variorum and Definitive Edition of the Poetical and Prose Writings of Edward FitzGerald,* edited by George Bentham, ix–xxviii. New York: Phaeton, 1967.

———. *Father and Son.* New York: Penguin, 1982.

Graña, César. "The Private Lives of Public Museums: Can Art Be Democratic?" In *Fact and Symbol: Essays in the Sociology of Art and Literature,* 95–111. New York: Oxford Univ. Press, 1971.

Graves, Robert, and Omar Ali-Shah, trans. *The Original Rubáiyát of Omar Khayyám.* Garden City, N.Y.: Doubleday, 1968.

Greenblatt, Stephen. "Resonance and Wonder." In *Literary Theory Today,* edited by Peter Collier and Helga Geyer-Ryan, 74–90. Ithaca, N.Y.: Cornell Univ. Press, 1990.

Greenwood, Thomas. *Museums and Art Galleries.* London: Simpkin, Marshall, 1888.

Guides to the South Kensington Museum. 1857–96. National Art Library, Victoria and Albert Museum, London.

Hagstrum, Jean. *The Sister Arts.* Chicago: Univ. of Chicago Press, 1958.

The Handbook of 1840: A General Description of Sir John Soane's Museum. London: Shaw and Sons, 1840.

Haraway, Donna. *Primate Visions.* New York: Routledge, 1989.

Harbison, Robert. *Eccentric Spaces.* New York: Knopf, 1977.

Hardy, Thomas. *The Complete Poetical Works of Thomas Hardy,* edited by Samuel Hynes. 5 vols. New York: Oxford Univ. Press, 1984.

———. "The Fiddler of the Reels." In *Life's Little Ironies.* New York: Harper and Brothers, 1893.

———. *The Mayor of Casterbridge.* New York: Penguin, 1985.

Hart, John E. "Ritual and Spectacle in *The Man of Property.*" *Research Studies* 40, no. 1 (1972): 34–43.

Hay, John. "Address." In *Rubáiyát of Omar Khayyám.* New York: Brentano's, n.d.

Haydon, Benjamin. *Autobiography.* Oxford: Oxford Univ. Press, 1927.

Hayter, Alethea, ed. *FitzGerald to His Friends*. London: Scholar, 1979.

Hazlitt, William. *The Collected Works of William Hazlitt*. 12 vols., edited by A. R. Waller and Arnold Glover. New York: McClure, Phillips, 1902–4.

Heffernan, James. *Museum of Words: The Poetics of Ekphrasis from Homer to Ashbery*. Chicago: Univ. of Chicago Press, 1993.

Heron-Allen, Edward. *Poetical and Prose Writings of Edward FitzGerald*. New York: Phaeton, 1967.

Hill, Octavia. *Homes of the London Poor*. London: Frank Cass, 1970.

Hitchcock, Alfred. *Blackmail*. London: British International Pictures, 1929.

Hitchens, Christopher. *The Elgin Marbles: Should They Be Returned to Greece?* London: Chatto and Windus, 1987.

Hobsbawm, Eric, and Terence Ranger, ed. *The Invention of Tradition*. New York: Cambridge Univ. Press, 1984.

Holroyd, Michael. *Lytton Strachey*. New York: Farrar, Straus, Giroux, 1995.

Hooper-Greenhill, Eilean. *Museums and the Shaping of Knowledge*. New York: Routledge, 1992.

Houghton, Walter, and Robert Stange, eds. *Victorian Poetry and Poetics*. 2d ed. Boston: Houghton Mifflin, 1968.

"The House and Museum of Sir John Soane." *Penny Magazine* 6, no. 363 (1837): 457–64.

Hudson, Kenneth. *Museums of Influence*. New York: Cambridge Univ. Press, 1987.

Huntington, John. *The Logic of Fantasy*. New York: Columbia Univ. Press, 1982.

Hutter, Albert D. "Dismemberment and Articulation in *Our Mutual Friend*." *Dickens Studies Annual* 11 (1983): 135–75.

"An Immortal Idea." *Punch*, January–June 1851, 63.

Impey, Oliver, and Arthur MacGregor, eds. *The Origins of Museums: The Cabinet of Curiosities in Sixteenth and Seventeenth Century Europe*. New York: Ursus, 1996.

Inventory of the British Water Colour Paintings in the Fine Arts Collections at South Kensington. With an introduction by R. Redgrave. London: Eyre and Spottiswoode, 1860.

Jack, Ian. *Keats and the Mirror of Art*. Oxford: Clarendon, 1967.

James, Henry. *The American*. New York: Penguin, 1981.

———. "Americans Abroad." In *The American*, edited by James W. Tuttleton, 357–62. New York: Norton, 1978.

———. "London." In *English Hours*. Temecula, Calif.: Reprint Services, 1992.

———. *A London Life*. New York: Oxford Univ. Press, 1989.

———. *The Spoils of Poynton*. New York: Oxford Univ. Press, 1983.

James, Louis. "Tom Brown's Imperialist Sons." *Victorian Studies* 17 (September 1973): 89–99.

Jameson, Mrs. Anna. *Companion to the Most Celebrated Private Galleries of Art in London*. London: Saunders and Otley, 1844.

Jewett, Iran B. Hassani. *Edward FitzGerald*. Boston: Twayne, 1977.

"A Journey round the Globe." *Punch*, July–December 1851, 4.

Jukes, Peter. *A Shout in the Street*. Berkeley: Univ. of California Press, 1991.

Karp, Ivan, and Steven Lavine, eds. *Exhibiting Cultures: The Poetics and Politics of Museum Display*. Washington, D.C.: Smithsonian Institution Press, 1991.

Karp, Ivan, Steven Lavine, and Christine Mullen Kreamer, eds. *Museums and Communities: The Politics of Public Culture*. Washington, D.C.: Smithsonian Institution Press, 1992.

Keats, John. *Complete Poems*. Edited by Jack Stillinger. Cambridge, Mass.: Harvard Univ. Press, 1982.

Kermode, Frank. *Continuities*. New York: Random House, 1968.

Kerney, Michael. Biographical preface to *Rubáiyát of Omar Khayyám*, by Edward FitzGerald. New York: Caldwell, 1900.

Kerr, Robert. *The English Gentleman's House*. London: John Murray, 1864.

Kipling, Rudyard. *Kim*. Edited by Alan Sandison. New York: Oxford Univ. Press, 1987.

Kirby, R. S. *The Wonderful and Scientific Museum*. 6 vols. London: T. Keating, 1803.

Krieger, Murray. *Ekphrasis: The Illusion of the Natural Sign*. Baltimore, Md.: Johns Hopkins Univ. Press, 1991.

————. "The Ekphrastic Principle and the Still Movement of Poetry; or *Laokoön* Revisited." In *The Play and Place of Criticism*, 105–28. Baltimore, Md.: Johns Hopkins Univ. Press, 1967.

Langbaum, Robert. *The Poetry of Experience*. New York: Norton, 1963.

Laurie, Thomas. *Suggestions for Establishing Cheap Popular and Educational Museums of Scientific and Art Collections*. 1885. British Library.

Layard, Austen Henry. *Nineveh and Its Remains*. 2 vols. New York: Putnam, 1849.

Lee, Rensselaer. *Ut Pictura Poesis: The Humanistic Theory of Painting*. New York: Norton, 1967.

Lefevere, Andre, ed. *Translation/History/Culture*. New York: Routledge, 1992.

Levine, Lawrence. *Highbrow/Lowbrow: The Emergence of Cultural Hierarchy in America*. Cambridge, Mass.: Harvard Univ. Press, 1988.

Lipking, Lawrence. *The Ordering of the Arts in Eighteenth-Century England*. Princeton, N.J.: Princeton Univ. Press, 1970.

Litvak, Joseph. "Charlotte Brontë and the Scene of Instruction: Authority and Subversion in *Villette*." *Nineteenth-Century Literature* 42 (March 1988): 467–89.

Lodge, David. *The British Museum Is Falling Down*. 1965. Reprint, New York: Penguin, 1981.

Loftie, W. J. *A Plea for Art in the House*. Compiled by John Hullah. New York: Garland, 1978.

Lutchmansingh, Lawrence D. "Archaeological Socialism: Utopia and Art in William Morris." In *Socialism and the Literary Artistry of William Morris*, edited by Florence S. Boos and Carole G. Silver, 7–25. Columbia: Univ. of Missouri Press, 1990.

Lysons, Daniel. *Collectanea: Public Exhibitions and Places of Amusement*. 5 vols. Strawberry Hill, U.K.: Thomas Kirgate, n.d.

Macaulay, Thomas. *History of England*. In *Prose of the Victorian Period*, edited by William Buckler, 55–82. Boston: Houghton Mifflin, 1958.

Mainardi, Patricia. "Postmodern History of the Musée d'Orsay." *October* 41 (summer 1987): 31–52.

Malraux, André. *Museum without Walls*. Garden City, N.Y.: Doubleday, 1967.

Marryat, Florence. *Life and Letters of Captain Marryat*. 2 vols. New York: Appleton, 1872.

Martin, Loy. *Browning's Dramatic Monologues and the Post-Romantic Subject*. Baltimore, Md.: Johns Hopkins Univ. Press, 1985.

Martin, Robert Bernard. *With Friends Possessed*. New York: Atheneum, 1985.

Martin, Robert K. "Edward Carpenter and the Double Structure of *Maurice*." In *Literary*

Fictions of Homosexuality, edited by Stuart Kellogg, 35–46. New York: Haworth, 1983. First published in *Journal of Homosexuality* 8, nos. 3–4 (1983): 35–46.

Marx, Karl. *The Communist Manifesto.* New York: International, 1980.

Mayhew, Henry. *1851: or, The Adventures of Mr. and Mrs. Cursty Sandboys.* London: David Bogue, 1851.

————. *London Labour and the London Poor.* Vols. 1 and 4. London: Griffin, Bohn, 1861.

McClellan, Andrew. *Inventing the Louvre: Art, Politics, and the Origins of the Modern Museum in Eighteenth-Century Paris.* New York: Cambridge Univ. Press, 1994.

McClure, John. *Kipling and Conrad: The Colonial Fiction.* Cambridge, Mass.: Harvard Univ. Press, 1991.

————. "Problematic Presence: The Colonial Other in Kipling and Conrad." In *The Black Presence in English Literature,* edited by David Dabydeen, 154–67. Dover, U.K.: Manchester Univ. Press, 1985.

McConnell, Frank. *The Science Fiction of H. G. Wells.* New York: Oxford Univ. Press, 1981.

McCormack, Kathleen. "*Middlemarch:* Dorothea's Husbands in the Vatican Museums." *Victorians Institute Journal* 20 (1992): 75–91.

Metz, Nancy. "The Artistic Reclamation of Waste in *Our Mutual Friend.*" *Nineteenth-Century Fiction* 34 (June 1979): 59–72.

Meyer, Susan. "Colonialism and the Figurative Strategy of *Jane Eyre.*" In *Macropolitics of 19th Century Literature,* edited by Jonathan Arac and Harriet Ritvo, 159–83. Philadelphia: Univ. of Pennsylvania Press, 1991.

Millar, J. H. "Review." In *Kipling: The Critical Heritage,* edited by Roger Green, 269–71. London: Routledge and Kegan Paul, 1971.

Millenson, Susan Feinberg. *Sir John Soane's Museum.* Ann Arbor, Mich.: UMI Research Press, 1987.

Miller, D. A. *Narrative and Its Discontents.* Princeton, N.J.: Princeton Univ. Press, 1981.

Miller, J. Hillis. *Illustration.* Cambridge, Mass.: Harvard Univ. Press, 1992.

Mirollo, James. "Sibling Rivalry in the Arts Family: The Case of Poetry vs. Painting in the Italian Renaissance." In *So Rich a Tapestry: The Sister Arts and Cultural Studies,* edited by Ann Hurley and Kate Greenspan, 29–71. Lewisburg, Pa.: Bucknell Univ. Press, 1995.

Mitchell, W. J. T. *Iconology: Image, Text, Ideology.* Chicago: Univ. of Chicago Press, 1986.

Morris, William. *News from Nowhere.* New York: Penguin, 1993.

"Mr. Wyld's Globe in Leicester-Square." *Illustrated London News,* 29 March 1851, 248.

"Mr. Wyld's Model of the Earth." *Times,* 30 May 1851, 8.

Muensterberger, Warren. *Collecting: An Unruly Passion.* Princeton, N.J.: Princeton Univ. Press, 1993.

Mumford, Lewis. *The City in History.* New York: Harcourt, Brace, and World, 1961.

Nesbit, Edith. *The Story of the Amulet.* In *The Five Children.* New York: Coward-McCann, 1930.

A New Description of Sir John Soane's Museum. 7th ed. London: Trustees, 1986.

"A New Use of the Globe." *Punch,* January–June 1851, 103.

Newhouse, Victoria. *Towards a New Museum.* New York: Monacelli, 1998.

Newton, Judith Lowder. *Women, Power, and Subversion: Social Strategies in British Fiction, 1778–1860.* Athens: Univ. of Georgia Press, 1981.

Nietzsche, Friedrich. *On the Advantage and Disadvantage of History for Life*. Indianapolis: Hackett, 1980.

Nord, Deborah Epstein. *Walking the Victorian Streets: Women, Representation, and the City.* Ithaca, N.Y.: Cornell Univ. Press, 1995.

The Official Descriptive and Illustrated Catalogue of the Great Exhibition. 3 vols. London: Spicer Brothers, 1851.

"Open House at the Crystal Palace." *Punch,* January–June 1851, 43.

Owen, Richard. Miscellaneous Manuscripts. Owen Collection, Natural History Museum Library, London.

———. "On the Extent and Aims of a National Museum of Natural History." London: Saunders, Otley, 1862.

Owens, Craig. "The Birth and Death of the Viewer: On the Public Function of Art." In *Discussions in Contemporary Culture,* edited by Hal Foster, 16–23. Seattle: Bay Press, 1987.

Paracelsus (Theophrastus Bombast von Hohenheim). *The Archidoxes of Magic.* Kila, Mont.: Kessinger, 1992.

Parrinder, Patrick, ed. *H. G. Wells: The Critical Heritage.* Boston: Routledge and Kegan Paul, 1972.

Pater, Walter. "The Child in the House." In *English Prose of the Victorian Era,* edited by Charles Harrold and William Templeman, 1469–78. New York: Oxford Univ. Press, 1938.

———. *The Renaissance.* Edited by Donald Hill. Berkeley: Univ. of California Press, 1980.

———. "Sir Thomas Browne." In *Appreciations.* New York: Macmillan, 1901.

Paxton, Nancy L. "George Eliot and the City: The Imprisonment of Culture." In *Women Writers and the City,* edited by Susan Merrill Squier, 71–96. Knoxville: Univ. of Tennessee Press, 1984.

Perl, Jed. "Pieces of the Frame." Review of *The National Gallery Complete Illustrated Catalogue. New York Times,* 11 February 1996, 16.

"Pictures for the Exhibition of Industry." *Punch,* January–June 1851, 42.

"A Plea for Collecting." *Herdman's Miscellany* 5, no. 50 (1898): 1.

Pollock, Griselda. "Vicarious Excitements." *New Formations* 4 (spring 1988): 25–50.

Porter, Roy. *London: A Social History.* Cambridge, Mass.: Harvard Univ. Press, 1995.

Pound, Ezra. *ABC of Reading.* New Haven, Conn.: Yale Univ. Press, 1934.

———. *The Letters of Ezra Pound.* Edited by D. D. Paige. New York: Harcourt, Brace, 1950.

Preziosi, Donald. "Collecting/Museums." In *Critical Terms for Art History,* edited by Robert S. Nelson and Richard Shiff, 281–91. Chicago: Univ. of Chicago Press, 1996.

Pritchett, V. S. "The Upholstered Prison." In *E. M. Forster: The Critical Heritage,* edited by Philip Gardner, 447–50. Boston: Routledge and Kegan Paul, 1973.

Reed, John R. *The Natural History of H. G. Wells.* Athens: Ohio Univ. Press, 1982.

Report from the Select Committee on the South Kensington Museum. Ordered, by the House of Commons, to be printed. 1 August 1860.

Report of Proceedings at a Deputation to His Grace the Duke of Marlborough on the Subject of the East London Museum. London: Willis and Sotheron, 1868.

Richards, Thomas. *The Commodity Culture of Victorian England.* Stanford, Calif.: Stanford Univ. Press, 1990.

————. *The Imperial Archive: Knowledge and the Fantasy of Empire.* New York: Verso, 1993.

Rischin, Abigail S. "Beside the Reclining Statue: Ekphrasis, Narrative, and Desire in *Middlemarch*." *PMLA* 3, no. 5 (1996): 1121–32.

Ritvo, Harriet. *The Animal Estate.* Cambridge, Mass.: Harvard Univ. Press, 1987.

Rossetti, D. G. "The Burden of Nineveh." 1870. Reprinted in *The Pre-Raphaelites and Their Circle.* Edited by Cecil Lang. 2d ed. Chicago: Univ. of Chicago Press, 1975.

Rothenberg, Jacob. *"Descensus Ad Terram": The Acquisition and Reception of the Elgin Marbles.* New York: Garland, 1977.

Roy, Parama. "Unaccommodated Woman and the Poetics of Property in *Jane Eyre*." *Studies in English Literature* 29, no.4 (1989): 713–27.

Rubinstein, David. *Victorian Homes.* North Pomfret, Vt.: David and Charles, 1974.

Rugoff, Ralph. "Beyond Belief: The Museum as Metaphor." In *Visual Display: Culture beyond Appearances,* edited by Lynne Cook and Peter Wollen, 68–81. Seattle: Bay Press, 1995.

Rushdie, Salman. *Shame.* New York: Vintage International, 1989.

Ruskin, John. *Deucalion: Collected Studies of the Lapse of Waves, and Life of Stones.* Vol. 1. New York: John Wiley and Sons, 1886.

————. "Of Queens' Gardens." In *Sesame and Lilies: Three Lectures.* New York: Mershon, 1865.

————. "Picture Galleries: Their Functions and Formation." In *The Complete Works of John Ruskin.* New York: Chesterfield Society, n.d.

————. "The Use of Museums." In *Selections from Writings.* London: George Allen, 1905.

Said, Edward. *Culture and Imperialism.* New York: Knopf, 1993.

————. *Orientalism.* New York: Pantheon, 1978.

"Sales in Progress of Exhibits." *Times,* 15 October 1851, 4.

Schenker, Daniel. "Fugitive Articulation: An Introduction to *The Rubáiyát of Omar Khayyám*." *Victorian Poetry* 19, no. 1 (1981): 49–64.

Schulte, Rainer, and John Biguenet, eds. *Theories of Translation: An Anthology of Essays from Dryden to Derrida.* Chicago: Univ. of Chicago Press, 1992.

See, Fred G. "Henry James and the Art of Possession." In *American Realism,* edited by Eric J. Sundquist, 119–37. Baltimore, Md.: Johns Hopkins Univ. Press, 1982.

Shea, F. X. "Mr. Venus Observed: The Plot Change in *Our Mutual Friend*." *Papers on Language and Literature* 4, no. 2 (1968): 170–81.

Shelley, Mary. *The Last Man.* Vol. 4 of *The Novels and Selected Works of Mary Shelley.* Edited by Jane Blumberg. London: William Pickering, 1996.

Sherman, Daniel. *Worthy Monuments.* Cambridge, Mass.: Harvard Univ. Press, 1989.

Sherman, Daniel, and Irit Rogoff, eds. *MuseumCulture.* Minneapolis: Univ. of Minnesota Press, 1994.

Silverman, Debora. *Selling Culture.* New York: Pantheon, 1986.

Simpson, William. "Omar Khayyám's Grave." In *Rubáiyát of Omar Khayyám.* New York: Houghton, Mifflin, 1888.

Skoblow, Jeffrey. *Paradise Dislocated: Morris, Politics, Art.* Charlottesville: Univ. Press of Virginia, 1993.

Smiles, Samuel. *Self-Help.* Boston: Ticknor and Fields, 1859.

Soane, John. *Crude Hints, Towards an History of My House.* 1812. Sir John Soane's Museum, London.

———. *Description of the House and Museum*. London: James Moyes, 1830, 1832; London: Levey, Robson, and Franklyn, 1835–36.

"The Soanean Museum." *Mirror,* April 1833, 209–14.

Speke, John Hanning. *What Led to the Discovery of the Source of the Nile*. London: William Blackwood and Sons, 1864.

Spielberg, Steven. *Indiana Jones and the Last Crusade*. Hollywood, Calif.: Paramount Pictures, 1989.

Spitz, Ellen Handler. "Psychoanalysis and the Legacies of Antiquity." In *Sigmund Freud and Art,* edited by Lynn Gamwell and Richard Wells, 153–71. Binghamton: State Univ. of New York, 1989.

Stamp, Gavin, and Colin Amery. *Victorian Builders of London, 1837–1887*. London: Architectural Press, 1980.

Stearn, William. *The Natural History Museum at South Kensington*. London: Heinemann, 1981.

Steegman, John. *Victorian Taste: A Study of the Arts and Architecture from 1830 to 1870*. Cambridge, Mass.: MIT Press, 1970.

Steiner, George. *After Babel*. 2d ed. New York: Oxford Univ. Press, 1992.

Steiner, Wendy. *The Colors of Rhetoric*. Chicago: Univ. of Chicago Press, 1982.

Sternlicht, Sanford. *John Galsworthy*. Boston: Twayne, 1987.

Stewart, Susan. *On Longing: Narratives of the Miniature, the Gigantic, the Souvenir, the Collection*. Durham, N.C.: Duke Univ. Press, 1993.

Strachey, Lytton. *Queen Victoria*. London: Chatto and Windus, 1969.

Summers, Claude. *Gay Fictions: Wilde to Stonewall*. New York: Continuum, 1990.

Taine, Hippolyte-Adolphe. *Notes on England*. New York: Holt and Williams, 1872.

Tennyson, Alfred. "Ode for the Opening of the International Exhibition." London: Edward Moxon, 1862.

———. "Ode on the Opening of the Colonial and Indian Exhibition." London: William Clowes and Sons, 4 May 1886.

———. "The Palace of Art." In *Tennyson's Poetry*. Edited by Robert W. Hill Jr. New York: Norton, 1971.

Terhune, Alfred, and Annabelle Terhune, eds. *The Letters of Edward FitzGerald*. 4 vols. Princeton, N.J.: Princeton Univ. Press, 1980.

Thackeray, William Makepeace. "Mr. Molony's Account of the Crystal Palace." *Punch,* July–December 1851, 171.

Thompson, E. P. *William Morris: Romantic to Revolutionary*. New York: Pantheon, 1977.

Thwaite, Ann. *Edmund Gosse: A Literary Landscape, 1849–1928*. London: Secker and Warburg, 1984.

Tintner, Adeline R. *The Museum World of Henry James*. Ann Arbor, Mich.: UMI Research Press, 1986.

Torgovnick, Marianna. *Gone Primitive*. Chicago: Univ. of Chicago Press, 1990.

Valéry, Paul. "The Fabre Museum." In *The Collected Works of Paul Valéry*. Edited by Jackson Matthews. Vol. 12. New York: Pantheon, 1960.

———. "The Problem of Museums." In *The Collected Works of Paul Valéry*. Edited by Jackson Matthews. Vol. 12. New York: Pantheon, 1960.

Venuti, Lawrence, ed. *Rethinking Translation: Discourse, Subjectivity, Ideology*. New York: Routledge, 1992.

Vergo, Peter, ed. *The New Museology*. London: Reaktion, 1989.

Wainwright, Clive (deputy curator of Furniture and Woodwork Collections at the Victoria and Albert Museum). Interviews with author. London, August 1990.

Walkowitz, Judith. *City of Dreadful Night: Narratives of Sexual Danger in Late-Victorian London.* Chicago: Univ. of Chicago Press, 1992.

Wallis, Brian, ed. *Hans Haacke: Unfinished Business.* Cambridge, Mass.: MIT Press, 1986.

Weintraub, Stanley. *Victoria: An Intimate Biography.* New York: Dutton, 1987.

Wells, H. G. *The Croquet Player.* New York: Viking, 1936.

———. *Experiment in Autobiography.* New York: Macmillan, 1934.

———. *The Time Machine.* New York: Penguin, 1979.

———. *Tono-Bungay.* New York: Duffield, 1926.

Wells, Richard. Preface to *Sigmund Freud and Art,* edited by Lynn Gamwell and Richard Wells, 11–13. Binghamton: State Univ. of New York, 1989.

Welsh, Alexander. *George Eliot and Blackmail.* Cambridge, Mass.: Harvard Univ. Press, 1985.

Weschler, Lawrence. *Mr. Wilson's Cabinet of Wonder.* New York: Pantheon, 1995.

Wiesenfarth, Joseph. "The Greeks, the Germans, and George Eliot." In *Browning Institute Studies: An Annual of Victorian Literary and Cultural History* 10 (1982): 91–104.

Wilde, Alan. *Horizons of Assent: Modernism, Postmodernism, and the Ironic Imagination.* Baltimore, Md.: Johns Hopkins Univ. Press, 1981.

Williams, Raymond. *The English Novel from Dickens to Lawrence.* London: Chatto and Windus, 1970.

Wilson, Angus. *The Strange Ride of Rudyard Kipling.* London: Secker and Warburg, 1977.

Winner, Viola Hopkins. *Henry James and the Visual Arts.* Charlottesville: Univ. Press of Virginia, 1970.

Witemeyer, Hugh. *George Eliot and the Visual Arts.* New Haven, Conn.: Yale Univ. Press, 1979.

Wood, J. G. "The Dulness of Museums," *Nineteenth Century* 21 (March 1887): 384–96.

Wood, Robin. *Hollywood from Vietnam to Reagan.* New York: Columbia Univ. Press, 1986.

Woodring, Carl. *Nature into Art: Cultural Transformations in Nineteenth-Century Britain.* Cambridge, Mass.: Harvard Univ. Press, 1989.

Wrentmore, C. Quaritch, ed. *Letters from Edward FitzGerald to Bernard Quaritch: 1853–1883.* 1926. Reprint, Folcroft, Pa.: Folcroft Library Editions, 1973.

Wright, W. Aldis. *Letters and Literary Remains of Edward FitzGerald.* 7 vols. New York: Macmillan, 1903.

Wyld, James. *Notes to Accompany Mr. Wyld's Model of the Earth.* London: Model of the Earth, 1851.

Yonge, Charlotte. *The Daisy Chain.* London: Virago, 1988.

———. *Heartsease.* London: Macmillan, 1902.

Zipes, Jack. *Fairy Tales and the Art of Subversion.* New York: Wildman, 1983.

Index

Victorian Literature and Culture Series

DANIEL ALBRIGHT
Tennyson: The Muses' Tug-of-War

DAVID G. RIEDE
Matthew Arnold and the Betrayal of Language

ANTHONY WINNER
Culture and Irony: Studies in Joseph Conrad's Major Novels

JAMES RICHARDSON
Vanishing Lives: Style and Self in Tennyson, D. G. Rossetti, Swinburne, and Yeats

JEROME J. McGANN, EDITOR
Victorian Connections

ANTONY H. HARRISON
Victorian Poets and Romantic Poems: Intertextuality and Ideology

E. WARWICK SLINN
The Discourse of Self in Victorian Poetry

LINDA K. HUGHES AND MICHAEL LUND
The Victorian Serial

ANNA LEONOWENS
The Romance of the Harem
Edited by Susan Morgan

ALAN FISCHLER
Modified Rapture: Comedy in W. S. Gilbert's Savoy Operas

EMILY SHORE
Journal of Emily Shore
Edited by Barbara Timm Gates

RICHARD MAXWELL
The Mysteries of Paris and London

FELICIA BONAPARTE
The Gypsy-Bachelor of Manchester: The Life of Mrs. Gaskell's Demon

PETER L. SHILLINGSBURG
Pegasus in Harness: Victorian Publishing and W. M. Thackeray

ANGELA LEIGHTON
Victorian Women Poets: Writing against the Heart

ALLAN C. DOOLEY
Author and Printer in Victorian England

LINDA H. PETERSON
  Traditions of Victorian Women's Autobiography: The Poetics and Politics of Life Writing

GAIL TURLEY HOUSTON
  Royalties: The Queen and Victorian Writers

LAURA C. BERRY
  The Child, the State, and the Victorian Novel

BARBARA J. BLACK
  On Exhibit: Victorians and Their Museums